HANDS
of an
ANGEL

HELEN PARRY JONES

arrow books

Published in Great Britain by Arrow Books, 2012

2 4 6 8 10 9 7 5 3 1

First published in paperback in Ireland 2011 by Arrow Books

Arrow Books
Random House, 20 Vauxhall Bridge Road,
London SW1V 2SA

www.randomhouse.co.uk

Addresses for companies within The Random House Group Limited can be found at:
www.randomhouse.co.uk/offices.htm

The Random House Group Limited Reg. No. 954009

A CIP catalogue record for this book
is available from the British Library

ISBN 978-0-099-56905-3

The Random House Group Limited supports The Forest Stewardship Council
(FSC®), the leading international forest certification organisation. Our books carrying
the FSC label are printed on FSC® certified paper. FSC is the only forest certification
scheme endorsed by the leading environmental organisations, including Greenpeace.
Our paper procurement policy can be found at:
www.randomhouse.co.uk/environment

Printed and bound by CPI Group, Croydon, CR0 4YY

I dedicate this book to
my husband Richard,
my children, Blake, Curtis, Fiona and Anthony,
and to the loving memory of my parents,
Colin and Judy.

Acknowledgements

This book is brought to you with the help of some people who all deserve a special acknowledgement. Everyone who has helped me carries importance in my thoughts and the order of my thanks has no bearing on the level of my gratitude.

My thanks firstly goes to my friend Andrea Hayes, radio and television presenter, who managed to focus my endeavours and point me in the right direction in a world alien to me – the world of the media.

Thereafter, there are to two special souls, Patricia Scanlan and Aidan Story who guided me to Random House. Sample chapters were sent by email to Random House at 8.30am one morning in May 2011 and at 9.01am the publishers had made the decision my voice needed to be heard! Soon after, Patricia's spiritual heart guided me directly to Sheila Crowley, who is now my agent and has taken me under her very professional wing to ensure my voice is heard loud and clear.

My thanks next extend to the Random House team: Gillian

Holmes, my editor, who stepped in when Kate Elton moved on and has helped to make my voice clearer and more succinct. To Claire Round, Jen Doyle and Najma Finlay whose enthusiasm matched mine when it came to marketing and publicising the book, and my Mr Dan Dare aka Andrew Sauerwine who I will never forget after our first hilarious meeting. In production and design, Linda Hodgson and Rachael Ludbrook took the book on to publication. . . . Thank you team.

I would especially like to thank my Cousin Debbie, Aunty Joan and Aunty Connie who gave their help in clarifying some of my family history facts.

On a personal level, I would like to thank Jackie and Robert Ryan-Beswick, John and Diane Beaumont and Margaret Grey (my second mum), who over many years have listened without complaint to my ideas, thoughts and escapades. Also to Margaret Medley for her help with family matters when the boys were much younger and I was away from home doing what had to be done.

A thank you list wouldn't be complete without mentioning the encouragement some of my clients have offered me, but the list is too long to mention each and every one by name but your support has been greatly appreciated.

To my mother-in-law Elsie who is now one of my greatest fans. Our meeting changed both our lives beyond recognition.

I need to thank my darling children who listened patiently for countless hours throughout their childhood while I talked to complete strangers about the spirit world, and who made no demands when Dad and I had to be away from home. Your patience is endless and my love for you is immeasurable.

Last but not least, I want to thank with all my heart, my soul mate Richard, whose help and love has been my strength. We are twin flames working on a parallel journey: you have been my worst critic and my best ally with all that I endeavour to do. Thank you my darling for the best of my life.

Contents

x

Introduction

As a professional healer, people often ask me: 'Helen, what is it that you do?'

I believe that all my work falls into the category of healing. That the people I come into contact with are sent to me in order that I can fill them with positivity and healing energy, so they can face whatever challenge lies before them.

Whether I am administering hands-on healing to alleviate a physical illness, or giving you a message from your family in spirit or from one of the many Guides, Guardian Guides, Angels or Arch-Angels that I am able to see, or even if I send you absent healing from many miles away . . . it all comes under the auspices of healing.

This gift has been given to me from the highest of all energy sources and I welcome the opportunity to share it with you. I have noticed in my work that when communication is involved, I become the equivalent of a telephone line between two dimensions; when physical healing is performed I become a transformer, to enable spiritual energy to pass quickly into the earthly body.

What I have learned is that LOVE is the key. It is through this invisible force that everything flourishes. It is the nourishment necessary for our spiritual growth. We cannot prove love's existence but we can feel it. In the same way, it is possible there are other realities far beyond our grasp or understanding.

So many people glibly state that there is no such thing as the spirit world. Well, I say to those people: prove that it does *not* exist.

Prologue

My husband Richard and I arrived at Dublin's Sunshine 106.8 radio station in Bray, to be serenaded by howling winds and pelted with rain. The radio station was based in a small, plain industrial unit, but it's the magic created inside it that inspires everyone to tune in in search of familiar voices and music.

As we entered the building, I was so excited to be arriving to prepare for my very own, first of a kind, *Helen Parry-Jones' Sunday Session*. Like any budding celebrity I had my entourage with me, all eager to offer their advice when the broadcast began; however, my backup was from the realms of spirit and quite invisible to the Sunshine staff who were already hard at work.

The two-storey warehouse was filled with sound-proof studio booths plus an open-plan area for admin and technical teams. The whole place seemed to buzz with youthful energy as shows were being prepared or going out live on air.

After welcoming smiles from the receptionists, we climbed up a wooden spiral staircase to the top floor where we met glamorous Andrea Hayes, a regular voice on radio and television, and best-known for being the presenter of the highly successful *Animal A&E*.

While other people might concentrate on securing their own fame and fortune, Andrea is a special soul, spiritual in her own right, who at every opportunity tries to help other people excel in what they do best. In my case that was bringing the gift of spiritual healing in its many forms to a mainstream radio audience.

Andrea is a true professional in all that she does and I was so grateful that she was now helping me to mould the programme into shape as 'running orders' and 'time radio schedules' were all new to me: there was so much to learn and so little time available.

Before we began Andrea organised the ritual mugs of tea, courtesy of Karen, producer of the Lynsey Dolan breakfast show, who kindly found the least wobbly chair for me to sit on before she went downstairs on tea duty. There was no standing on ceremony in this office. Instead all the staff, whatever their job title, pitched in and did whatever had to be done.

The steep, narrow spiral staircase leading to the upstairs studios was pretty hard to negotiate in flat shoes and with two hands free for balance. So the sight of the very slim and beautiful Karen tippy-toeing up the wooden risers in her ultra-high-heeled shoes, while also balancing three mugs of boiling hot tea, was worthy of a place on YouTube!

As Karen gingerly negotiated the last of the spiral steps, she said, 'Phew! I didn't think I was going to make it this time.' We all laughed and it certainly seemed to break the ice. What was meant to be a serious meeting about the content of the programme, quickly developed into a girlie teatime chat about my spiritual work. Karen offered me her hand, to introduce herself formally, and that's when the spiritual explosion happened!

'Oh, my goodness, Karen,' I exclaimed. 'You really do need to speak to me.'

She looked puzzled, but as it was the first time the lovely girl had ever been exposed to my work, or to me, Andrea smiled knowingly and said, 'Don't worry, Helen is just picking up some messages for you.'

Some time before this Andrea's dear father had died and had communicated through me with her, confirming that he was indeed still alive in spirit. Andrea knew at first hand how accurate the messages I passed on could be. I believe it was her true belief in the spirit world and the faith she had in me that motivated her to make sure this new radio show became a success.

As we all sat down, huddled in a girlie circle around the office desk, my spiritual entourage were jumping for joy at the prospect of speaking to Karen. This always happens when I meet people in need: the spirit world has an uncanny knack of helping in whatever way it feels is required, no matter where I am or what else I am doing.

This spiritual outpouring of healing has been part of my daily life for as far back as I can remember. Like the biblical verse says: 'Ask and ye shall receive.' So when we are troubled in our daily life and have a true desire for guidance, our guides in spirit will always offer support. Sometimes it doesn't come in quite the parcel we would like . . . but that's another subject, for another time.

The conversation soon developed into a full-blown discussion of my work and the way I handle it. Our laughter soon aroused interest from the other people in the office and it wasn't long before a general furore of chatter erupted. Despite many people asking me for messages, the spirits were determined to single out Karen as the main recipient. It was Andrea who eventually called time-out. She and I were due to start our radio session together within the next hour, so Karen was allowed to have a quick ten minutes alone with me, and Andrea shooed all the other spectators away so as to give us some privacy.

My spiritual entourage suggested that I give Karen a sort of mini-sitting and that we should record it for use in the programme – calling the segment 'Out and About with Helen Parry-Jones'. A fabulous idea!

Karen was delighted by the prospect of having some time alone with me, although she did admit to being a little nervous. I explained what my Guides had suggested and she agreed that it was a good idea to tape the mini-sitting as she was only too pleased to showcase my work on radio. We moved to a quieter area, which was a feat in itself. However, what happened next changed Karen's life and that of her family in such a wonderful way.

Sam, my ever-faithful Guardian Guide, very kindly brought members of Karen's family from spirit to communicate with me. They explained that her nana was ill in hospital with a serious chest complaint. In fact, it was so serious the doctors were doubtful she could recover from such a severe bout of infection, especially as she had the underlying condition of emphysema. I felt really sad for Karen as her nana obviously meant the world to her, so I offered to send some of my absent healing to her directly.

'What's absent healing, Helen?' she asked.

'Absent healing is when you receive spiritual healing though the healer is not physically present with you. I become a little like a radio broadcasting station,' I explained. 'I send out healing energy waves, and the person receiving them becomes like a radio set as the waves reach them and trigger the healing to take place. Even though I won't be there in person with your nana, don't underestimate the power of absent healing. The positive physical and emotional changes can be as dramatic as if I were there in person.'

Karen seemed relieved to hear her nana might find some respite, having heard only that morning that her grandmother's condition was worsening.

Listening to my Guide Sam, I relayed to her an update of her grandmother's condition after the absent healing. 'Your nana will soon come out of hospital, but her condition is still serious. Don't waste time. When she comes out, do all the things you need to do with her.'

Karen was amazed. 'How did you even know she was in hospital? My mother will be so pleased to hear you sent some healing to Nana.' Tears had started to trickle down Karen's face and her eyes were red-rimmed from crying – not at all the composed, professional look most people in the office were used to seeing when they looked at her as she was always beautifully groomed. 'Oh, Helen!' she continued. 'Thank you so much.'

With my next intake of breath, I started to talk about her work and personal life. Each new message caused Karen's jaw to drop in disbelief. Her other grandmother, on her father's side, then popped in and Karen was shocked to the core as this grandmother in spirit relayed details of her own death five years before.

When I had finished Karen stood up and hugged and hugged me, telling me how wonderful our impromptu consultation had been. She felt it had charged her with a positive new energy and filled her with so much happiness. She couldn't believe the accuracy of the information.

What was particularly interesting was that I had mentioned to her that I could see her being filmed on TV in connection with health but on a natural level, maybe something to do with fitness. She gasped as it had been a closely guarded secret that only she and a production crew knew about, but she had in fact just been chosen to appear on *Celebrity Salon*. I could see why because of her Demi Moore-style looks.

Afterwards Andrea listened to the recording and was captivated.

'Oh, that's fantastic!' Andrea smiled, when she heard how positive Karen now felt. 'We'll have to let the listeners hear that. It will show them what Helen can do when they invite her to their place in the "Out and About" segment.'

Andrea then leaped to her feet and rushed my Dictaphone over to Dave, the technical wizard at the station, to make sure my meeting with Karen was transferred on to the station's digital equipment for broadcasting later. If the corporate world could bottle Andrea's efficiency and energy, believe me, there wouldn't be a recession right now!

We were soon gathered back around the meeting table. Richard had joined us as this time we had to discuss the 'promo' for the show: that's the little advert that is broadcast during the day to promote the show. As Andrea played it to us, we both noticed it didn't specifically say I was a healer or what I actually did. It made no open reference to the fact I was going to offer live spiritual communication and healing on air.

'Good point,' Andrea conceded when we raised it. 'We have a problem. It's called censorship. Unfortunately we have our hands tied.'

Such statements really are like a red rag to a bull, especially to Richard.

'What? We can't say the simple words "Helen is a healer"! Ridiculous!' he fumed.

But it was an obstacle we were all too familiar with – see my Note on Censorship at the back of this book for an indication of the difficulties many healers and empathists face in reaching a wider audience. Now that I had been given my own platform on radio in the form of *The Sunday Session with Helen Parry-Jones*, my objective was to reach out to as many people as possible and tell them how the spirit world appears to me, and how the wonderful gifts of healing I have inherited can help so many people in need.

I checked my watch and saw my show was due to begin in ten minutes. 'Relax,' Andrea had advised, so I closed my eyes and started to do an absent healing on myself as the walk up the spiral staircase had triggered my back pain. I'd had an accident about four years before, slipping on the bathroom tiles and landing hard on my back. The fall was so severe it broke two vertebrae and slipped two discs. The surgeon I consulted at the time said I was lucky not to have been paralysed. After twelve months of home rest and hours of absent healing, I managed to recuperate enough to return to work. However, some days are still so bad I rely on my absent healing sessions to keep myself fit and mobile.

I blanked out all the noise and distraction of the busy office around me and thoughts of previous landmark occasions flickered through my mind. All I could hear was the hypnotic effect of the wind howling outside and the drumming of the rain on the corrugated roof: with no effort at all I was entering into a healing trance. As I relived an event from my past, I was still aware of Andrea and Karen preparing for the forthcoming show while in my mind I wandered back in time . . .

In the here and now Andrea called to Karen: 'Be ready in three minutes, please!'

In my mind, I'd travelled back twenty-one years and was listening to a tinny voice from the Chester Gateway Theatre's dressing-room intercom.

'Three minutes, please, Miss Parry-Jones . . . Three minutes!'

It had just dawned on me, like a bolt of lightning, that there were people actually sitting in the auditorium out there who had paid good money for their tickets to see me. Events were unfolding just as Sam, my spirit guide, had predicted in the late-1970s.

Going in front of any large audience is always a leap of faith, especially when it is live and you don't know what you are about to say, but I was about to step on to the stage and offer the general public proof of survival after death. It might very possibly be the first time in their lives they had experienced such an event, so I prayed and prayed that my visitors from the spirit world would not let me down at this crucial moment.

Then as now Richard was with me in the dressing room, pumping me up with his energy and enthusiasm. He introduced me on stage and ran around the audience taking the radio-mic so that anyone I needed to pass a message to could reply for all to hear.

This was a special night for me because although I had appeared in town halls and large auditoriums, this was the first traditional theatre I had worked in. The prospect set my heart thumping in my chest.

For me the Gateway Theatre was in a different professional league to anything I had done before. There was a team of highly qualified assistants and lighting engineers buzzing around, all of whom took their job very seriously. I think they found it strange pandering to the needs of a spiritual empathist, but they treated me with great respect. In fact I believe I was *the* first spiritual lady to grace the stage at The Chester Gateway Theatre.

Now it was time for Richard to leave the dressing room and take up position on stage for my grand entrance. As always, before leaving me he told me how beautiful I looked, and kissed me tenderly on the lips for moral support. As he walked through the door he turned quickly back to face me and gave me a smile. 'Break a leg!' he shouted, his eyes held fixed on mine for a one second hold of deep love.

Nervousness started to take hold of me. Get yourself together and be strong, I told myself, remembering the advice that Sam my Guide had always given me. I told myself I had nothing to prove. My faith in myself, my Guides, Angels, and my God-given gifts, was as strong as ever.

It seems to me that giving a message from a spirit loved one is as valuable and important as giving actual hands-on spiritual healing, because if a spiritual communication brings peace to the recipient, and allows their life to move forward positively, that in itself is another form of healing.

Yet doubt crept into my mind like a hidden dagger. What if the messages didn't come through . . . what if I froze?

'Get thee behind me, Satan!' I murmured under my breath.

The attention of the audience was focused straight ahead on the centre of the stage when I walked in from the back of the auditorium behind them, something they had not expected. They seemed openly surprised when I touched as many hands as I could before ascending to the stage amidst rapturous applause.

No going back now, I told myself. I was on my own . . . but hopefully not for long. The applause from the audience sounded like a thousand galloping horses.

Messages were soon flooding through to the theatre audience. As usual they were full of natural humour, love and compassion for all the people present. I was able to give them the best and truest gift . . . the knowledge that life in spirit continues for those loved ones who have gone before us. Are messages a form of healing? Yes, I do believe they are.

My peace was disturbed as Andrea's bubbly voice announced that it was time for us to go into the studio. I opened my eyes slowly as though waking from a deep meditation.

'Helen! Are you OK? You were deep in thought there for a while. It's time . . . we should go into studio,' Andrea said with a hint of trepidation in her voice. 'The big guns are listening,' she continued. 'I don't usually get nervous, but I am tonight. Something wonderful is about to happen . . . I can feel it all around us.'

We walked into the studio together, putting on our head-phones in anticipation; the 10 o'clock news had just finished and our music intro started – 'Calling All Angels' by an American group called Train. We smiled at each other with a sisterly love that had developed in recent months, and as the intro faded Andrea introduced *The Sunday Session with Helen Parry-Jones* to its Irish audience.

I glanced down at the show's running order, typed out on a sheet of paper before me, just a blur of words. Not a problem – you can't script the spirit world.

And then I thought: At last, Sam has arrived! There could be no show without him. And Andrea's voice slipped into her natural broadcasting tones: 'Tell me, Helen, how did all this start?'

1
A Gift Or a Curse?

My earliest recollection of being different, having what you might consider a special ability, was at the age of four when I would visit my Granddad Joseph and Nana Ada's house. Despite its being a pet-free home, every time I went to visit my grandparents, there would be a fat ginger cat and a black-and-white moggy curled up on the sofa. Sometimes I wanted to play with them, but they would run away into the kitchen or up the stairs; sometimes they would disappear altogether. Whenever I spoke about the cats to Nana, she would laugh lovingly and tell me: 'Oh! Don't worry about them, Helen my dear, that's just Tigger and Arthur. They were Nana's cats which died years ago. I'm glad they are still here – I feel better for having them around me.'

Home for me at that time was a ground-floor flat in an area called Hoole, on the outskirts of Chester. The flats had two upper storeys, gardens to the front and a back yard, but unfortunately none of the neighbours looked after either area.

When I was sent out to play in the concrete yard at home, I remember on many occasions sitting on a piece of old linoleum (which apparently protected my bare legs from the cold cement), and watching all sorts of different cats and dogs in spirit playing alongside my very own dog and companion, Gyp, a crossbreed bearded collie, which had been part of the family longer than I had.

Gyp was a big softie: a grandfatherly presence thanks to his bearded, whiskery face. One day I asked my mum if she knew the names of the other two dogs that happened to be there with him. I received a blank stare from her, and was told not to be so silly as there were no dogs in the yard other than Gyp. On one occasion I remember insisting I could see some animals playing alongside him, and that's the first time I remember being scolded for telling lies.

So, from the outset, I found accepting who and what I was a bit of a dilemma. I soon learned that describing reality as I saw it to my mum and dad was likely to end in tears, as when I spoke about the people and pets I could see, my parents thought I was a liar, or at best a silly dreamer, and I risked being shouted at or made to go upstairs to my bedroom as a punishment for being naughty.

Even as an adult, knowing that you can see people others cannot is pretty daunting; accepting this ability in yourself from an early age is very difficult. It's not perceived as a wonderful gift, like having an ear for music and performing on the piano like a little princess while your parents look on adoringly, encouraging your every move. In fact, referring to my own special abilities was soon completely forbidden in our household.

In retrospect, my gift of healing must have been quite strong even back then as my mother often commented to people that she couldn't believe how many of the neighbours' dogs and cats would gather around me when I was playing outside.

On one particular day I remember her taking a photograph of me in the yard with two stray dogs lying beside me. That might sound like a pretty mundane picture, but these two were villainous, snarling creatures that would terrify everyone in the vicinity and occasionally bite the postman – just for fun! I can remember that day like it was yesterday, despite being so young at the time. It is locked in my mind for eternity.

An adult now, I understand that the two stray dogs must also have felt the presence of the spirit animals for ever at my side. And they were responding to the healing energy I was transmitting through my displays of affection, which in turn would have calmed them down. Also, I probably fulfilled a need in them for attention as they were starved of love. They rolled over and let me rough and tumble them as though they were puppies. These two savage canines would even stay still long enough to allow me to dress them up in my dolls' clothes before I would make them share tea and biscuits with me from my little tea set. They lapped up all the love and attention I had to offer them.

My mother used to call me (totally unaware of her statement) *their* guardian angel. Pretty ironic don't you think?!

I was born at Chester Royal Infirmary, to Judith and Colin Sparrow. My father was in the Army at the time, serving his country, so my mum cared for me for the first couple of years of my life at my Nana Ada's house, her family home. Although my dad visited my mother and me at the hospital when I was born, apparently it wasn't until I was nine months old that I met him for the second time.

My father was always very close to his own mother and we would often, at his insistence, go and visit her on Sunday afternoons. To be honest, I didn't much like going to Grandma Lilly's. (Everybody else called her Ethel, though she was christened Lilly

Ethel Levinia. But for some reason I called her Lilly, and to me she was always Grandma Lilly.) For starters, we lived on the outskirts of Chester in one direction, and she lived right on the other side. It seemed to take ages on the bus to actually get there. And when we did visit, I used to have this overwhelming feeling that Grandma didn't like my mum and me very much. One Sunday I remember telling Mum: 'You know Grandma doesn't like us, Mummy.' On that occasion, although Mum told me not to be so silly, at least I wasn't called a liar!

Another reason I didn't like visiting my grandma's was because there was always a man sitting there in Army officer's uniform, usually in a chair directly opposite my grandma's. He told me his name was Stanley and that he was my granddad. I couldn't really understand at first why Grandma Lilly and my dad and mum never spoke to him, especially as he was my granddad. Perhaps that's why I never really said much to him either. Eventually my mind associated the cats at Nana Ada's with Stanley at Grandma's: they had all died – and I could see them. I learned some years later that Granddad Stanley, who had achieved the rank of Major, died six months before I was born, from tuberculosis at the age of 53.

Around this time I noticed another man who seemed to be around me wherever I went. No matter where I was or what I was doing, he would be there in the background – just watching. I don't remember him speaking to me for a good while. In fact, I was rather glad he didn't, because I felt a little frightened of him. Firstly he was very tall, and secondly he was very black.

In and around Chester in the early 1960s, I can honestly say I can't remember ever seeing any other black men so I naturally thought he was the Bogeyman that my friends often spoke about. Sometimes at night I would see him watching me in my bedroom, and of course I would climb out of bed to find Mum and tell her:

'I feel frightened, Mummy, the Bogeyman is in my bedroom watching me sleep.'

You probably already know the response my mother gave to that: 'There's no such thing as the Bogeyman, Helen. Stop being so silly and go back to bed.'

But I wasn't being silly, and he was there in my bedroom. Why wouldn't anybody listen to me?

This large black spirit figure must have sensed when it was time for me to know more about him, and took the opportunity to speak to me one day when I was at my Auntie Joan's house.

Auntie Joan didn't have an inside toilet. Theirs was outside, next to the coal-shed, just as in thousands of other tenement houses at that time. I spent my penny, pulled at the long piece of string hanging to the side of the cistern, and left the toilet cubicle . . . and there, several feet in front of me, was this large black figure sitting on the kitchen step. There were only two steps, so as he sat there with his backside so low to the ground, his knees seemed to be taking up all the available space. I had no option but to walk past him to make my way back inside. The man smiled, showing a remarkable display of white teeth, perfectly graduated so as to give him the most flawless of smiles. Oddly, I didn't feel frightened. In fact, I had a strange feeling I was meeting an old friend, despite the fact I didn't know who or what he was. I stood there, waiting to climb the steps to the back door.

'Hello, Helen – I am here as your friend!'

His deep voice was gentle and full of warmth; he spoke with an accent I had never heard before. He went on to explain that he wasn't the Bogeyman but my Guardian Guide. He formally introduced himself and said I could call him Sam.

'Hello, Sam,' I whispered with as much friendliness as I could muster when speaking to a stranger for the very first time.

'Don't fear me, chile. I am here to protect you,' this large black Sam answered.

I stood still and listened closely while he spoke. It seemed to me the most natural thing in the world.

Sam went on to say I was to think of him as a teacher, helping me to learn new subjects, like at school. He said he knew I wouldn't follow everything he was saying right now, but as I grew up I would understand more and more of what he was trying to teach me about the world and people of spirit.

I asked him: 'What are spirit people?'

It was then that Sam taught me my first lesson. 'Well, Helen, my chile . . . they are people who once lived here but have died and are now living somewhere else, somewhere often called the spirit world.'

He then continued his first lesson by telling me that everyone has a Guardian Guide, like he was to me, but that these should not be confused with Angels. Each Guide's purpose was to assist, educate and protect their ward, leading them to a higher spiritual awareness. In most cases people couldn't see their Guides but they were always there, standing by them. He explained that there are many much more powerful energies in spirit, ranging from Guardian Guides like him to Higher Guides, Angels, and ultimately Arch-Angels. He went on to tell me that Arch-Angels are Seraphim who are linked to the highest of all energy, the source. Our families who have passed in spirit are on a very basic level of understanding, but I was very different apparently. Not only could I see him, I would come to understand in time the reason why I had my gifts.

In conclusion of this first lesson, Sam added: 'I will visit and teach you more when I feel it is right for you.'

I tried to understand and remember everything he had said, but felt that it was not necessary to worry as he would always be there to help me find answers whenever I might need them. There was one specific question on my mind, one that troubled me considerably: 'Why do my mummy and daddy say I do not see you?'

Sam gave me a kind smile then, one I knew meant that he cared for me in a very special way: 'It is because they do not understand your gift and fear what they do not understand. One day they will learn there is nothing to fear other than fear itself.'

When Sam stood up he towered over me. I noticed he was wearing a long robe, made from a smooth, light-textured fabric that hung loosely from his body. I felt comforted to hear that I was under his protection. He waved his hand as if to tell me to go to my family. I opened the door and ran in as if nothing had happened, even though deep inside I was trembling after finding out about my new friend. How could I ever explain to my mum about the person I had just spoken to?

Over time, I have grown to think of Sam as a good, honest and loyal friend, one who has only ever shown me kindness and understanding, and has explained to me the complexities of life, here and in spirit. He explained that each person has the ability to have some consciousness of spiritual awareness. You see, we are all sensitive to seeing and hearing spirit to some degree, but most of us are taught from a very early age to block out our natural spiritual abilities.

I learned very quickly that my Guide Sam radiated true love. During one of his lessons, Sam advised that soon Angels would come calling on me. When they did, I would learn that it was one of their roles actually to administer love by bathing those who came in contact with them in floods of affection, asking nothing in return. He explained to me that Angels have a special way to touch your heart, which is why people often feel uplifted in their presence.

On reflection, actually seeing my first angelic-looking spiritual visitor other than Sam happened around my sixth birthday. I went on holiday with my mum's sister's family: Auntie Joan, Uncle Bob, their two boys David and Peter, and their daughter Debbie, who was a little younger than me. I loved being with my Auntie Joan's family. The boys were always playing because they had loads of toys and Uncle Bob just adored me, treating me like another daughter.

I didn't see my own dad much as he now worked for the County Council as a plumber's apprentice by day, and by night as a barman, in The Piper's Arms in Hoole. We always seemed to be very poor but money was never a problem for Uncle Bob as he worked as a foundryman in Shotton steel works; in those days, that was a very well-paid job and the foundrymen always seemed to have plenty to spend.

It seemed a long drive from Auntie Joan's house in Queensferry, on the Welsh border, to our holiday destination, the Sunnyvale Holiday Camp in sunny Rhyl. How exciting it was when we eventually drove through the town. We passed a big open-air roller-skating rink. There was an expansive harbour filled with all types of boats; a lake with a little train going around it; a massive, brightly coloured fairground making all sorts of loud noises that were music to a child's ears . . . and it all smelled absolutely delicious. You could almost eat the air which was full of the scents of doughnuts, candy floss, ice-cream, chips and hot dogs: sugar and grease – in just the right proportions! We had found a children's paradise.

Our journey continued over a large iron bridge and within minutes we found the holiday camp's entrance. It seemed such an adventure, walking about trying to find our two chalets. Actually they were more like little garden sheds, but I thought they were absolutely fantastic. We four kids had one of our own, and Auntie and Uncle had the other.

Before we'd even unpacked our brown cardboard suitcases, I made my Uncle Bob roll up his trousers and take Debbie and me to the paddling pool where a big plastic elephant sprayed water all over us. I remember thinking life couldn't get much better than this!

By bedtime Debbie and I were tucked up in our bunk beds. The boys were allowed to play cards with each other and listen to the radio in the adults' chalet next-door, while their parents went out for their nightly drink. It was the boys' job to keep an eye on us girls.

I must have fallen asleep for a while because when I woke up the room was substantially darker. The boys must still have been in the next-door chalet as I could hear the radio playing, but I was a little disorientated and wanted my mum. I started to cry. My cries soon turned to sobs. I remember sliding down from the top bunk and wandering around the chalet. I climbed on to a chair and peeled back the net curtains, to see if I could see Auntie Joan or Uncle Bob outside. I knocked on the wall to try and make the boys hear me. Finally I tried to fiddle with the main door, but it was locked from the outside. Debbie was still fast asleep so I sat on a plain wooden chair facing the door, resigned to the fact that no one was going to come. My cries subsided to quiet sobs.

The room was dim rather than dark as the summer evening was retaining the light for as long as it possibly could. Gradually the chalet started to fill with a low blue light, rather like an old fluorescent tube being switched on. I noticed that the source of this blue light seemed to be coming from behind me, so I turned around and saw a young woman standing there. How did she get in when I couldn't get out? I could see the outline of her body through a transparent layer of some sort of shimmering material, gold-like in colour but translucently so, that sheathed her body from shoulder to floor. She wore simple flowers in her hair, which was blonde and long. She was angelic-looking.

She spoke to me then, simple words but reassuring: 'They won't be long. They're not far away, they will be here soon.'

As she moved her arms, her gown shimmered and the room became filled with a strong white light that seemed to radiate from her body.

I was transfixed when I saw this bright light and it took all my fear away. I sensed this woman was different from others in spirit I had seen. For some reason she felt purposeful and loving, but not like any love I had received from my family. I have now learned a Guide of such brightness is from the higher realms within the world of spirit. Some people with less spiritual under-standing might even believe she was an Angel. Love from such a high-up Guide cannot be compromised in any way; it is pure and clear, it has no boundaries. It is an endless, engulfing sensation of total safety and entire purity.

In that room I felt safe and secure. I felt loved.

Aware of the sound of a key in the door latch, I instinctively turned to face the door and the light disappeared. The door opened and Auntie Joan came in, looking surprised to find me sitting upright on a wooden chair, facing the door. I tried to tell her about the woman, but Auntie Joan was adamant that nobody could get in. The boys came in then and she told them off for not hearing me cry.

Soon we were all put to bed and sleep overcame me.

At such a young age I obviously didn't know where my visitors originated or why I was being visited. No wonder I found it hard to express all that I could see and hear. On reflection, the gift was no doubt inherited at least partly from my Nana Ada: she was a gifted intuitive herself, and felt a need to nurture the bigger gift that seemed to be revealing itself in me.

Our back yard felt huge to me when I was small. A wire fence cordoned off the concrete yard outside from the allotments sprawling all the way down to the railway lines that ran along the bottom of the communal land. I was forbidden to think about visiting the train lines, and absolutely forbidden from going anywhere near the fence. Looking back, I can imagine how worried my mother must constantly have been at the danger that lay just beyond that wire enclosure.

My parents were as poor as church mice; my dad's wage was so low that my mum never had any money in her pocket and half the time would go without food so as to provide for me. Of course, I didn't know that at the time. It was only years later in conversation with her that I learned these facts.

She would walk for miles into the city centre, propelling my push-chair until her arms ached, just to save bus fares. Another piece of information I later learned.

Even so, despite our meagre resources I remember her cleaning up the back yard and planting rose trees outside in the front, given by an elderly neighbour, in the vain hope of creating a more cheerful and happy home environment for herself and the other residents of our block of flats.

She could not work full-time in those days because she had me to care for, but she would often take in ironing or clean neighbours' houses to earn a little extra for us.

To my childish eyes our home never looked like a block of flats, but more like one enormous house. As a young child I never really gave the other people living there much thought; I just assumed it was 'our' house. Most of them must have been out working all day as I never saw anyone. I suppose by the time they returned home, I would have been tucked up in bed. The days were peaceful, with only my mother and me and the odd neighbour for company, it seemed like we were the only people in the world.

Next-door to our block lived a lady called Phyllis, an Irishwoman with a strange but lovely accent, who in my opinion lived in a much nicer house. I would often comment to my mother that her house was prettier because it was smaller than ours.

Although she was not a relative, my mum said I had to call her Auntie Phyllis. My mum and she were best friends and we would often spend time at her house next-door. I would play for hours with her children when they were home from school. Playing with her children was like having a football team of friends, as she had so many of them.

Unlike at our 'house', she had a back garden that sprawled all the way down past the allotments, right to the bottom end where the train tracks began. A high fence made of thick wire and concrete posts contained her garden, so my mum was always happy for me to go there as she felt I was safe.

Popping into Phyllis' house was a regular event for my mum, and they would chat for hours over cups of tea and cigarettes. Auntie Philly was always so kind to me and always had biscuits in her biscuit barrel – something we never used to have. In my eyes, hers was a life of sheer luxury.

Auntie Philly would always buy some shopping from the mobile van that travelled door-to-door around our local streets. Back in the sixties these vans seemed to be on every estate as an alternative to the corner shops. Ours resembled a well-stocked pantry on wheels and, when it stopped in the neighbourhood, the ladies would flock inside to buy bread, cakes, pies, crisps and biscuits.

Normally when the van visited my mother said we didn't need anything, which always left me feeling very disappointed. Auntie Philly, however, was different. She'd send her kids into the van for cake or bread, and if I were visiting hers at the time, she would let me buy something as well: she was always so kind to me. I still remember the sweet sugary smell of jam doughnuts wafting into my nostrils . . . heavenly.

In Phyllis' house there was always food around. If there wasn't cake on the table, she was making something on the stove to share: unlike my mum, she was always cooking. I absolutely loved it there – it was so friendly and homely.

I remember one particular day walking in through the door and seeing Auntie Philly ironing in the kitchen. Without hesitation or forethought, I said out loud: 'Gosh, Auntie Philly, why is all your hair going to fall out?'

When I heard messages in those days, they came into my head like a thought or a picture and I would repeat word for word what I could hear. Nowadays I tend to listen first and decide what best to say, in case it compromises someone. When you are young, you obviously don't think like that; it's just an uncensored, natural outpouring.

Phyllis stared at me, stunned at first, and then laughed out loud. With little regard for what I had just said, she told me to get a biscuit and sit inside with the other children while they watched *Blue Peter*.

It wasn't until two weeks later that I realised what my message had been about.

We heard a loud, piercing scream coming from next-door. My mum told me to stay inside our house as she went to see what was happening. A few minutes later Mum rushed back home and told me to stay with Peter, Phyllis' eldest boy, while she ran to the telephone box on the corner.

We hadn't a phone in those days and the nearest one was a good walk away, at the end of the road. I remember my mum running in sheer panic, as fast as her legs could carry her, to reach that red phone box.

What seemed like a long time later, the ambulance eventually arrived outside and all the neighbours stood huddled around the garden gate as they watched Phyllis being carried away flat on a stretcher in the back of the white ambulance.

It was all very upsetting because my mum and all of Phyllis' children were crying. I was infected by the emotion and started to cry as well. Phyllis' husband had been called home from his job, working for the local council on the roads, and been told to go straight to Chester Infirmary. My mum wept floods of tears as she ushered all us children back inside the house while the ambulance drove away.

It was a strange week and eerily quiet in the yard. Family members had taken Phyllis' children into their own homes while their mother recovered in hospital.

Eventually, about a week later, she returned home in yet another ambulance. She was still very poorly, according to my mum, and I was told not to go around trying to see any of the children as they were still staying with relatives until Phyllis was completely better. Her mother had travelled all the way from Dublin in Ireland to look after her. I remember thinking about what my mother had told me of the harrowing journey across the Irish Sea.

I learned that Phyllis had suffered a massive electric shock while ironing, as a result of a faulty cable. Apparently a huge surge of electricity hit her like a brick wall and threw her across the room. The doctors said she was lucky to be alive, but unfortunately afterwards she lost all her hair through alopecia because of the shock.

I really didn't understand what had happened. I didn't understand the seriousness of her injuries. I didn't understand why all my friends had disappeared.

Although in time Phyllis did recover, she never regained her lovely dark hair in its full glory, and always wore wigs from then on to hide the patches where it had become thin and not grown back properly.

Some time later her whole family decided to move back to their homeland, so Phyllis could be nearer to her mammy. In retrospect, she did seem to lose her pep after the accident, and her lack of hair seemed to have dented her usual self-confidence.

When they actually left, it was a sad day for me. I will never forget the large van leaving, full of chairs, the sofa, and all their belongings. The worst part came when I waved goodbye to Peter, the eldest boy, his nose pressed against the window of the car. He cried. We waved to each other. The car followed the van like a hearse down the road. This was a forever goodbye. I was heart-broken. I cried for a week.

I kept telling my mother I had special friends she couldn't see . . . why wouldn't she listen to me? Why wouldn't Auntie Philly listen? If only they had paid attention to what my spirit friends were saying, none of this need have happened and I would still be going next door to play. I felt guilty that my friend Peter and Auntie Philly had left. IF ONLY, I kept saying to myself.

After this incident I noticed more spirit people started to visit me. I remember they would come into my bedroom at night and keep me awake for hours, talking about families living in the neighbourhood. When I tried to tell my mother about this, she flew into one of her rages and started to huff and puff in exasperation.

On one particular occasion when I'd spoken to an old man called Jack from the spirit world, he told me he'd kept birds when he was alive and that he'd lived just up the road, in the house with the green door. He said his son had now taken over his aviary so I pestered my dad to take me up the road to visit the man with the large aviary and pigeon coops at the back of his house. I remember holding my dad's hand and him knocking on a green wooden door. A man came to answer it and my dad asked if we could have a look at all his birds.

The man was very welcoming and took us through to the outside yard where he kept them. After having a good look at all the colourful birds, I noticed the owner talking to my dad and he was holding a pigeon. The man kindly offered to let me stroke the bird, and as I ran my fingers gently down its wing, I told him that I had been speaking to his dad, Jack, and that this particular pigeon was going to be a prize bird. Although the man gave me a beaming smile, my father gave me one of his scolding looks.

This was around the same time in my childhood that I started to hear noises in the middle of the night from the corner of my bedroom ceiling. I would wake up and start crying, and my mum would have to get up and see to me or I would go and disturb her. When she asked me why I was continually doing this, I explained to her that every night an old lady would knock on the corner of my ceiling with what seemed to be some sort of pole, and shout my name. I don't know which was more disturbing to me: the old lady making the noise, or my mum's anger as once again she seemed to disbelieve what I was trying to tell her.

It happened so often and disturbed my sleep to such a degree that I eventually demanded not to sleep in my bedroom. Strangely, whenever my mum lay next to me there, the lady did not knock. That's why Mum thought I was imagining the noises, because she never heard them.

For a while, Mum put up with my constant complaining and nightly tears. Eventually, fed up of these regular upsets, she shouted at me one night that if I didn't stop imagining this lady calling out to me, she would take me to the doctor's for him to sort me out.

Despite being so young, I knew when I was being threatened,

and my mother not believing what I was saying seemed very cruel to me.

Undeterred, I reiterated the same information to her, over and over again, repeating that it was the woman upstairs who kept waking me up as she was continually asking me to fetch her things and to help her out of bed. It scared me that the old lady incessantly shouted out my name in the middle of the night, and I hated the fact that my mother didn't listen to me. I constantly heard the old woman droning, on and on. I had images of a wicked witch from my fairy-tale books and thought that at any moment a clawed hand was going to come through the ceiling and grab me.

I think the main reason I cried was not because the woman might be evil, but because I didn't understand what was happening to me. At a time when I should have been able to turn to my mother for security and support, she didn't listen. I felt desperately alone. On one particular night I became so frustrated with her as she tucked me back up in bed as if nothing were wrong, telling me that the noises were all in my imagination, that after she'd left the room I begged Sam to make the noises go away. To be fair, he instantly darted upstairs to where the woman was moaning and silenced her.

This same pattern continued for weeks until finally I managed to convince my mother that maybe it wasn't just in my imagination. She decided that she would pluck up courage to confront whoever lived above us . . . and give them what for!

My mother told me that a man lived in the flat directly above us. She'd seen him leaving one day as she was coming home from taking me to school. He always seemed to be coming back in the morning around ten so she thought his job must be a night one.

With a little bit of planning, Mum made sure she was looking out for our upstairs neighbour at his coming home time. Rather like an ambush, she stopped him just as he was about to go upstairs to his flat. He looked weary from his night's work but not unfriendly, so she felt it was the right time to discover what lay at the bottom of all of the banging and shouting.

'You live directly above us . . .' she began in her usual forceful manner.

'Yes, I believe I do,' he said. 'I'm just coming home from working nights.'

Mum continued with her interrogation. 'Well, I am Mrs Sparrow, I live down here . . .' She paused and then said in one long breath, 'The thing is . . . would you please ask the old lady who lives with you to stop pestering my little girl? Every night she keeps knocking on the floor and calling out my daughter's name. Helen's bedroom is directly underneath hers and she is being kept awake and becoming so nervous she can't sleep. The lady just keeps banging on the floor and calling out her name, night after night.'

With that the man stumbled a little and sat down on the steps leading to the upper floor. He looked pale and dazed, as if he had been given a terrible shock.

'What do you mean, Mrs Sparrow? There is no one else living in my flat. I'm sorry that your daughter has been kept awake, but it can't possibly be my mother. She died many years ago. She did live upstairs with me before she died, and was housebound in bed for a year or so prior to her death. But there's no one else living with me now so it must be someone else, in one of the other flats. Anyway, I work nights. I only arrive home at this time in the morning. I don't know what you're talking about.'

My mother's mind went into overdrive. How would I even know about the old lady? She had died before we'd moved in. My mother didn't even know this man had had an invalid mother, let alone that she had died. No one close to her had ever spoken about it.

They both stared at each other, totally bemused . . . and then turned and looked at me. I was standing watching the two of them while they stood there dumbstruck. I had walked home from school, opening the heavy iron gate – on my own, crossing a busy main road – on my own, and finding my way back – on my own. I was just a small child.

How did I do that? How did I even know how to find my home? And how did I do it just when my mother was talking to our upstairs neighbour?

My shocked mother didn't know what to say, she was literally speechless. So was the man from upstairs. They both stared at me. I don't know whether it was because of the revelation about the man's mother, me walking home on my own or the fact that I turned up unexpectedly when they were talking about me, but I will never forget the expressions of surprise on their faces.

My mum was furious with the school for not noticing I had gone, but I told her not to worry. Sam was walking with me, making sure I got back safely. I cheerfully announced to her, very matter-of-fact: 'I've had my milk, I've had my biscuits and I have had enough of school!'

My mum's face said it all. This was too much for her to handle. She scooped me up, left the neighbour outside and took me into our living room where she plonked me in front of the television, sat down in the armchair opposite, put her hands over her eyes and sobbed uncontrollably.

I suppose in such a small community word travels about strange goings-on! Soon Mrs Sparrow's daughter started to become the talk of the neighbourhood.

A day or two later, my mum made an appointment for us to

see the family GP, Dr Cornforth. His practice was in the heart of Chester, which meant I had to have a day off school to go and see him. It never felt like I was going to see a doctor as his surgery was in a beautiful Georgian terraced house. The few times we had consulted him before was for general coughs and once measles, so I didn't really know him. I felt nervous, especially as my mum kept saying 'my friends' were all in my mind and that there were definitely no noises going on in the night.

As I walked into his surgery, I remember the smell of surgical spirit and the sight of ladies in white uniform. On meeting him I thought he was a nice man. In fact, he looked a bit like Father Christmas, but with a smaller beard. What's more he was Irish, just like Auntie Philly, so I liked him immediately as his melodic voice soothed the ears and made me think of my friend Peter, Auntie Philly's son. I wondered what Peter would be doing right now back in Ireland . . . Funny the things you think of in times of stress. While I was looking about I know my mum was talking to the doctor, but I wasn't listening to their conversation. What caught my eye was Sam, standing beside the doctor's desk, concentrating on my medical notes.

The doctor coughed loudly which caught my attention and then he looked my mum straight in the eye and said in a much louder voice: 'Now, Mrs Sparrow, I don't want you to say a word. I just want to speak to Helen alone. I am going to ask my nurse to come in and I will examine Helen and ask her some questions, then I will ask you to come back in and she can wait with Nurse outside in the waiting room.' I was surprised; no one had ever managed to silence my mother so quickly!

He asked me about my spirit friends and about the detailed conversations I had with my 'imaginary' people. After a little while he used his intercom to buzz through his nurse from another room, and when she came in she held up my dress while he listened to my chest on his, what I called at that time, 'earphones'.

After he had completed his tests he said in a brisk voice, like my teacher's, 'You go and sit outside in the waiting room, Helen, for one minute, while I chat to Mummy. Nurse Jenny will wait with you, OK?'

I didn't learn until I was much older that Dr Cornforth had had a long chat with my mother and told her he believed there were sometimes people with special gifts who could quite possibly see spirits and heal the sick. He said that although scientifically it was hard to prove, he felt I might have such an ability. He had tested me and I showed no signs of being delusional or mad so it was just possible that she had a very special child with a very special gift.

I am quite confident this was not something my mother had expected to hear, and definitely not from her well-respected doctor. She apparently had a big argument with him, saying that he needed to give me something to calm me down because I could not sleep, constantly kept awake by sounds from upstairs which no one else could hear.

He gave her a prescription for Phenobarbital to help me sleep, and said that as my parents were in so much distress and anxiety about this bewildering situation, he personally would apply to the council for special dispensation for us to be allocated a new house somewhere else.

I can still see my mother's face as she left the surgery, red and tearful in her sheer incomprehension of what he had said to her. Despite what the doctor had said, I knew that she was still in total denial about my abilities.

All I wanted was for my mum to put her arms around me and understand. I wanted my mum to accept and simply love me, no matter what. I felt as if I had a dreaded illness; as though my ability was something to be ashamed of. And, more to the point, that my own family was ashamed of me for having it. At least the doctor had been nice to me. He did not dismiss my friends as fantasy, but just asked me questions about them and smiled.

Once I was old enough to reminisce about my childhood, I realised that I'd never had a chance to thank Dr Cornforth personally for supporting me that day. He must have been a spiritually minded soul, to be so open-minded and forthright with his answers to my mother. His Irish heritage still held dear the notion of people having the gift of healing and spiritual sight, but in those days very few would have spoken out in such a candid way about a world they could not see. I am forever grateful for his understanding, the more so because he didn't brand me as delusional or anti-social. Without such understanding, another doctor might well have prescribed ECT, a barbaric technique then popular with the medical profession. The treatment involved sending a searing blast of electricity through the brain in order to alter behaviour in adults and children who proved difficult for their family to handle.

As good as his word, the doctor sent a letter to the council offices and about twelve months later my parents were offered a brand new council house on a new cityscape being built just outside the Chester city limits.

Although by now I was seeing spirit on a daily basis, with Sam's guidance I came to understand that I must not let wilful spirits tire me out by monopolising my attention. As in so many other areas of life, I had to learn to say no.

At heart I was still an ordinary little girl, despite having a very extraordinary ability; and that ordinary little girl loved receiving a present when the opportunity arose. A present of any description was not a common event in our house, so when my dad came home one day with a lovely yellow budgie, this bird meant the world to me. I called him Peter after my friend who had gone back to Ireland following Auntie Philly's accident. I loved my budgie. Apparently Jack's son, the man who lived behind the green door and had the coops filled with birds in his back yard, had asked my father if he could give me a gift because, after I'd passed on the message about the prize pigeon, it had won first prize in a competition.

We would often let Peter the budgie out of his cage at night to have a fly around, mainly because I would plead with my mother, saying that the bird needed to stretch its wings and feel free.

Peter had a bit of a routine and would start chirping around the same time every night, almost as if he knew we would let him out of his cage for a taste of freedom, even if he was still confined to the lounge. He would come out of his open cage door and fly around the room, resting on the curtain pelmets and occasionally landing on my dog Gyp's skull. When he did Gyp never moved a muscle, just allowed the bird to perch happily on top of his head.

It was like a cartoon, but harmony between dog and bird really did exist in our small home and this routine went on for a long time. Then one day I had been messing around, having some boisterous fun with Gyp. The dog was pretty active that day, bounding around the lounge while I rolled over, thinking it was a hilarious game to watch the dog find me as I hid behind the sofa. I thought it would be even more fun if I let the bird out of the cage to join in.

After I'd let Peter out of his cage, he flew around the lounge while Gyp and I played chase around the furniture. Unfortunately, on this occasion Peter landed on Gyp's nose and not his head. In a reflex action, Gyp jumped up and bit the little budgie and the bird fell to the floor dead.

I couldn't believe my eyes as Peter lay motionless, the dog

sniffing nervously around its lifeless body, cowering and whimpering when he realised he had done something wrong. I screamed for my mum, who came rushing in from outside. She didn't know whether to shout at me first, for letting the bird out of its cage, or to scold Gyp as she looked at the dead budgie on the carpet. Carefully picking up the little yellow fluffball, she said: 'I am so sorry, Helen my love, Peter's gone – he is dead.'

'No, no!' I screamed, sobbing my heart out. 'Peter can't die. Give him to me, Mum. Give him to me.'

I held Peter's limp body in my hands for a few seconds and felt a warm sensation tingling within me, the same warmth that filled my body whenever Sam stood near me. I cupped my hands, making a sphere around the bird. I didn't understand what was happening within me, but I couldn't help but feel a burning sensation go through my whole body. My hands in particular felt like they were on fire.

Astonishingly, the budgie started to move his wings against my fingers. After a minute or so I opened my hands and the bird began to flap its wings and fly around the room again.

My mum nearly passed out and kept repeating: 'That's not possible . . . it's just not possible. It's been too long . . .'

I screamed in glee as Peter flew around the room a couple more times and then I coaxed him back into his cage. He was probably safer away from me! I smiled towards the corner of the room and my mother caught a glimpse of my eyes. 'Who are you looking at?' she asked.

'Sam, of course.' I smiled a broad smile. 'I am just thanking him.'

My mum looked as white as a sheet. She promptly sat down for a cup of tea and a cigarette.

Sam my Guide had given me the confidence to have faith that I could heal the bird. Together we had saved Peter. It was fantastic! It certainly became a story shared amongst many of my mother's neighbours.

Soon after that my mum decided it was time to get some maternal advice from her own mother. After a long chat about what I was getting up to, Mum spoke up loudly. 'Other six year olds don't do this, do they?' My nana just listened to her and smiled.

I went upstairs to find something to play with. Intuitively I always seemed to know when my mother needed space, apart from the more obvious fact that I was told to play somewhere else for a while so she could have a little chat with Nana. While I was playing, I encountered a friendly spirit called Fred: he was standing on Nana's stairs, and asked me how she was keeping.

In the warmth of Nana's kitchen, which smelled sweetly of baking, my mum had just sipped some tea when I burst into the room. She almost choked to death when I breezily told Nana that Fred was asking how she was keeping, and that he said hello.

Mum looked at Nana, Nana looked at Mum: then they both looked at me before looking back at each other. Apparently Fred was Nana's old lodger who had died four years before I was born.

'That's it!' my mother screamed as she stood bolt upright. 'I have had enough of this.'

'Oh, don't be so ridiculous, Judy,' my nana screamed back. 'It's only Fred!'

With those few words, she made the other world seem natural for me, like it was an everyday part of life – which, of course, it is. Without her loving influence and acceptance, I am sure it would have been even more difficult for me to come to terms with my abilities.

Reflecting on that time, I realise that my parents must have been terrified about the possible implications of me hearing these special friends of mine. And, obviously, it took me a while to accept this new spiritual dimension to my childhood world. But I began to realise that, no matter how many times I closed my eyes, they were still there when I opened them!

It wasn't until I was a little older that I realised I was different from other little girls, both in what I saw and in what I instinctively understood about my newfound abilities.

I now realise that most of the time my parents' actions could be considered well-intentioned; that they thought they were protecting me from harm. However, the fact is we are indoctrinated from an early age into refusing to talk about spirituality apart from that which is connected to our particular religious background. Society is only just starting to recognise that having the ability to see spirits is not a lifestyle choice; it is a part of what and who we are.

As a society we are conditioned as to how we should eat and drink, dress, be educated, and observe religion according to the cultural beliefs we are born into. These beliefs dictate what is acceptable or unacceptable in broader ways too. So, looking back on my childhood, it is no real surprise to me that my parents branded all my conversations about my spirit guides and spiritual visitors improper and unacceptable. They, like so many others at that time, failed to understand we are not human beings on a spiritual quest, but spiritual beings on a human journey.

I was constantly being told not to talk about my visitors, which forced me into an intolerable position. I wanted my mum and dad to recognise my gift and to give it their approval because they loved and trusted me. I wanted them to know I didn't tell lies to them; that I was telling the truth about my visitors, who were not figments of my imagination. I desperately wanted them to be proud of me, not flinching in embarrassment and denying there was any such gift. And, worse than that, by denying the spirit world they were turning their backs on their own nearest and dearest, which hurt them and cut deep into their hearts.

I believed the teaching I was receiving from Sam was a gift, but my parents seemed determined to view it as a curse. I was still far too young to have any hope of changing their minds. In sheer self-preservation I was learning to conceal most of the things I was being told by my Guide, until I was old enough to claim my independence. It's a dilemma, I know, but it is important to remember that it is not spiritual communication that is bad, but what is expected from that communication. If mutual communication is done through love then no harm can come to any recipient; it is a positive motive with a positive outcome.

So, you decide: seeing the world of spirit, is it a gift or a curse?

2

Primary Tears

My Primary school years were the saddest of years for me. Most of us look back on our childhood memories and can remember family laughter, happy holidays, or adventures into the unknown. Remembering my early life with my mother and father, I recall only isolation and sadness.

My mind takes me back to when we first moved into the new council house in the suburbs of Chester. Thanks to the re-housing request from the forward-thinking Dr Cornforth, twelve months later we could finally all have a good night's sleep, away from ghostly moaning and banging in the night. Or that's what my mum and dad thought!

Our new home was part of a huge housing project involving massive teams of builders and architects. Even though our house was ready for occupation, the completion of the whole estate was far from finished. As it happened, we were in the end-of-terrace house in the first block to be built in our sub-division. Dozens of similar blocks were planned, but not many as yet had reached even foundation level.

Life on the estate was sheer madness, there were so many gangs of workmen doing various jobs. Some were dashing around on dumper trucks delivering sand and cement; others were climbing ladders and scaffolding; while huge concrete mixers continually drove in and out of the estate, emitting clouds of dust.

Directly next-door to us work was in progress on the construction of a new block of four one-bedroomed flats for housing the elderly. The ground dropped so steeply from outside our back door that the council had built a low brick wall separating our path from where the excavation had taken place for the lower level of the new apartments.

Standing outside my back door, facing the new building, I was directly opposite the neighbouring first-floor front door. The drop from the top of our little wall to the path below was a massive three metres at least.

On one particular day when the construction work was in full flow, I sat on the wall watching the various workmen weave in and out of the downstairs floor, taking in fresh plaster to complete the walls. The scene was a hive of activity and the workmen would often ask my mother to boil water for their mugs of tea. 'A few biscuits would be nice, love!' they would always shout – but my mum never gave them any. I don't think they realised we had none to give.

The builders were always nice to me. They whistled while they worked, and I loved to watch them chat and laugh during their tea breaks. Often they would make me feel very special when they would sneakily give me chocolate biscuits they had coaxed off other residents on the estate. My mother allowed me to talk to them, providing I kept out of their way and stayed on my side of the wall.

I would rest my arms on top of the bricks, looking down at the sheer precipice below. I don't know if my mother ever considered the wall a risk, but Sam certainly did. He constantly nagged me to be careful and not to sit on top of it or even to run down the path, in case I fell over. He always looked so alarmed when I went near the wall, I would tell him to stop worrying as I was a big girl now.

Even though we were still poor, my parents seemed happier than they had done previously. The thought of making a new home in these surroundings gave them fresh enthusiasm. They believed the troubling experience with the noisy neighbour was now well behind us. My mother even bought a sewing machine and started to make clothes and curtains. Cooking was definitely not her forte, so through her needles and threads she found a new way to show that she too could compete with some of the other mothers' household skills. Both my parents constantly kept telling me in a reassuring way that living on the new estate was a fresh start for all of us. Dad even smiled these days!

Whenever my mother chatted to me in this manner, I smiled sweetly back. To encourage this new togetherness we shared, I refrained from speaking about my spirit visitors altogether and, as if to reinforce their disappearance from my life, Mum kept repeating the same statement, reminding me my invisible friends were 'just a figment of my imagination'. But no matter how many times she told me this, my spirit friends kept multiplying and were going nowhere! The old lady might have stopped calling me each night from the flat above, but there were many more spirit voices and visitors to replace her.

Fortunately every night Sam would call into my bedroom as I struggled to sleep. Spirit visitors seemed to like it best when the rush of the day was over. Maybe it was because I was alone and quiet that they most often chose this time of day to show themselves. Sam had a natural authority. He reminded me of the way my teacher spoke to our class at school as he firmly directed the spirit visitors out of my room, asking them sternly to leave me in peace so I might be allowed to rest.

I asked him once why he didn't say something to them sooner, especially when the old lady had woken me so often in our last home, and he smiled a cheeky smile and said: 'Well, chile, you needed a new home, didn't you?'

It comforted me to know he was always at hand, tucking me up at night and keeping the many visitors at bay. As I became older his accent, which at first sounded strange and unfamiliar, became more what you might call proper Queen's English, but I have to admit that when he is excited or being affectionate he sometimes reverts back to his old-style English. Sam's watchful presence helped me feel secure, and he explained that I was not to be scared about what I was learning or about all the spirit people I was seeing as I was becoming a clear link for them to speak through, and those over in the spirit world were very excited about this.

'Don't worry,' he soothed. 'I will teach you how to protect yourself and how to decide who to speak to and who it is best to leave well alone. Just like your mother explains that you must not speak to strangers in the street, so you will learn who are safe spirit visitors to talk with and who are not.' Naturally I felt a little scared by his words. But something inside me instinctively knew that he was another guardian, similar to my mum and dad, and of course my ever-faithful Gyp.

I asked Sam once if he was a Guardian Angel and, smiling, he replied: 'No, chile, I am your teacher – and also your Guardian Guide. As I have told you before, everyone has one.'

On one particular night I remember him taking a little longer to rid the bedroom of unwanted visitors. He chatted to me as he 'cleaned' the room (that was the expression he used about the process of ushering out chatty spirits from my bedroom at night! As a young child I found this ritual very comical to watch). Sam explained why there was an increasing number of spirit visitors gathering around me each day. He said that I was a little like a brand new radio station that the spirit world had discovered, and they wanted to broadcast to the world! According to him I had caused quite a stir in the spirit world and they were excited about the future potential of my ability to communicate for them. They wanted to touch, talk, feel, look – anything they could, just to be near me. I thought this very strange and laughed out loud.

Sam told me that when I was older he would explain more and more about the spirit world, but for now I was to think about resembling a radio, and soon when I was bigger I would be more like a telephone. Being like a radio, I could receive voices. And then, when I was like a telephone, people could chat with one another through me. He explained: 'You will be so fast and so quick that you will be able to speak to many people all at once!'

To be honest, I couldn't understand what he was trying to say, but I did understand that it meant the people from the spirit world were going to keep calling. Tiredness overwhelmed me. My eyes started to close on the sight of Sam dusting the very last person in spirit from my room. Once again my little haven was peaceful, and eventually sleep enveloped me.

During another of our bedtime conversations Sam explained that soon many more 'teachers', different from him, would visit me. They would be doctors, surgeons, musicians, writers, who had once lived with us here before they had died, and wanted their life's work to continue to benefit others. Some would be family members who needed me to help their relatives in this world recover from their grief. However, from time to time there would be some who were very special: these wonderful beings would be Arch-Angels.

Sam explained that I must not be fearful of them, and said I would be amazed how they could help me in my life by sprinkling their love around me. He said I needed to grow up some more and then I would understand better about the special gifts that all Angels and Arch-Angels bring. But for now it was enough for me to know that the Angels had so much to give. He continued by saying: 'You have much to learn, but for you, Helen, it is as natural and as easy as breathing.'

I was always grateful to Sam for keeping all the spirits away from me at night, but he never mentioned the day! What about then? I thought.

Now we had settled into our home, I had to start at my new school, Dee Point Infants. I only wished Sam could have taken away my first-day nerves as I held my mother's hand, walking up to the school gates for the first time. The prospect of making new friends seemed very daunting. My parents thought I was now sleeping peacefully at night; they presumed my invisible spirit friends no longer played any part in my life and that therefore it would be easier for me to acquire new schoolfriends.

Children have an uncanny knack for knowing things they are not supposed to! Especially as the previous night I had cried myself to sleep after overhearing my parents talking about how relieved they were that the nonsense with the invisible friends and the strange noises now seemed to be out of my system. Once I started school I would have no time to think about them. My mother had often said as much to me, but somehow overhearing my parents talking about me like this had shocked and upset me. Why would they not believe me? And how could I ever talk about anything with them if they refused to listen?

With my confidence low, I found it difficult to make new friends. Children are very intuitive and my new classmates must have sensed that I was not quite the same as them. Especially after an incident that happened not long after I had started school when one of them, Gary, fell off the monkey bars, causing his head and knee to bleed quite badly.

Before the teacher could reach Gary, I noticed a bright light next to him as he lay on the floor. Other children were shouting for the teacher, but she was far over on the other side of the playground. I instinctively ran over to Gary and told him I would take his pain away. I put my hand on his head and a glow appeared around his body. He immediately stopped crying even though the blood was still oozing from his knee. I felt a tingling sensation enter my body and hands as warmth penetrated them. Gary said he felt tired, and asked if he could lie down. When the teacher arrived at the accident scene, she asked me what I was doing as she examined his head and knee.

I replied, 'I am making him better, of course,' as if the answer was obvious.

The fall had torn his trousers, exposing a deep cut to his knee. The bruise on his head looked like half an egg protruding and seemed to be swelling by the second. Gary sat up again, staring at me as the teacher told me to let go of him. She would now take over and look after him. Smiling at me, she remarked in a milder tone: 'Quite the little Florence Nightingale, aren't we?'

I smiled back and said: 'I am putting love into him, to stop him from feeling scared and so he will know everything will be all right.'

She looked mystified as Gary then said he saw a big bright light around me.

'Oh, gosh!' she commented, looking worried. 'You must have bumped your head really badly. Let's get you inside, Gary, and we may have to take you to hospital to get you checked out . . .' Either way, the teacher passed off my intervention as nothing of any importance, but at least Gary had stopped crying. In retrospect, I now know that my aura had appeared to him. In fact, I could see his aura and he could see mine, and the light beside him was his Angel protecting him.

That same evening, Sam lit up my room with a warming glow as he sat down on the edge of the bed. 'I was proud of you today, helping Gary. Despite all the blood, you showed no fear and helped to calm him when he was frightened and in pain.' Sam made me feel good inside with his words of praise. I only wished my own father could have done the same. If only I could sit on my dad's knee and tell him how I'd made Gary feel better by putting my hands, tingling with heat, on his cuts and bruises. But I knew that if I did he would dismiss the whole experience or, worse, become angry with me.

Feeling my despair, Sam told me softly, 'Don't worry, chile, one day your parents will understand. You are a special girl and you are loved more than you will ever know – here on earth and indeed in spirit. You may not think your parents love you the way you want to be loved, but they love you very much, in their own way. I will always protect you, and even when you feel you cannot see me, I will still be there, standing by your side. When you need help in a different way, you always have the Angels to call upon with their special gifts. You will have assistance and love surrounding you, Helen, you will never be alone.'

I loved the thought that I was loved and not alone, but naturally this made me feel very inquisitive. 'What type of Angels, Sam? Are they like the Bible pictures at school?'

'Oh, there are so many wonderful angels, my chile, and throughout your life they will visit when they feel the need. You might even unknowingly have seen one already. They all look a little different from each other, although there is a common bond they share. They all glow brightly, Helen. Sometimes they glow so bright it would burn your eyes, so they dare not show themselves in their truest form. They seem to have a special way of connecting with people. The main thing to remember is that they automatically know when you need help.'

I looked at him in awe as he spoke of them to me.

'There is something special I want to explain to you tonight,' he announced as he gesticulated to a man who had appeared and was standing beside him. I felt a bit uncomfortable having a stranger in my bedroom, but this man was different. He was wearing a white doctor's coat which reached to his knees. I stared at the stranger, my mouth open. The white-coated stranger never said a word, but gave me a kind, reassuring smile.

Sam maintained a serious tone. 'Without my asking, you automatically felt the need to heal your friend and you intuitively knew what to do. You are now ready to develop your natural healing potential. As time goes on and you grow up, I will explain everything I can to you. You have such a long path ahead of you and it is not possible, even in your whole lifetime here, to know all there is to know. Now stop worrying yourself, little chile. I am always here to protect you, no matter what. I know you will ask when you are ready to learn more.'

I didn't know what he was talking about. I was becoming a tad nervous as usually he made everyone leave my bedroom at night, so why was he bringing this strange man to me? Who on earth was he? I thought. I had a feeling he was important, or going to be important to me in my future. It was as though Sam was showing me off like a proud parent.

'Is he a doctor?' I asked, pointing at the man. 'Why is he here?'

As I finished my sentence, Sam turned to the stranger and gave one of his wide smiles: 'Yes, he is a doctor. His name is Dr

Clarke and he is going to help you, chile. He is going to teach you in ways I cannot.' His voice was soft and comforting but I was confused. I didn't understand what he meant.

Quite out of the blue, Sam told me to climb out of bed and fetch a plain piece of paper from my little homemade wooden desk which stood against the wall. I always had wads of paper there because I loved drawing – just like my dad. As I picked up the paper from my desk, Sam continued: 'Now place it on the bed in front of you and tell me what you see?'

What was he talking about? What did he mean – what could I see? So I told Sam exactly what I saw: 'I see an empty piece of paper.'

To this day, I don't know if it was in the physical plane or through my spiritual eye that I saw a faint outline appearing on the page. At first, it was like a shadow.

Sam prompted me to look harder: 'Chile, what do you see?'

To my astonishment, from the page started to emerge the outline of a skeleton, just as if the paper had become an Etch A Sketch. Once the body shape had formed, the full image of a skeleton followed. Sam whispered: 'Can you see it?'

I thought it was amazing. Not only could I see the skeleton, but bold ticks and crosses had appeared on certain parts of the image.

'What does it mean?' I gleefully enquired.

'Speak to me quietly and I will explain it a little more.' Sam spoke in a strong, calm voice. I was totally intrigued; after all, it's not every day you see skeletons appear before your very eyes, albeit in picture form.

He was concentrating just like my teacher when she looked at me through her thin-rimmed glasses. 'Now, first, what can you see on the picture?'

Like a new game, I explained in detail about the skeleton and the position of all the ticks and crosses on it. Suddenly a name began to appear at the top of the page . . . It said COLIN! I was shocked as I recognised the name. I pointed to the picture. 'That's my daddy's name,' I whispered to Sam, one hand pressed to my mouth to contain my excitement.

'Yes, chile, I knows,' he confirmed, but still he demanded more from me. 'What else do you see on the picture? Is there a mark on any particular part of the body?'

Looking hard at the piece of paper again, I saw there was a big cross over the left side of the skeleton's body. By chance, my mum and I had been looking at a children's book about anatomy recently; books that showed human organs and body parts completely fascinated me. I noticed that two crosses were situated on the area occupied by the heart and lungs. Proudly, knowing the answer to his question, I announced that it was where we breathe from. I was very satisfied that I had remembered about the book and thought I was revealing a new fact to Sam.

Sam bent his head close to mine, smiling a beam of pure delight as he stroked my hair. 'Dear chile, you are so good to remember what your mummy told you.'

As I looked down at the skeleton picture again, it had five ticks at various places on the body and there were TWO BOLD CROSSES. I wondered what they were for.

'What you must remember when you see this picture is that the ticks mean that part of the body which is well, and the crosses mean the area that is ill. These two crosses are over your dad's lungs and heart and you need to know what I have to tell you. Your father needs you to heal his chest. His lungs are very sick.'

Heal my dad's chest? What did Sam mean? I was very confused.

He continued: 'Well, you have special hands that send energy

– or, as you have started to call it, love – into sick people when you touch them.'

This was all too much to take in and I remember my eyes starting to fill with tears. But determination not to cry came over me. I wanted to be strong in front of Sam and Dr Clarke even if I was just a little girl. I nodded my understanding and noticed the way that Sam's voice had stimulated the tingling feeling in my hands. This must be the energy he was talking about, I thought. My mood lifted. I felt elated and confident, a sense of inner peace coming over me. I now know this was as a result of the healing energies flooding through my body.

Sam reminded me then about my experience with my little yellow budgie. 'Soon you will know when a person is ill. You will feel it inside you.'

I didn't like the sound of feeling ill inside so I screwed up my nose. 'Does that mean I will be sick too?' A very logical question, I thought at the time.

Sam smiled again: 'Oh, my chile, you have much still to understand and learn, and it will be my privilege to help you discover what is locked away inside you. Remember our lesson today. *You* have to put your hands on your father's chest. Tell him you want to send him love because he coughs too much. When you do this for him, he will feel great warmth from your hands, and you will feel them tingle with the energy being given. This will seem strange at first, but soon you will become more confident and it will be natural for you. Remember when you first learned to ride your bike and turn those big pedals? Well, your healing lessons will be the same. They will become easier and easier for you each time, and you will feel a lovely warmth inside yourself as the Angels will be smiling upon you.'

Gosh, I thought, when am I going to meet all these Angels? To me they sounded so lovely and pretty. Sam continued: 'After you have held your hand on your dad's chest, I will ask you what you felt.'

Naturally, I didn't properly understand what he wanted me to do, but it seemed a good thing to try and help my dad. I loved him, so if his chest was poorly and Sam said I needed to make it better, I had jolly well better do the job as soon as possible.

As if Sam understood my thoughts, he replied without me even having to speak: 'Choose a moment to heal Daddy when he is happy and quiet, and tell him you want to touch his heart to send your love inside him.'

He smiled at me again as I yawned. 'Time for you to go to sleep, chile. Think happy thoughts. I am very proud of you.'

Then in a change of tone he gave me a strong warning: 'And remember, be careful! You are going to have an accident if you don't keep away from that wall!'

I know I have to be careful so there's no problem, I thought to myself.

Quiet came. I felt consoled as Sam hummed a tune, as though it was some sort of lullaby, but I didn't recognise it. I fell asleep.

The next day I went to school as normal. When evening approached, I sat down to our evening tea with my mum and dad. I was very excited. There was Sam's visit to talk about, the way he'd made my hands go tingly, the skeleton picture on the paper appearing right in front of my eyes and the silent man in the white doctor's coat – Dr Clarke – who was going to teach me to be like him. In my excitement I forgot that my parents had reached the conclusion I no longer had any sort of invisible visitors. This was different, this was fantastic, I was convinced my mum and dad would be excited to hear this! Sam had made me feel very grown up, answering his questions, and I thought Mum and Dad would be equally as pleased to listen now.

Mum had just taken a forkful of rosy-red tomato when I started to tell them both that Sam was worried about the boundary wall and had warned me to take care. Hearing his words of wisdom, she started to choke. Undeterred, I continued to talk about Sam as I thought this would prove he was with me and they would be happy this time to hear what he had to say. The choking sound stopped and everything went still . . . I never had a chance to explain about the exciting things I had witnessed as there was a sudden loud clashing sound when my mother's fists hit the table, making the knives and forks bounce and clatter off the dinner plates.

Oh-oh! Am I in more trouble? I thought.

As quick as a flash my mother frowned at me and said I was talking good sense by mentioning the need to be careful near the garden wall, but I must have heard it said by someone else . . . maybe one of the builders. She paused to draw in a deep, steadying breath. It was as if she intended to take in enough to blow down the three little pigs' house. After she had gently exhaled she told me in a very angry tone that I should stop talking about Sam and my so-called invisible friends right NOW. That I knew only too well it was plain common sense not to play on the wall outside as it was obviously dangerous.

Do little children really think like that? I only know I did not – until Sam pointed out the danger to me.

Nevertheless, the predicted accident didn't take too long to happen. One summer's evening I sat nonchalantly on the wall, swinging my legs.

The dog heard the doorknob rattle as my mum took out the bins. Gyp innocently thought he was about to be given some food and he ran past me up the concrete path in a bid to reach the door as fast as he could. My mother carried on with her chore oblivious to us both. Unfortunately, as he sprinted past me, he brushed against the bottoms of my feet, which were dangling off the ground. In a split-second reflex I lifted them up, unbalancing my centre of gravity. I tumbled backwards Humpty Dumpty fashion, landing on the solid concrete path three metres below.

By now new neighbours, an elderly retired couple, had moved into the ground-floor flat next-door. They heard me scream as I fell. Apparently they rushed out to my rescue and shouted for help as I lay motionless. Hearing them, my mother also rushed over, to find me covered in blood and completely unconscious.

To this day I don't know how long it lasted. When I came to, I was surprised to see Sam, a paramedic, another very tall spirit person and my mother, all huddled into the back of the ambulance as I was being rushed to hospital. It must have been quite a squeeze! I thought. Thankfully all I had to have done, according to the doctor there, was seven stitches plus several X-rays – which thankfully showed no fractures. I did, however, have to take it easy for a good while with a week off school, as my head seemed to throb continually with a massive headache. The doctors said I was lucky to be alive. A child of my age could easily have fractured their skull dropping from such a height as it was the equivalent of jumping out of a first-storey window. They reckoned that because I fell backwards it must have softened the fall in some way. I knew different! My spirit folk saved me.

As I went to bed that night, I cried to Sam because I had not had a chance to give my dad his healing, as I'd promised to do. Sam never became angry with me. Now he smiled, his big white teeth gleaming out of his shiny black face. 'I was hoping that it was time, dear chile.'

'Time for what?' I asked, not understanding what he meant.

'Time for your parents to accept your gifts, my dear,' he replied.

I still didn't understand.

'Are you upset with me for not putting my hands on my dad's chest?' I asked.

With the look I had seen many times lighting up his loving face, he answered: 'No, chile, never angry with you. Just sad that those closest to you cannot see, hear or feel you as yet. You are here with stitches in your head, yet you worry over your father.'

I closed my eyes, feeling a little confused but happy that I had not upset my Sam.

Strangely, after my accident, we had never seen a new brick wall built so quickly. The three-foot barrier down the side of our house grew overnight to about five foot. After hearing of my accident, the council made sure the wall was built so high I could never climb it again. I believe it was thanks to my mother's nagging.

Hundreds of new houses were being built in this new area known as Blacon. They ranged from terraced properties, apartment blocks, schools and shopping precincts to an old people's nursing home with pretty gardens. My mum and dad felt very blessed to have been allocated their new two-bedroomed terraced house with its own private garden and shed. There were even flowerbeds filled with roses, as a courtesy from Bee's Garden Nurseries. Nowadays the estate has a bad reputation, but back in the early-1960s nearly every person moving into one of the new houses was excited and grateful at the prospect of living in a fresh new home. They were all decent working people with a sense of pride in their surroundings. After all, these were not just a few new houses being built; this was going to be a brand new cityscape!

Dad was now working in the day on the production line of the Vauxhall car factory in Liverpool. He hated the job but said it was a means to an end until we got on our feet financially. He was still studying to pass his City and Guilds exams in master plumbing. I felt sorry for him, working so hard. I barely had the chance to see him. He was always either too tired to play or else heading off to work.

Originally he had wanted to go to art school as several people in his family were very talented artists. His dream was eventually to teach art in a college, but he didn't have the money to study with a wife and daughter to support. So despite only being in his early twenties at the time, he assumed adult responsibility and put his family before his dreams.

I respected and loved my dad, who genuinely was a very good man, but I felt that he had little patience with me. His temper always seemed to flare up at the least little problem. With age and hindsight, I now know that these are the signs of extreme stress. I wish I could have my time with him over again as the healer I am today, so that I could take that feeling of stress away. Back then in my tender years it was hard to understand the complexities of adult responsibilities. A child sees only rejection and lack of love when an adult shrinks into themself through stress and depression.

My mum started to work part-time at the huge garden nursery about half a mile away from our house. Bees of Chester was situated on the Sealand Road, not far from the famous RAF Sealand base. It nestled out of sight of the main road, amongst the open fields where massive greenhouses stood. Row after row of roses and lavender bushes filled acres of land with their sweet aromatic perfume in the summer months when they were in full bloom. It was truly a beautiful sight to behold.

Originally, years before I was born, my mother had worked as a computer punch-card operator for a company called Williams & Williams. Not having worked in that profession for a few years, she needed a refresher course to keep up with modern-day technology and that sort of retraining was expensive. The only way she would be able to return to office work was if a large company would support her financially while she could complete the course, so her options were slim. Plus she had me and my dad to look after.

Despite his reluctance for my mother to work at all the reality was they needed more money, so Mum convinced Dad that she should take any job that was close to home and fitted in with my school hours. Bee's Nurseries seemed an obvious choice to her. What made it even more appealing was that the company picked up their workforce by mini-bus and would drop them off again in the evening. My mum thought this was manna from heaven, especially as it would more or less fit in with my school hours.

She worked in the greenhouses and fields, packing thousands of roses for UK distribution and foreign export. In fact, even at my then young age, I became aware of many of the names of rose varieties as my mother packed and labelled many thousands at home in the winter evenings.

I thought it was fun, helping her to stick identification labels to the boxes in the kitchen while she crammed the soaking wet roses into the delivery packets. It seemed like a great way to earn extra money on something my mother called 'piecework'. Every time she packed a different variety of rose she made me say the name over and over again, to make sure I would remember it. To this day I can still remember the rose 'Ena Harkness' as being one of her favourites. It had a beautiful strong perfume and a deep crimson colour, with petals that looked and felt like velvet.

After we'd finished our evening's work I can remember how my mother soaked her hands in hot soapy water and Dettol for hours, and then sat painstakingly picking the thorns from her fingers with a sewing needle, wincing with pain.

After working in the greenhouses for over a year, she managed to secure a job in the offices at the site and went back to her original career of computer programming. She was very happy as it was quite a prestigious job and the company agreed to finance her refresher course. Computers were progressing at that time from punch-card to computer programming on tape. Anyone involved with them felt excited by the endless possibilities they afforded. At that time the master computer was housed in a huge air-conditioned room where the reels of tape were processed, rather like a massive old-fashioned tape recorder. This room was sealed and dust-free; all the technicians there wore white laboratory coats as if they were doctors. My mother was lucky enough to be in the right place at the right time to secure herself a good job. The new office work gave the family some extra money and at last allowed her poor battered hands to recover.

One day my dad had time off work and picked me up from school (a rare treat). We drove to Bee's in his new, very well-used Vauxhall Viva. At the time I remember thinking I was riding in a golden chariot as my dad's car was, in my opinion, the best on the road.

Once we arrived at Mum's office she came out to meet us and suggested showing us round the place. Dad declined and said he would wait in the car while she proudly took me by the hand and showed me off to her work colleagues. I felt very important and loved the fact that *my* mum wanted to show *me* off!

During our walkabout she introduced me to her boss, let's call her Pam, who was much younger and had very long, straight red hair. Sam stood by the side of me, saying that she had just got engaged to one of her seniors in the office. She bent down so that her head was about six inches from mine and stroked my long blonde hair. I remember her saying, 'Oh, you are a pretty little girl,' and without thinking I replied that I hoped she would be happy when she got married to the man in the other office. I pointed over to some glass doors at the back of the room.

I noticed that her cheeks were turning redder than her hair! She turned to my mother and said, 'I didn't realise the office girls talked about Phil and me being together?' My mother did one of her huffing noises and said: 'Honestly, we don't. I have heard nothing. Don't listen to Helen, her imagination is always running wild.'

Pam smiled ruefully and swore under her breath: 'Well, that's it . . . Our engagement is out of the bag now!'

My mother dragged me a little way off, jerking my arm. I felt I had said something I shouldn't, and wanted to cry because my mummy was cross with me. How was I to know it was a secret about Pam and her boyfriend? Sam never said that when he told me!

As we rapidly made our getaway we bumped into, let's call her Sakra, an Indian girl I had heard my mother talk about at home. She smelled of spices and was dressed in bright clothes but looked very pretty in her Indian costume. I suppose my mum had no option but to stop and make conversation with her. Sakra seemed like a really nice lady, but I could tell by the way my mother was speaking hurriedly that she wanted us to leave quickly.

Sakra seemed upset, not with mum but about something else as she started to whisper in my mum's ear. Even I could tell she had been crying because her eyes were red and swollen. My mother's urgent desire to leave suddenly dissolved, and seemed to have waned altogether after their whispered conversation. She started to talk in a quieter, softer tone.

'Go and sit on that chair over there, will you, Helen?' my mum said, pointing out the black swivel chair behind one of the desks. I thought, Oooh, this is a step in the right direction. There was no anger in her voice now. I couldn't hear the conversation as they spoke to each other in hushed tones across the room. It was obviously a secret chat, and as I had had it drummed into me on numerous occasions that 'children should be seen, not heard', I continued to swivel round and round on my new toy, the office chair.

Both my parents were sticklers for good manners. They said that they cost nothing and meant the world. My generation was brought up to wash their hands before eating and always to be well behaved in other people's company. I thought I was a good girl as I tried to listen to my parents and please them, but they always seemed upset with me when I talked about people they could not see, so at least by being good and behaving well in public I could offer them something they would understand. It was my way of winning their affection.

The conversation finished as I quietly twirled round one more time on the office chair. I wished I had one of these at home. My mother kissed Sakra on the cheek and gave her a hug as the poor woman broke down in tears yet again.

'I have to go,' my mother apologised, walking over towards me. 'Colin is waiting in the car. Will you be OK?' she asked Sakra, who once again wiped her eyes with a soggy tissue.

'Sorry, Judy, I know you have Helen with you. I didn't mean to spoil her visit to the office, but I had to tell you.' I wondered just what was so important that they'd had to whisper, but it was obviously hush-hush.

Sakra bent down as she approached me and said, 'Oh, you are a such a good girl, sitting there so quietly.' She gently touched my shoulder, and as she did Sam told me to tell her she shouldn't have to marry the man in the photograph. So that's exactly what I did! She promptly burst into floods of tears once more as my mother looked on, gritted her teeth and frowned. I remember feeling a fluttering in my stomach and sensing that I was once again in trouble.

As we climbed back into the car, Dad asked how we'd got on. My mother said that her friend Sakra was upset because, due to her culture, her family were making her marry a man she didn't know. She never mentioned to Dad what I had said to the ladies, maybe to avoid him getting into one of his moods with me. We sat in silence on the way home.

I suppose accidents are very much part of any child's life, and in this respect I was no different. My next recollection of a scrape was when I catapulted over the handlebars as the brakes on my bicycle jammed and I flew into the air, breaking eight of my front teeth as I landed flat on my face on the concrete path in front of our house. I was very poorly after having a general anaesthetic and eight teeth removed. My face was bruised, my top gum all bloodied and my head so sore I couldn't eat anything solid for weeks, only slurp my favourite tomato soup from a straw. The dining arrangements seemed to be the best part of my accident really, because Mum made me jellies, ice-cream, and my favourite fruit squashes. At last she had found something she managed to cook well! The moment my Auntie Joan and Uncle Bob heard about my accident they made a special journey up to see me and Uncle Bob gave me eight brand new shiny half crowns, one for each tooth missing, and another two for good luck, just to cheer me up!

Every cloud has a silver lining . . . because of the accident I was now rich, proven by the silver coins gleaming in my hand.

'That's a lot of money for a little girl,' my mother said loudly, and gestured with her index finger towards my piggy bank waiting on the sideboard in what we called the lounge. I reluctantly put the coins inside, fearful that she would need them to pay the electric bill or some other unexpected household expense and I would never see them again. Fortunately, despite this period now being known as my toothless goofy stage, the teeth I'd lost were baby teeth, so new ones replaced the yawning gap some months later.

Once I was feeling better and my gums had healed, my Auntie Joan invited me to stay at her house for the weekend. I still had my pocket money from Uncle Bob and thought I would share some of it with my cousin Debbie. I'd managed to save most of it in my piggy bank, but as this was a special occasion I took two half-crown pieces with me when I went to stay. Debbie and I were going to have a great time at my sleepover at hers! When I stayed at Auntie Joan's house, it was always fun as we were allowed to stay up longer at night and watch TV. My older cousins Peter and David would babysit while my aunt and uncle went to the Legion for their nightly drink.

After my arrival it didn't take long for Deb and me to trot off to the local grocer's shop to buy some sweets and snacks to enjoy later that evening. We walked home from the shop laden with our stash of tuck. Fizzy pop was sold in glass bottles then and these were quite heavy. Out of the blue, I heard someone shout my name from behind. It scared me so much that I dropped every-thing on the concrete path, shattering the pop bottles we had just bought. The voice had sounded like my Great-aunt Rhoda's. She had died a few months before but I'd recognised her very distinctive high-pitched tone. I looked around but there was nobody there. Or at least I couldn't see anybody there!

I was so upset that I had broken our precious pop bottles, I burst into tears and cried. Debbie, though, two and a bit years younger than me but of sound practical sense, thought the owner of the shop was a nice lady and would replace the bottles if we took all the bits of glass back to prove what had happened.

I don't know how or why Deb had the notion we might be given fresh pop, as now I realise no shopowner in their right mind would replace broken bottles! Strangely, though, as we walked back to the shop with the broken bits balanced carefully in our hands, trying not to cut ourselves, I saw Sam chuckling and heard him say 'OK, OK' as though about to grant a wish.

The wooden slatted shop, shed-like in appearance, was full of local people buying the odds and ends they needed. Comically, we arranged the glass pieces on the counter-top, along with shards of a bottleneck with the top still attached as in our minds that proved we had not opened and drank them! In stereo, Deb and I explained to the shopowner the story of me breaking my teeth and being given the pocket money, then buying our tuck, then breaking the bottles because I was startled by a shouting voice. The lady shop-keeper, her elbows leaning on the counter-top, listened intently. Finally she laughed and without hesitation she loudly told us, so that everyone in the shop could hear, that she would replace the bottles, then she told us *not* to drop these and to go straight home with them – carefully! She was still laughing as we shut the door.

We were so happy that we had our 'goodie bags' of tuck back in one piece. As we reached the back door of Debbie's house, leading directly into the kitchen, Sam had already arrived and was leaning against the doorframe. I love his smile; it lights up any room. I could hear my mother and my Auntie Joan laughing indoors, and couldn't wait to tell them what had just happened.

Sam said briefly: 'When you have dropped off your shopping and told your mothers about your adventure, why don't you go and pick some wild flowers for them?'

I didn't think that was a bad idea. So, always the organiser, I told Deb once we'd put our shopping in the kitchen that we were going to go flower picking.

Before we left to go in search of flowers, we were pleased to tell our mums about our amazing good luck at the grocery store. Before the excitement in the room had even begun to settle, Debbie and I scampered outside in search of some flowers. No matter how hard we looked, though, we couldn't find any wild flowers to pick. All the best blooms were in people's gardens and we knew we couldn't take them, as that would be stealing.

'Let's try and find some daisies or buttercups,' I said as we scoured the long grass in the fields near the house. Buttercups seemed to grow in abundance there and it wasn't long before we had quite a handful, but they were very small and we agreed they wouldn't look like much once we had put them in a vase.

Before too long we found ourselves at the local church, which bordered on to a piece of empty ground where the local kids often played. Some vivid orange asters caught my eye, peeping through the Vicarage's chain-link fence.

'Come on, Deb, let's pick those orange flowers over there. They are gorgeous and our mums will love them. Look, there's loads of them and we're not going into the churchyard grounds to pick them, they're peeping through on this side of the fence.' In my opinion this made them fair game to be picked. We weren't taking something illegally. So, in my innocence, I led my young cousin off to help me claim our bounty.

We thought our flower-picking idea was brilliant, just what we wanted, as the Vicarage garden was in full bloom, albeit on the other side of the fence, with massive borders full of beautiful bright flowers. I thought the few escaping through the fence wouldn't even be missed, so we merrily kneeled down and picked them to our hearts' content.

Suddenly we heard a man's deep voice booming out from the other side of the fence. 'What do you two girls think you are doing?' the Vicar demanded in his powerful voice. A little scared that we were now in trouble, we both apologised and told him that we were just picking flowers for our mums, to take home and make them happy.

'Well, these are privately owned gardens and you can't pick these flowers!' he shouted in a very angry tone. Within a second Sam stood next to me and demanded I repeat his words, saying *'Let the little children come to me and do not hinder them.'* I didn't know what else to do or even what Sam actually meant. Not thinking, I blurted out what I thought he had said to me, but the Vicar reddened and shouted at me again in an angry tone: 'What did you say, girl? Are you trying to be clever?'

I was dumbstruck. I didn't know how to answer him. After all, priests and vicars were very important people, or so I had been told. Debbie stared at me, looking for moral support. I was the elder child. I was supposed to be looking after her. But neither of us knew what to say so we continued to babble to the Vicar that we were only taking a present to our mums and did not intend to steal the flowers.

I don't know what happened next but the tone and the demeanour of the Vicar suddenly changed. He smiled at us. 'Don't take too many then, and make sure they are only from that side of the fence – OK?'

We both nodded. Wow, we thought, that was a close shave!

Sam smiled back at me and I heard him speak in my thoughts: 'Good girl. Now you can go home. The priest has finally remembered his vows!'

3

Growing Pains

My school days were starting to improve, and as I started to make more friends I became much happier at my new Infants school in Blacon. I had even been put into the top set of the class as my teacher told Mum I was a bright little girl. That particular day I felt absolutely wonderful as I saw my mother's face light up with true pride.

Normally she never arrived home from work until 4 p.m. at the earliest. We finished at 3 p.m. so a friend of my mum with children in the same school usually walked me home. The walk was lonely and usually made in silence as her children were much younger and wouldn't readily talk to me. We would reach our house by about 3.30 p.m. as it was quite a hike for a young girl of my age and the other two smaller kids. My mum's friend would stand and watch me let myself in through the front door. Every day she would tell me to wait quietly until Mum returned, which still meant that I had to wait a short time in the house alone.

Some people might say it's not a long time – half an hour – for a child to be left alone without adult supervision. But, having had a family of my own, I now cringe at the thought of leaving an eight year old to let themself into an empty house for any length of time.

I used the half-hour to do some housework. If I didn't, my mum would become very angry with me. To avoid any confrontation I would work as fast as I could to make the most impact, which meant I usually tidied away the breakfast mess first. Sometimes, when my mum walked in, she would give me a lovely smile – then I really felt the hard work was well worth it.

On one occasion, my mother walked into school looking very stressed. Walking by her side was my Guide Sam: something had to be *very* wrong. There was no reason that I knew of for her to be there. Why was she coming into school to speak to *my* teachers and *my* Headmistress when she should have been at work? What had I done wrong now? More to the point, why was Sam beside her?

Within moments of her arrival, I was summoned into the Headmistress's office by my teacher and told to sit down and listen carefully to what Mummy and she had to say. I gulped in air: this was not going to be good. The Head explained that the authorities had made a terrible mistake and put me in the wrong school year. Seemingly I was meant to have started at the Junior school that September, but because my birthday fell in August they had made an error and put me in the Infants. Apparently I had been put in the wrong class all along: I was meant to have been a year higher, which would have made me one of the youngest there. I started to cry at the prospect of moving, especially the thought of having to make new friends all over again. My mum explained to the Headmistress that making new friends was difficult for me as I was very shy, and compensated by creating invisible friends to talk to all the time.

Once again I could feel my inner self shrinking into a corner somewhere in my subconscious where no adult could hurt me. Yet again my mother was making references to me 'imagining' my spirit friends. I was so miserable that she *couldn't*, or should I say *wouldn't*, understand that Sam could tell me what was going to happen to people and that the spirit friends I spoke to were real to me.

Looking rather disgruntled, Sam stood by the two women, offering no help to me whatsoever. Why didn't he speak up? Why didn't he say something so I could tell them his words now? Instead he looked me in the eye and put a finger over his lips, like children do when they are told to shush and be quiet. Was he upset with me too?

Although the Juniors section was independent from the Infants department, the schools' playground and sports fields were communal. The Headmistress took one look at my sad face and tried to appease me by saying I would still see friends from my old class during breaktimes as we shared a playground. Old class! I thought. She already has me moved. No matter how she tried to convince me, I knew different. I knew my current classmates would distance themselves once I'd moved from their classroom. Yet again I felt so alone, so unheard. Sam glanced across at me and smiled, whispering, 'Don't worry, dear girl, it will sort itself out.'

This time my mother was genuinely upset for me as she could see that leaving the cosiness of my present classroom was going to be very distressing. She demanded to know why it had taken the authorities so long to realise I was in the wrong year. The Headmistress shrugged her shoulders and blamed it on the Education Department in our last area of Hoole.

That was it then. It might have seemed straightforward to an adult to accept this change, but to me it was devastating. All the other children in Juniors had settled into their new classrooms and school at the start of the September term. They were now in the middle of their work and I had to catch up. It was the end of November and having to make new friends all over again was a daunting prospect. But Sam said it would be all right – so I supposed things would be.

Reluctantly I had to collect my coat and walk over to the other school, there and then, with my mother and Headmistress, to meet my new teacher and classmates. No matter how I struggled to hold my tears inside me, eventually my lip quivered and I couldn't stop the flow of emotion.

Arriving at the bigger school, I was put into Mrs Yates' class and thought what a nice lady she was with her bright red lipstick and sweet-smelling perfume. She didn't look like my other teacher; she had a less officious look, with a big smile and a kind voice. This won't be so bad, I thought to myself, but as I sat in one of the little wooden chairs, even at my tender age I knew in my heart there was something different about this class of children. I couldn't put my finger on what it was yet, but I felt it was all wrong. Plus I saw Sam tutting in the corner saying, 'This will never do,' so I could tell he was not best pleased either.

As the days went by, I didn't understand why the other children spoke differently from me and used baby words. I tried to settle in with them, but found that when we did our lessons, whether it was Maths, English or Science, they seemed not to understand anything, whereas I found the lessons to be easy and would often say so to Mrs Yates.

After what seemed to me to be a couple of days, she asked me to stand next to her and read aloud to the class. She frowned as I read, and to this day I can still experience the smell of that room: a mixture of Dettol and beeswax. In my mind's eye I can see myself standing there looking at the Janet and John books with the bold printed words underneath the pictures and the various colour codes on the front of the book, which showed how well you were progressing.

'Hmm,' Mrs Yates said. 'I will have to go and talk to someone about you, Helen dear.'

I thought I was in trouble again, and my stomach churned over and over like it did when my parents were cross with me. She left the room so that she could talk to the Headmistress about me, and a student teacher, Jenny, was left in charge. Mrs Yates was gone for what seemed ages, but I was happy because Sam had decided to join me and he walked around the room scrutinising the pictures on the wall. Then he went over to twin boys who were playing at the sand table, a sort of square metal trough on wooden legs filled with about six inches of sand, and held his hand over their heads for a few moments. He seemed to be fascinated, watching the twins playing with the sand, letting it flow freely through their fingers, and after about ten minutes joined me back at my table where I was working alone with my reading book. 'These little dear souls,' he said, smiling. 'So much love in their hearts.' He didn't say any more, but smiled and watched and kept me company.

About half an hour later Mrs Yates burst back into the room with a beaming smile on her face. She walked over to me and gently touched my shoulder. 'Collect your belongings, Helen, and follow me. We are going into a new teacher's classroom.'

So it seemed I was on the move yet again! As instructed, I gathered my stationery together. I could feel myself wanting to cry. Sensing my distress, Mrs Yates smiled at me. 'Do you want to hold my hand, Helen?' she offered. She took my hand in hers as we left the room, leaving her assistant in charge once more.

'Now don't you worry, Helen, you have done nothing wrong. I merely think you might be better suited to Mrs Jones' class.'

I liked Mrs Yates; she had such a soft face and a kindly disposition. Together we walked closer to Mrs Jones' room. We could hear the happy chatter of children's voices as we approached. They were reciting their times tables and I could tell at once that Mrs Jones had a busier classroom with more children in it than Mrs Yates had. We knocked on the door, entered, and all the children stood up in silence. 'Sit down, class, and carry on quietly with your work,' Mrs Jones said in a commanding voice.

Her class had a different feel about it from Mrs Yates'; everything about the room looked different. Again I couldn't comprehend what it was but I recognised that in Mrs Jones' classroom there were many more detailed pictures and lots of stories lining the walls, all produced by the children. Pupils had completed projects, and their paintings were arranged in an organised collage depicting a woodland scene. Mrs Yates had also had children's pictures on her walls, but theirs were more like the ones I produced when I was three or four.

Sam winked at me from where the teachers stood and put his thumb up to signify all was well. Then he came to my side and said: 'Everything is OK now, dear. Sorry, but I had to get through to Mrs Yates and make her bring you into this class.' What did he mean? Had she seen him? I thought. Did he actually speak to her too?

Sam and I have a sort of mind connection that means he rapidly answers any question I ask, even if it is just a thought. Sometimes I get answers from him to the idlest thoughts at the back of my mind. He had clearly put thoughts about me into Mrs Yates' mind, and she had responded by independently deciding that I was indeed in the wrong class.

Mrs Yates whispered into Mrs Jones' ear as she kept a watchful eye on her class, doing two things at once. Once she had finished, Mrs Jones told me that I was to settle down at one of the tables as I would be joining her class. Why was I changing again? I thought. As if in answer to the question in my mind, the new teacher said she would give me a letter to take home for my mother to explain everything. Mrs Yates smiled her lovely warm beam and I knew I was staying. That was that, I had a new class. I never argued with a teacher's decision, and nor do most pupils; that's what kids do – they just accept.

I later discovered that Mrs Yates' class was for children with 'special needs' and learning difficulties. Fortunately she had spotted that I was bright and decided to take responsibility for my education on her own shoulders, by swapping my class there and then. She had also apparently written in my notes that the Council authorities had got it wrong *again*. Why they put me in her class to begin with, among the 'special needs' children, I will never know. As an adult I can only speculate that my mum had said too much to the teachers about my 'vast imagination and imaginary friends', and the educational system had translated this as meaning I was a child in need of special assistance. Thankfully for me, Mrs Yates realised different.

After all this changing around at school, my mother must have had a chat to her bosses asking them to release her early from work, as my friend's mother could no longer walk me home because her children were still in the Infants section and they finished half an hour before the Juniors' later finish time. I loved it because my mother would now be home in time to pick me up, so no more time alone. I loved walking home with her. We always chatted together and she sometimes bought me a treat like a packet of crisps because I was always starving hungry. My life had begun to move up a notch on the happiness scale.

I think out of my entire childhood those few years in Junior school were the ones in which my mother and I truly became close. I no longer had to let myself into the house and she was there to make tea for me as soon as I got home, the same as my other friends' mums. As far as I was concerned, she was now a real and proper mother.

Christmas came quickly and, to try and help me fit into the class, Mrs Jones gave me the role of an Angel in the school nativity. I thought it hilarious that I was going to act like one of my spirit friends. Sam saw the funny side, too, as I stood in the back row dressed in my white robe and a halo made out of a bent metal hanger covered in silver tinsel! I don't know who was prouder, my mum or my Guide Sam.

What child doesn't love Christmas? It is the most magical time of year, with glistening fir trees laden with fairy lights, coloured tinsel and shiny baubles. During schooltime there was always a continuous flow of happy faces and excited chatter in anticipation of Christmas presents to come.

This year I was really, really excited, because I had left Santa so many letters, placing them on the hearth before the fire every night before I went to sleep. By morning they had gone. He must have magically taken them while I was asleep, so at the back of my mind I had no doubt at all that this year would be the BIG one and he would remember the two gifts I wanted above all else. How could he not?

I still secretly felt that Santa actually existed, although my new friends were starting to make me doubt this, so in order not to miss out on any presents I decided to hedge my bets and believe. I was so excited as I counted down the days on the chocolate advent calendar in the kitchen, which my mother had reluctantly bought at my prompting.

Every year we had a real tree delivered by my Uncle Tom a few weeks before Christmas. He wasn't a real uncle, but I was told to call him by that name. Tom was a rotund jolly man with whom my father had made friends during his time in the Army.

Actually, Tom finished his military service before my dad. During the early years of their marriage, my mum was left alone with me at Christmas, so Tom had made a pact with my dad that he would deliver a Christmas tree every year from then on.

Without fail, every Christmas he kept his word and continued this tradition until I was in my twenties. It always arrived to a ceremonial toast of mugs of tea and mince pies, as Tom was completely tee-total, after which my father would decorate the house with paper garlands and put tinsel and lights up at the windows. Oh, I just loved this time of year!

I remember once being invited to Tom's home where he still lived with his ageing parents. I had thought our house was decorated beautifully but I remember thinking how differently theirs was adorned. Our decorations were nice; theirs were magnificent! Their tree was overflowing with presents, and the living rooms were decorated like Santa's grotto.

That particular year I had been dreaming night after night about finally having a Mousetrap game and a Space Hopper. I talked of nothing else to anyone who would listen, and of course Santa had had my gazillion letters so he had to know how important they were to me. I thought I had been a good girl, and good girls always get the presents they wish for. I had only asked for two, surely that must be possible for Santa to bring.

In addition, I had dropped daily hints to my parents and grandparents so everyone in the family knew too. Earlier that week I had been to my Grandma Lilly's and, when she'd sent me to look in her bedroom for a scarf of hers, I had by accident opened a different cupboard from the one I should have done and that's where I saw it!

There it was . . . I could see my prize sitting there on the shelf. I couldn't believe my eyes: the colourful box so shiny and bright, the detailed picture on the front, the big letters stating SPACE

HOPPER. Whoopee! I thought. Grandma Lilly really does love me after all and has listened to what I really, really want. I was so excited. In my mind, my Grandma Lilly had bought this for me and Santa was going to bring me the Mouse Trap game. Oh, wasn't this going to be the best Christmas ever?

As I turned around to leave the room, I noticed my Granddad Stanley standing upright to attention by the side of the door, in full Army uniform. I remember looking at the medals on his lapel and thinking how colourful they were. Although I had often seen him around Grandma's house, this was the first time he had ever properly spoken to me. Sam was also standing in the room. Was I in trouble because I had seen the Space Hopper? Instead of being scolded, however, what was said left me feeling a little bewildered. Sam spoke first, saying that my granddad needed to say something to me and that the message came with great love.

Granddad looked deep into my eyes. 'I always wanted a grand-daughter and I am sorry that I wasn't here for you when you were growing up. You need to know how proud I am of you, and that things would have been very different if I were still alive. I am sorry, my love, but Grandma has always had lots of boys in her family and her affections have always centred on them. It's just the way your granny is – you have to forgive her. She misses me so much. If I were alive everything would be different because I would have spoiled you so very much. Please tell your father I am very proud of him.'

I nodded, but had contradictory thoughts – how could I ever tell Dad when he wouldn't believe his father still existed?

As if in reply, I heard Sam say it was because my dad was fearful of the spiritual and my mother was openly in denial so as not to aggravate him, though inside she was starting to embrace the truth.

My Granddad Stanley continued: 'I knew when your mother

was pregnant that she was having a girl. She came to visit me in hospital to tell me she was pregnant when I was very ill. I told her she would have my first grand-daughter but that I would never be able to hold you in my arms. So, my dearest girl, I want you to know today how much you truly mean to me and how much I will always love you.'

My granddad's words were sincere and I felt he was sending me a different kind of Christmas wish.

In an instant both Sam and my granddad had gone. I turned back to the cupboard, bursting with excitement. My Grandma Lilly had never bought me anything like this before. Usually I had a pack of knickers or a box of white handkerchiefs from her for Christmas, so this year I thought she truly loved me after all. I quietly closed the door of the cupboard, making sure no one heard my mistake, and as I walked back down the stairs I was barely able to contain my excitement. I went into the lounge where Mum and Dad were talking to her. I ran over, threw my arms around Grandma's neck and gave her a huge bear hug.

'What's that for?' she said in a very puzzled way.

With my arms firmly around her shoulders, I said with adoration in my eyes: 'Oh, nothing, Grandma. It's because I love you.'

My dad smiled a sunbeam smile, radiant with pride and love because I had hugged my Grandma Lilly, something I didn't usually do voluntarily. I suppose like every normal child my affections were easily bought.

I nearly told him about his father coming to speak to me upstairs – but decided against it, just in case it spoiled the day and then I might not be given the Space Hopper.

Christmas Eve arrived. Although we were not a religious family, my mother voluntarily went to take Holy Communion every Christmas Eve with my Nana Ada at Holy Trinity Church in Blacon. I always wanted to go with them, but they said it was far too late at night for me to go, so Dad stayed in to watch me. As many children requested annually, I made Dad promise to leave a drink and a mince pie for Santa and some carrots for Rudolph on the tiled hearth. Even though our chimney was blocked by the gas fire, Dad assured me Santa would magically find his way into the house.

I couldn't sleep as thoughts of opening my presents drifted through my mind. In my imagination I could already see myself bouncing on my Space Hopper and playing my Mouse Trap game with Mum and Dad.

Naturally I drifted into sleep, at least for a while. When I opened my eyes the darkness of night was still evident. It was only 4 a.m. but the prospect of opening my longed-for presents was too much for me. I slid out of bed, tiptoed across the landing, and one step at a time walked down the staircase. Once downstairs, I saw the white pillowcase filled with colourfully wrapped presents standing by the Christmas tree. There was also a selection of other parcels thinly spread out underneath it. With great excitement I shouted upstairs to my parents, 'He's been, he's been! Wake up.' Without hesitation, I firmly gripped the pillowcase and dragged it upstairs one step at a time. It was heavy . . .

Finally, after dragging the pillowcase across the landing, I reached my parents' bedroom and struggled to fling the heavy sack on to their bed. 'Wake up! Wake up!' For my parents, there really wasn't another option. I was bubbling with excitement as I climbed between them into the middle of the bed. This was going to be the Christmas of all Christmases.

My parents reluctantly wiped the sleep from their eyes. My mother sat upright while my father lay immobile and horizontal and said the exact same words that are heard in a million homes throughout the country on Christmas morning: 'It's far too early, go back to sleep for a while.'

My mother smiled at him. 'Oh, Colin it's just one day . . . don't be so mean. Let her open them.'

No sooner had Mum given me the go-ahead and her smile of approval than I was on a mission. Paper was ripped impatiently from the parcels as I hauled them out of the white cotton make-do Santa sack. Each present I opened was not what I was expecting, but despite being pleased I was eager to continue until I found what I really wanted. I kissed my parents enthusiastically for each parcel I unwrapped, thanking them as I went along, cooing how nice this or that was. Finally I got to the end of the sack where only a few sweets and oranges were clinging to the cotton corners.

My swelling eyes must have said it all. Lovingly my mum put her arm around me and cuddled me to her side: 'What's up, my love – why you are so upset?' Naturally, I couldn't hide my feelings of disappointment from my parents, but not wanting to seem ungrateful, I said everything was fine. My mother smiled warmly. 'Well, there are some more presents under the tree, but you can't open them just yet, my love. You will have to wait until later, when it's the proper time to get up. Go back into your bedroom and play with what you have opened until your dad and I have had a couple more hours' sleep.'

Whooooppeee! Mum's kept the best until last, I thought, barely able to contain myself. My excitement was beyond bounds. In happy anticipation, I did as she said and played in my bedroom until I heard my parents stirring a couple of hours later.

Finally my dad rose and we gathered around the tree in the lounge. Dad had a mug of tea and a cigarette in his hand as he sat down to be entertained by his child's excitement. There were three biggies under the tree and a few smaller packages. I knew they were for me because I had already checked the labels several times before my parents came downstairs. They each had my name on them. Now I could open my long-awaited and already beloved Space Hopper and Mouse Trap.

Dad stubbed his cigarette out and grandly announced: 'I am going to play Santa. You sit by Mum and I will hand the presents over to you both.'

One by one, Dad read the labels and I opened the gift. First Nana Ada and Granddad Joe, then Auntie Joan and Uncle Bob, finally Grandma Lilly . . . only it wasn't a big present as I'd expected but a tiny parcel. Trying to work out in my mind why it was so small in comparison to the box I'd seen in the cupboard, I concluded that the only logical explanation was that Grandma Lilly had been cunning and taken my Space Hopper out of the box. Quite unnecessary – but devious nonetheless! If there wasn't air in the Space Hopper then it would look like a big flat balloon until it was inflated. My reasoning was faultless. That had to be the answer. I eagerly took the present and thanked Dad with a smile that caused his face to light up. That's strange, I thought, this doesn't feel like a Space Hopper, this feels soft and floppy. However, not giving it a second thought, the wrapper was torn into shreds and, lo and behold, there they were – like pieces of sliced white bread piled on a plate . . . two pairs of white cotton knickers and two white cotton vests.

Where was the Space Hopper? Where had it gone?

Without any self-control, I started to cry. My parents looked at each other; even Dad seemed upset and put his arm around me. As if to justify his mother's Christmas gift to her oldest grand-daughter, he offered an explanation without knowing what it was I'd expected: 'Grandma has gone to a lot of trouble and given you something useful that you really need, like she always does.'

Through sobs of disappointment, I rubbed my eyes with the

palms of my hands: 'But, Dad, I saw my Space Hopper in her house. When I was upstairs, I accidentally opened Grandma's cupboard door, looking for her scarf, and it was there . . . she was hiding it from me! What has she done with my Space Hopper?' My eyes widened and the tears started to trickle down my face unhindered.

Dad scooped me up and gave me a huge cuddle. 'Oh, I am so sorry, my love, Grandma sent that to your cousin in Germany. It went to Ian at your Uncle Denis's house. Did you think it was for you?'

Slowly, I nodded. In abject disappointment I held my head low, looking at my toes. With tear-filled eyes, barely able to utter the words, I dutifully replied: 'Yes. I thought it was for me.'

In an attempt to break the solemn mood, my dad went down on all fours and scampered under the tree to find me another present. He made me laugh. Despite feeling hollow inside, I tried to stay optimistic. My tears stopped as I realised I still had another biggie, didn't I?

I had my Mouse Trap game to open!

My mum looked worried and my dad also seemed to be a little furtive as he passed me the final present. What was wrong? The biggie was eventually handed to me – only this didn't feel right either. I opened the parcel a lot more slowly and carefully, dreading to see what was inside. It was a doll. My eyes filled up again but I swallowed my tears. Nevertheless my parents saw my distress. My mother knew what I really wanted that Christmas, she had heard me talk about it enough times: 'We couldn't get you a Mouse Trap, darling, Santa hadn't made enough this year. He will bring you one next year, I'm sure.'

I looked at Sam who had stood there all morning watching me. His reassuring smile filled me with an indescribable strength. 'That's OK, the doll is lovely. Can I go upstairs and play, please?'

I gave both my parents a hug and a big kiss, thanked them for my presents and disappeared upstairs.

Once I was there, I lay on my unmade bed and cried into my crinkled-up pillow to muffle the sound of my sobs. I wasn't crying because of not having what I really wanted, though it was of course a major disappointment, but because I now knew for sure what I'd felt all along. My Grandma Lilly didn't love me as much as she did her other grandchildren.

My tears were short-lived, though. My mood lifted with the realisation that I had just received a nice new doll and a Scrabble game. Really, I was a lucky girl to have any presents.

I decided to wash my hands and face and cool my red eyes, and then I went back downstairs to ask my mother if I could help with dinner. I loved my parents and wanted us all to have a happy day. As I entered the lounge, with the cosy gas fire belting out heat and the familiar smells of Christmas dinner filling the air, my father ran over to me, picked me up and held me tight in his arms. He hugged me in a way he had never hugged me before. For the first time in my life I felt really close to him – truly loved. This feeling was worth a thousand Mouse Trap games. I closed my eyes and this time cried from happiness.

Dad put me down and I could tell he too was upset, not angry. He said softly in my ear: 'Helen, my love, in this envelope is some pocket money Santa left you under the tree. I didn't see it at first when I was giving out the presents.'

In fact, neither had I. And I had scanned that tree for everything, in, around and under it!

My dad's mitigating story began: 'Santa doesn't want you to be unhappy. He knows you really wanted that Space Hopper, so as soon as we see one in town, he's left you enough money to go and buy one. Wasn't that thoughtful of him?'

A child can only be fooled some of the time, and on this

occasion my dad didn't fool me at all. From then on I knew that there was no Santa, as much as I wanted to believe it, because even the youngest child knows he doesn't leave money – he leaves presents! I went along with the illusion anyway, happy that I could at least buy my Space Hopper when the time for the next shopping trip came around.

What made my day was the feeling Dad gave me when he picked me up and held me in his arms. The love I felt from him at that moment has become a freeze-frame memory from my childhood: treasured forever.

Sam smiled. From tears of disappointment came the true joy of feeling my father's love for the first time. Sam too works in very mysterious ways.

It wasn't until many years later, in adult conversation with my mother, that it emerged that my dad had a massive argument with his mother about the way she always treated me so differently from her other grandchildren at Christmas and birthday times. Apparently, my mother explained to me, her reasoning was that as Denis was a Major in the Army and doing very well for himself financially, his children would naturally expect more!

Needless to say, from that time on I never talked to my Grandma Lilly about what I wanted for Christmas. I knew it would be knickers, vests, handkerchiefs or tights. After all, I needed them.

School life in the New Year of 1969 started in just the same way as usual. The bareness of the classrooms was disappointing as the Christmas decorations had been boxed away by the authorities for another year. The class dutifully knuckled down to its studies and we all made friends with the new children who had joined that term. However, there was one new girl in the class that particular term who didn't seem to like anyone and was continually causing the other girls to cry by being nasty, especially to me. Her name was Stacey – how could I ever forget! For some mysterious reason she never seemed to get into trouble with the teachers, despite her bullying tactics. It was as though they were oblivious to our complaints about this awful new pupil.

On our walks home, I explained to Mum many times that this new girl, Stacey, was always spitting at me, punching me, and often called me very rude names. My mother's attitude was that 'sticks and stones may break my bones but names will never hurt me'. The ditty stuck in my mind, but it certainly didn't help the situation. If that didn't work, I was advised to ignore her. However, if this girl ever hurt me, I must tell either my teacher or my mother.

So, dutifully, I turned the other cheek when the girl once again started to call me names. My ignoring her inflamed her temper even more, and she started to pinch me, harder and harder, every time she came near me.

Finally, after enduring weeks of relentless bullying, I could take no more and decided enough was enough. The girl was making my life hell as no matter how hard I tried to ignore her, she kept coming straight back, hitting me again and again. So I told her what my mother had advised. That I was going to tell the teacher *and* my mum that she was physically hurting me.

After that the girl left me alone: so that was that then. The plan had worked as my mum had said it would. I thought that was the last of it so I carried on with my schoolwork. A few minutes later, the teacher came over and dragged me out of the room firmly by one arm, ordering me to march to the Headmaster's office with her straight away.

I was sobbing. I had no idea what I had done wrong. Despite my pleas, the teacher refused to tell me. Once inside the Head's office, she accused me of biting the new girl's arm! The

Headmaster stared at me grimly and said that there was no tolerance shown towards bullying. I flatly denied the accusation, explaining that in fact it was the other way around and that the new girl had been bullying *me*. I said that she had been pinching and punching me during lessons when we were working together, and how she'd called me nasty rude names my mother said were crude and vile. I even told the Headmaster that I had told my mother about the way the new girl had been bullying me, and again I flatly denied touching or biting her.

The girl was brought into the office and she defiantly displayed her arm to the Headmaster, so that the teacher and he could see where the teeth marks were: all red and bruised-looking. I once again pleaded that I didn't do anything wrong, but the two adults decided I must be to blame as Stacey swore that it was my doing.

'We cannot have this sort of behaviour, Helen. I will not tolerate your lies. Your records show you are prone to making up fanciful stories. I just won't stand for anyone thinking they can get away with such acts of aggression in this school.' The Headmaster spoke fiercely to me.

For some reason none of the staff wanted to upset Stacey or confront her in any way and so straight away I was considered guilty of biting her in retaliation for her calling me names. Stacey was asked to leave the Headmaster's office and I was left standing with Mrs Jones. Naturally I kept protesting my innocence, which only seemed to make the Headmaster angrier. My mind raced with questions. Why did the teachers not believe anything I said? What was it about me? Even my own parents didn't trust what I said, so no wonder the teachers did not. They thought I was a liar, too. Mum had told them that I was always imagining things – which I wasn't!

Sam drew my attention as he stood at the far end of the office.

Not a word from him to help me. Why? It was hard for me not to cry.

Determined to mete out the appropriate discipline, my Headmaster walked over to his desk, opened a drawer and pulled out a very thin cane about thirty inches long. I remember wondering how he could have pulled something so long from a narrow drawer, but as he bent it I could see its flexibility. From the look on Mrs Jones' face I could tell she was not entirely comfortable with the impending punishment. However, I had been found guilty and sentenced with little opportunity for self-defence. Sam was there, of course, standing watching: our eyes met. No last-minute words to save me then? The Headmaster invited me to hold the back of a wooden chair that stood to the side of his large desk. Without so much as a warning, I heard the cane crack against the back of my leg, right inside the knee joint. Then the stinging began. Before I could draw breath to cry out, I heard the second crack and another sting started to burn and itch intolerably.

Punishment over, I was dismissed to stand in shame outside the Head's office for the entire last session before going home.

Sam crouched beside me, lowering himself to the same height as me. 'That was a wicked experience, Helen. When you go home, tell your mum it was not your fault and see what happens.'

His words were little comfort to me when the backs of my legs stung with pain.

Thankfully I didn't have long to wait before the end-of-lessons bell rang and I could go home. The Head said I had to wait until everyone else had more or less gone, so they could see me standing in shame, and only then would I be allowed to leave. My mum arrived to pick me up from school, waiting at the school gates, but became concerned when I didn't show up with all the others, as normally I would be among the first out. Eventually the

Head agreed I could go, so without running I walked as fast as I could to collect my coat and headed for the exit doors.

As the fresh air bit my face I saw my mother walking through the playground towards me. I ran as fast as I could towards her and started to sob uncontrollably.

'Whatever is the matter?' She instinctively threw her arms around me.

'I am never coming back to this school ever again,' I shouted. 'Please, Mum, take me away from here.'

'What's wrong? Let's go back in and tell a teacher,' my mother pleaded.

'NO! NO!' I screamed. 'I am never speaking to my teacher ever again. I just want to go home.'

My mother didn't know what to do, but she realised no amount of persuasion on her part was going to make me go back into school at that moment in time.

It's amazing how a cup of tea and a warm fire help to comfort you. Eventually, after much coaxing, my mother found out what had happened. I explained what the new girl had accused me of and how the teachers didn't believe me, and then how I was caned in the Head's office and left to stand in shame outside his office on my own until the end of school.

My mother stared at me almost in disbelief, making me swear that I had not bitten the girl. How could she even for one moment consider me capable of doing such a thing? It was bad enough my parents not believing my stories about Sam and the others, but not to believe me about this incident was the final straw. I shouted at the top of my voice that the girl in my class was constantly bullying me and now I had been caned for something I DID NOT DO. How difficult was it for my mother to understand that? I had already talked to her several times about this girl and her constant jibing. At that moment I hated my mother; in fact I hated both my parents. I felt that as usual they doubted anything I had to say. Immediately that thought came into my mind, Sam stepped in: 'Don't you ever think that of your parents. They are growing and learning, as you are!'

In my rage I ran upstairs to my bedroom, slamming the door. In my haste to leave the room I had spilled my cup of tea over the chair where I'd been sitting, so by the time my mother had mopped it up and climbed the stairs after me, Sam had gone.

'I am so sorry, darling.' My mother shed tears herself. 'I had no idea things were this bad for you. I am going in to school to sort it out tomorrow – don't you worry.'

In the morning, despite the fact I never wanted to set foot in the school again, my mother promised me that everything would be fine. She tackled the Headmaster in his office and made me swear an oath on the Bible that I did not bite the girl or cause her any harm at all. In fact, she said that she would bring the police into school if they didn't get to the bottom of what Stacey had done to me.

Once the word 'police' was used, the Headmaster started to take my mother's suggestion more seriously. He appeased her by saying he needed a little time to try and get to the bottom of the problem, and he pleaded with her not to bring in the police. My mother told him he had one day – then she was coming back.

The next day arrived and we were ushered into his office. He had now interviewed Stacey at length and also spoken to her parents. Eventually, under sustained questioning, Stacey admitted she had bitten herself in order to receive some attention from the teachers and to make sure I was in trouble.

My mother was furious when the Headmaster relayed his findings. He explained that Stacey was from a 'difficult' home and needed help and support. My mother's only agenda at that moment was to make the Head apologise in front of the whole school in her presence at the main assembly the next day. She also told him he was lucky she didn't press charges against him.

I was just happy that at last she believed in me and knew I had told the truth. Stacey had been making my life hell since her arrival ten months ago, so I was pleased that it had now come out into the open.

About a month later, the drama teacher gave me the lead part in the Christmas play; I was to be the Princess in *The Golden Goose*. In retrospect I see this was probably to appease my mother and ease the school's guilt for punishing me when I was innocent. After the disappointing Christmas last year without my Mouse Trap, it was positively refreshing to have the excitement of the school play to look forward to, especially as I was to play the Princess.

One morning during rehearsal time in the school hall, the kitchen staff started to set up for school dinner while we practised our forthcoming play. At the back of the hall, one of the dinner ladies was carrying a trayful of squash glasses to put on the lunch tables. She paused for a moment to catch a glimpse of me doing a solo piece centre-stage, then out of the blue let out one almighty scream and dropped the tray on to the wooden floor.

The dinner lady pointed directly at me and shouted out loud for all to hear: 'There was a man in an old Army uniform standing right next to that little girl!'

So much fuss, I thought. It was only Granddad Stanley coming to watch me rehearse.

I wished my mum had been at the rehearsal to witness what had just happened. Maybe then she would have known that I'd spoken the truth about Sam and my many spirits too.

No such luck!

4

Tinkle, Tinkle, Little Star

Stacey was moved on yet again. After her disappearance, school life improved for me as I felt more secure with the bullying incident behind me. As Sam reminded me many times, there is no future in looking to the past, only to what lies ahead. I just hoped no one else would be harmed by Stacey's lies, and still felt a pang of sadness for her as it was obvious she needed more care and understanding than she'd so far received.

From time to time we made a visit to my dad's sister, older than him by about ten years, Auntie Connie, and her husband, Uncle Eddie. My auntie lived in a lovely area overlooking the famous River Dee in one of the most prestigious areas of Chester. The entrance to her beautiful terraced home was via a set of steps up from the road, where you were instantly greeted by the scents and colours of her window boxes and ceramic pots gloriously overflowing with flowers. Prettily painted walls were lined with hanging baskets crammed with colourful blooms.

Once, when I walked into my Auntie Connie's house, I could

see a spirit lady standing in the hallway, dressed in rather frilly old-fashioned Victorian clothes with an apron over the top of her long white gown. I could tell she was a proud, albeit humble lady because, having seen period dramas on TV, I knew she was more working-class than gentry.

Auntie Connie's was a happy house full of homely comforts. However, every time I visited, this lovely spiritual vision of a lady appeared. The spirit lady was never stern and always smiled at me tenderly, almost as though she was welcoming me into her home and not my aunt's.

Inside, the house was on many different levels. The kitchen and dining areas were up a couple of steps, travelling to the back of the house. It was in the kitchen that I would see the spirit lady the most; she seemed to walk beside me whenever I was in that area of the house. It wasn't until Auntie Connie gave birth to Gary, my cousin, that I fully understood why the lady's spirit was there.

Gary was born in August, nine years after me. When I visited my auntie a short while after his birth, naturally she wanted to show us him as he slept in his cot, quietly and snugly, upstairs. My aunt had waited a long time to have a child and, in her mature years, Gary was going to be her one and only pride and joy. She was blissfully happy and wanted to show him off to anyone and everyone. I remember distinctly bending over to see him in his little cradle, and how he smelled of gorgeous baby products.

On this particular occasion, I noticed the lady in spirit sitting beside baby Gary in the nursery chair, almost as though she was keeping watch on her own child. I noticed that she also had a spirit baby in her arms and was cradling the child as it slept peacefully. She smiled a lovely warm gentle smile as I peeped into the crib, in acknowledgement of the two beautiful bundles she guarded so carefully. I didn't dare tell my aunt or my parents what I could see. My parents had threatened me so many times about speaking out about my 'imaginary' visions. As my aunt and I tip-toed back out of the room, my baby cousin slept and the lady in spirit waved goodbye to both of us.

As I returned to the lounge my aunt smiled at me and said: 'Wasn't he a lovely little boy?' Of course I had to agree; he really was a beautiful baby and I would have loved so much to have a brother just like him.

One day my aunt went to collect Gary out of his cradle upstairs after his nap when she noticed the ghostly form of a lady standing at the top of the steep stairs. She described the figure to me in detail and she was dressed in the same long white dress as I had seen. My aunt said that the lady smiled at her and she had the feeling that the lady in white was connected to the house in some way. Sam explained to me that the lady had died along with her baby in childbirth and that they were together in spirit. My aunt's home had been hers previously and she had wanted to share her bundle of joy with my aunt because she too was so proud of becoming a mother. It was a message of love, Sam said, between two mothers who adored their new babies. After that visit the spirit lady was never seen again.

Some months later my aunt told the whole family of her own spiritual experience. She was not prone to fanciful ideas so when they heard the story about the ghostly lady, they listened with great astonishment and believed every word she said. Strangely, my parents never called her a liar or said she had an over-active imagination.

During the school year, like many children, I had become very interested in music. Intriguingly, every time a teacher played classical music on the school record player it was as though waves of emotion ran through my body. Each time music filled the air Sam would sit near to me and listen, his eyes would close and he would sway to the rhythm.

Mozart became my favourite composer. During one of our chats, I asked Sam if Mozart was in spirit with him, still composing music. Sam smiled and reacted in a way I was not expecting. 'Oh, chile, you really are growing up. Music is such a vital element in the spirit world! There are great opportunities for all creators like Mozart to continue their work. Maybe it's time to remind you of the existence of the Great Halls of Learning there.'

From my earliest recollection it had always been Sam who taught me and guided me through life. However, I had absolutely no idea what he was talking about now. I knew nothing about the Great Halls of Learning, let alone remembering them! Sam saw my puzzled expression and announced: 'You see, Helen, in the spirit world we have a massive campus as big as any city, full of many great buildings more stately than you have ever seen. They are surrounded by gardens that are beautifully cultivated, with perfect colours and scented with perfumes you would find hard even to imagine.

'These buildings house all the knowledge known to the universe and are devoted to the pursuit of all study and learning at every conceivable level. They teach their subjects using every available sense: so, for instance, if you listen to music, it is not just the sound you listen to, which in itself is immeasurably purer in tone there. It is also represented by every colour of the rainbow, and every conceivable tone and shade of those colours. Colour and music become as one – and the perfect combination of them is perfect harmony. In spirit, music is part of our very existence. One day, when your understanding is more developed, we will talk more about these wondrous halls.'

So, inspired by the existence in the spirit world of a Great Hall of Learning full of music, my piano-playing began one wet winter's day during break-time, when my music teacher noticed me trying to tap out a tune and offered to help me by giving me half an hour of free instruction after school. Seeing my enthusiasm, my teacher was kind enough to continue lavishing any spare time she found on helping me learn, and I constantly practised. Soon I began to read music and had started to play the piano during school breaks and assemblies. I certainly wouldn't say I was accomplished, but I did seem to be able to knock out a relatively good tune for a child of my age and my teacher seemed to think I made a good enough job of it to play at morning assembly.

After a few months, I managed to tap out a selection of hymns and carols. My teacher begged me to ask my parents about having private lessons as I wanted to become an accomplished player. I loved the piano and thought my parents would be pleased that I showed an interest. Broaching the subject to my father one night, I explained that some private lessons would really help me improve. I didn't think he would refuse, seeing that the music teacher was taking such an interest in me. How wrong I was. Despite my pleading desperately for two hours with my dad, he remained adamant that private piano lessons were far too expensive. My tears must have softened him a little because he did agree, after much pleading from me, to look for a piano I could practise on. I was ecstatic and said that I was happy to have it as a Christmas present if they were expensive. In my mind I cherished a vision of him choosing something modest but modern, a bit like the piano at school.

Dad had given up his job at the Vauxhall factory, having passed his exams to be a master plumber. In his new job at Bromborough, based in Burma Oil's research department, he erected refinery scale models, complete with technical piping and valves. The laboratory scientists and chemists would test out refining techniques in the miniature constructions my dad set up. I say 'miniature' but they were actually pretty large working mock-ups of the chemical installations the company were about to build.

One of the chief lab technicians had asked Dad to do some plumbing work at his home and that's where the piano came from. As my dad fitted the new boiler for their central heating in the garage, he noticed the old piano shoved against the back wall, neglected and covered in cobwebs. Being friendly with the owners by then, he asked if he could buy it for me, but they were so grateful that someone was at last taking it off their hands, they gave the old Joanna to him for free, explaining that they had a more modern one indoors.

I was so excited I couldn't wait to see my beautiful new piano, so I went with Dad and his friends to pick it up. I had no idea what it looked like and had visions of the grand disclosure of the shiny white piano keys. On our arrival at their beautiful detached house, the couple were very polite and invited Dad and me inside, leaving the two friendly removers to wait inside the van. There I saw the modern upright sitting in the corner, polished and glistening, and I cried out with glee, saying: 'Oh, Dad, it's beautiful! It's just the one I wanted and so much like the one at school, but even nicer. Thank you for such a wonderful Christmas present.'

My father's eyes dimmed and the lady of the house frowned. What was wrong? I thought. This *was* my piano, wasn't it? Dad didn't know where to put himself as he squirmed uncomfortably and I knew there was disappointing news on the way. He explained that the piano we were going to collect was in the garage.

Sam appeared then. He almost always knows instinctively when I need him. He must have known that my heart was sinking right then or why else would he have arrived?

We went into the garage. I was stunned into silence as the three men wheeled the piano out of the darkness at the back. An old blanket had been thrown over the top to protect it a little from the ravages of time, but it looked dead and lifeless, its wood all dull and drained of its once former glory. Had my dad brought me all this way to collect this ravaged antique?

The lady of the house could see my sadness as the woollen shroud was taken away and almost apologetically asked me if we still wanted it. My dad smiled as he cheerfully said, 'It will do for now, won't it, love? Helen will probably get fed up of playing in a month or two, so it's pointless spending a lot of money on something I'm unsure she will stick to.'

How could he even think that? Wasn't this supposed to be my Christmas present? The piano was heaved up and loaded into the back of the van as the men moaned that it weighed a ton.

I tried to talk to my father quietly, saying that it wasn't quite what I was expecting, but in his usual way when cornered he started to grow angry. I always knew when my father's own decisions were frustrating him. I think he often meant well with his impulsive actions, but if anyone thought differently from him he would blow up angrily.

I think the piano's previous owners were happy to see the back of it. However, they politely gave Dad the telephone number of a piano tuner. He looked surprised as they handed him the number; obviously he had not realised that it would need any work and took the card in bemusement as the lady explained to him that it was badly in need of repair. He optimistically announced: 'Don't worry, Helen, I'll call the tuner tomorrow and he'll make it as good as new for you.'

My mother was at home making room for the surprise. It was to be placed against the wall in the dining area.

To be honest, it wasn't quite the Christmas present I had hoped for. But I thought, oh, well, it *is* a piano, and like an old car after a good tune-up it will be as good as new. Then it would be my new pride and joy and I could practise to my heart's content.

My mother had a huge row with my father as he tried to manhandle the scruffy old thing off the van with the other two men. 'Why have you brought such a monstrosity home?' So that confirmed what I already suspected . . . it was in such bad condition it would never be much use.

While the piano stood at the front door, I lifted the dusty lid to reveal a row of amber-coloured keys and tried to play my first tune. The order in which I played the keys with my fingers didn't represent the sound that came out: the tune sounded as if Liberace's blind dog was attempting to perform it.

Sam stood nearby. I knew he was thinking the same as me. Not quite the flowing quality of musical tone I was expecting.

Every Christmas was starting to feel like a disappointment of some sort. As the build-up to the main day arrived, any thoughts I'd had of playing 'Jingle Bells' in the lounge, with doting parents and friends singing joyfully aloud, were dashed. My ambition of becoming an accomplished piano player was sunk.

Eventually, after the last of the turkey had been eaten, my father decided to call the piano tuner. Actually, I think he couldn't cope with the off-key sounds I was making a moment longer! The man arrived and was much older than I'd imagined he would be. He took one look at the piano and asked my father if he was kidding, then shook his head from side to side, tutting in disapproval. Judging by the expression on his face this was going to be a huge job. He rolled up his sleeves and asked my mother to leave him alone as it was going to take some time. Sam stood and looked on, watching his every move.

After about an hour, the piano tuner called my father from the other room, his face grave as he explained the magnitude of the job. He showed my father that the pads had worn away on the keys internally and the structure inside had rusted due to damp. 'You are lucky to get any tune at all out of this old girl,' he said reverently. 'Mind you, she would have been a corker in her day. Unfortunately she's long past her best. Sorry, Mr Sparrow, it will cost you a small fortune to renovate her. It would have been better if you had invested in a more modern upright. This old dear has not been cared for in a long time.'

I was devastated. This was my Christmas present he was talking about.

'Surely it'll be good enough for Helen to practise on?' my father pleaded, almost in an apologetic manner, to exonerate himself. The man shook his head and my father's embarrassment mounted. Dad left the room to have a cigarette outside as he was upset, and asked my mother to see the man out.

The tuner wouldn't even take any money from my parents for trying to salvage the old dear. As he said to my mother when he left: 'If you have a child who wants to play music, then like any gift it should be nurtured and invested in.' Sam smiled at the man who was voicing his own thoughts. Did my mother hear or was this said to deaf ears? I am not sure.

In one of our nightly conversations, Sam told me there was a lesson to be learned from my father's actions. By trying to do things cheaply, ultimately he had nothing to show for it. Sam was starting to teach me about life choices.

Nevertheless, as this was the only piano I had, out of tune or not, I was determined to play my old Bessie at night when I came home from school. I would sit and finger the notes, and try to imagine what colours and shapes these sounds would make if I were playing in the spirit world in the Great Hall of Music. Something inside told me my attempts to create sound might be harmonious, but the results coming from this piano certainly were not!

At school, I continued to play during lunchtime or whenever my teacher had some spare time. Eventually she decided that unless my father paid for the extra lessons, she couldn't carry on, as reaching a higher standard required a greater commitment from both of us. I had no option but to practise at home and try to teach myself.

But my piano-playing skills weren't completely wasted. A year or so before my mum had enrolled me in the local Sunday School, maybe she thought it would help me forget about my spirit visitors. Or perhaps it was her bid to have a few hours to herself on a Sunday. Either way, I voluntarily made the short walk every week to the church hall.

While I was at Sunday School I would tinkle the keys of the piano during breaktime. When I explained my predicament with my father to a nice lady from the church, she offered to teach me a little more. I was so happy I trotted along to Sunday School every week after that, feeling joyful at the prospect of playing on another piano, with the help of a caring musician.

Actually, I loved Sunday School as I felt that the clergy surely ought to understand my ability to see spirits. When the Vicar, Father Whetter, told us stories from the Bible and described how Angels would visit, I thought that at last someone felt the same way as me and could see the same things. I told him about my Guide and my other spirit visitors. While I spoke to him about my experiences, the Vicar would sit open-mouthed and listen without interruption. At least he didn't ridicule me or tell me to shut up when I raised the subject.

For once in my life I actually felt proud of my abilities and of all the people from the spirit world who visited me. I took great pleasure in explaining to Father Whetter about the different sorts of spirit people who came to me. There were the ordinary people in spirit related to those alive here who I would meet. They looked very much as they had prior to their death, but often younger. I normally saw them in colour, but I could never remember seeing any feet; their bodies seemed to disappear below the knee, although at times I could see only their head and torso.

I also explained about my Guide Sam, saying that often he had a glow about him, rather like watching the Readybrek advert where the people lit up after eating the warm cereal. As far as I could understand at that age, Guides from the higher realms had a brighter aura, but Sam had taught me they mustn't be confused with Angels who were different altogether. Father Whetter just sat quietly and listened to me. Although I told him that my Guides exhibited various levels of brightness, to make him feel a little more involved, I explained to him that some spirit Guides glowed with a light like people in the Bible pictures we studied at Sunday School.

To me it wasn't a school at all but a happy place where children coloured in pictures to take home. Mums and Dads came to the special church service with their children, and drank tea and ate biscuits with us afterwards. I often wondered why my mum too didn't come to church to have tea and biscuits with the other families, but when I asked her one day she said that she was far too busy.

When Sunday School finished, it was the one time in the week when Mum would cook a meal and we would sit down together as a family. This was my favourite time, although I have to say her cooking skills still had not improved.

Then I caught chicken pox. I was very ill with it and could not attend Sunday School for at least two weeks. Sam was worried about me as I even had spots around my eyes, and my mum had to take time off work to look after me. I thought it was heaven, having her pamper me all day, and wanted to be ill more often.

She was helping me complete a huge jigsaw one day when the

doorbell rang and the Vicar stood on the doorstep, asking if he could come in and see me.

My mother was a little nervous as she invited him indoors. I thought it was nice to see him. He said he had come because he was worried after not seeing me in church for a few Sundays, and wanted to know if I was well. He explained to my mother that I played the hymns on the piano during the service, something she didn't know, and the lady who helped him was also worried because it was unlike me to miss Sunday School. My mother was quite shocked when he seemed so concerned, and I was flattered that he was asking about me. After all he was a very personable young man. Someone older might even have thought he was good-looking under that starched white dog collar.

My mum told me to put the kettle on to make tea and to get the best cutlery out of the drawer. She had a cutlery set kept in a red velvet-lined box for such special occasions, so I knew she was trying to impress him. A clergyman was a rare visitor to our house, and vicars in the late-1960s were treated as VIPs, so this was indeed a special occasion.

Although it was only about 4.30 p.m., the lounge was becoming dark, so Mum asked me to turn on the lights while they talked. Pooof! Suddenly all the electricity went off. My mother was so embarrassed. How could that happen now? What would he think? Sitting in the dark, she realised that she had forgotten to top up the meter and began desperately to hunt for her purse.

The Vicar laughed out loud as she continuously apologised. Even in the dim light you could see Mum had gone bright red. Rummaging around in her purse, she finally found a shilling, but only one, so the Vicar gave her a couple more coins out of his own pocket and I was told to put them in the meter.

The priest shouted to me, 'How will you see, Helen? You'll

need a torch to see under those stairs, surely. It's very dark in here and it will be even darker under there!' Without hesitation I replied innocently: 'It's OK – Sam's here! He'll come in with me and show me where to put the coins.' Then, a few moments later, we had light again.

My mother told me to go into the kitchen and make tea for them both while she spoke to the Vicar privately. I didn't understand why I had to make the tea and leave the room, I was the one who was ill. He had come to see me, hadn't he? So why was I being ushered out? I didn't know what I had done to upset her, then I thought for a moment and realised . . . Oops! I'd mentioned Sam, hadn't I? I'd been warned not to talk about him in front of other people.

Mum told me to close the door to the kitchen behind me, so I could only hear their muffled voices when I tried to listen through the gap I had purposely left. I cursed the hissing water in the kettle. I could not make out the whole conversation, only snippets while they were having an intense chat about me. Despite my concentration, all I could hear was *Sam – spirit – lovely girl – Guides*! I quietly opened the door wide, pretending I wanted to ask about sugar in the tea, and then I heard: 'Where does she get all this talk from? Do you talk to her about this, Mrs Sparrow?'

After eventually making the tea, I carefully tried to carry a tray laden with the pot and three cups and saucers. The Vicar found it quaintly amusing when he saw that I had put tiny egg spoons on the side of the saucers rather than teaspoons, eventually bursting into laughter to relieve the tension.

While we sipped tea he never mentioned a word to me of what my mother had said to him, but smiled and told me that I was a special girl and that everyone missed me in Sunday School and to hurry back to them.

That was the last time my mother let me go there, and I never again had a piano lesson from one of the congregation. Sam said it was because my mother still couldn't accept I saw spirit, and maybe he was right. But I also understood that I had reached an age where I might be an embarrassment to her.

It was also the last time I saw kindly Father Whetter.

This was my final year at Dee Point Junior School. In the summer my class would leave and we would go our separate ways to various High Schools in the area. Where we went depended upon the results of our 11-plus exams. We had worked hard with our teachers to prepare for the forthcoming entrance exam, which gave a child like me the chance to receive a scholarship from the education authority – if I passed.

Fortunately I did succeed and was offered a scholarship at the prestigious Queen's School, Chester, set right in the heart of the city limits. Very posh, I thought, and loved the idea of attending this highly respected establishment. There were only forty free places given in any one year so I felt very honoured and excited to be given the chance. I felt proud to have accomplished so much; however, despite my achievement, my dad didn't seem too happy about the prospect, especially when he noticed the charges for school uniform, outings and the extra lessons listed. He made the decision that for me to go to Queen's would be far beyond his pocket. Besides, in his opinion, 'It's way too snooty for the likes of you to attend.'

So my parents agreed that I was to go to Charles Kingsley Girls' School in Blacon. At least it was a single-sex school with a good reputation and I was assured of a place in the grammar stream, my mother reasoned.

My dad had been talking about buying a house for some time and how we should all work hard to improve ourselves in the world, and yet here I was, being denied the chance of a better education. I never openly questioned why my parents didn't want me to achieve educationally, but it did cause me pain deep inside my heart.

My mother had taken on full-time hours again now that I had gone to secondary school, which meant that she was no longer home when I returned. Life fell into a routine of walking home to an empty house where I was expected to tidy up, wash the dishes, peel potatoes, prepare food, make the beds, feed the dog and take him out for a walk. All this had to be completed by the time my parents returned home at around 6 or 7 p.m. No wonder I would stop off at my nana's most nights for some little home comforts for an hour before I returned to the empty house to start doing housework.

Starting a new school is never easy, and like most people who are a bit different from their peers I had trouble with bullies. Bullying had always been a problem for me at school for as long as I could remember. It wasn't that I came home black and blue every night but, to a child, being pushed about, ignored and laughed at is certainly as painful as any bruise.

At my new school there was a group of three girls who were particularly nasty. Sam often said that when I looked at someone I could see through them like a piece of tissue paper, and this was certainly true of these girls. I could see right through their hearts and they were as yellow as custard!

He would often accompany me on my walks home from school when I was on my own, but on one particular occasion I was walking home with my friend Kim. The girls followed us along the road, holding sticks with dog-poo on them, goading us with them. Then, without provocation, they smeared the back of Kim's coat with the foul-smelling stuff. It was the final straw.

I stopped dead in my tracks, which caught all three of them

off guard. Without thinking, I spoke directly to one of them: 'You above all people should care more. You know how we feel because you are bullied at home, aren't you?'

The girl looked stunned and stared at her two bullying accomplices. 'How the f*** do you know that?' Tears welled up in her eyes as the message hit a nerve. She dropped her stick and ran off. Like two sheep, the other girls ran after her.

Kim looked bewildered but grateful that they had gone. 'My mum will kill me when she sees the mess on my coat.'

'No, she won't,' I reassured her. 'Just tell her the truth about what happened.'

All the same, I am grateful that my gifts were not so developed at that time as to make me even more conspicuous to the ignorant and fearful. Being singled out as something alien is not a pleasant experience for a youngster. Powerful gifts like mine can cause unnecessary fear in people and provoke a reaction in them.

Bullying was not just confined to the pupils. There were two teachers in that school who had a bad reputation for bullying: Mrs Hough the needlework teacher, and the science teacher Mr Garner. He was the worst but they both frightened the life out of me as they always threatened and shouted in class.

Mr Garner seemed to gain sadistic pleasure from being violent. He would slam a ruler across your head or throw one of the wooden chalk wipers at you if you didn't give him the right answer. His aim was so good he rarely missed a target. Many a pupil was left with a bloody nose or a bump on the head from his antics. Those chalk wipers carried a fair whack as they were hurled across the classroom.

In retrospect, I must admit Mrs Hough was only trying to do her job. She thought being nasty to us was a great motivator. It wasn't. For me the underlying problem was that I hated sewing. My lack of enthusiasm meant I rarely remembered my sewing homework as it was such a low priority to me.

One day I had to run home – yet again – for my sewing. I hadn't realised that my mum had taken a day's holiday from work. As I opened the door I found her ironing in the kitchen. I daren't stop and chat as I might be late back and be caught absent. If I was found to be out of the grounds during school hours, I would earn a detention.

'What are you doing home?' she said, surprised to see me too.

With no time to speak, I ran upstairs as fast as I could, grabbed my sewing bag and ran back down the stairs at lightning speed.

Fearing that Mum would shout because I was not meant to be home at that time, I rushed to the back door, telling her as fast as possible that I couldn't stop and chat, must get back as I had forgotten my sewing homework – Mrs Hough would have my guts for garters!

My mum laughed. I turned away to walk out and couldn't help but see Sam standing by my mother. His presence prompted a flash of enlightenment that hit me full force. The words just tumbled from my lips with no self-censorship.

'See you later,' I shouted. 'Oh, and by the way, Mum . . . one day I will be famous and then you won't have to iron!'

She laughed out loud again. I shouted some more: 'And we must look after Dad. He's going to be very, very ill. Sam says it's his chest and Dad should let me heal it for him!'

With no time to wait for her reaction, I raced down the garden path and back to school.

I am sure the teachers there did notice there was something different about me, even if they couldn't quite put their finger on what it was. I remember at one parents' evening my domestic science teacher remarked that I had an uncanny knack for knowing things in advance. This came about when I was doing her class one afternoon. 'We are going to cook fish pie,' my teacher, Mrs Cook, said. (Yes, her name really was Mrs Cook! She had a hard time from us over that.)

'Open your exercise books and copy out the recipe from your textbook for next week's lesson,' Mrs Cook ordered. When she noticed I wasn't following her instruction, she shouted across the classroom: 'Helen, are you immune to work?'

Well, that's not a very nice thing to say, I thought.

'No,' I told her. 'But I knew what you would be asking us to do, so I have already written it out.' True to my word, holding my exercise book up in front of her, I showed her a perfectly written recipe for next week's lesson. Needless to say she was dumbfounded as she had only just decided during the lesson to choose that particular recipe.

As a youngster, my close friends at Charles Kingsley School seemed to accept my gifts of empathy almost as a matter of course, in the way children often do. I always seemed to know things about them before they told me, which tickled their curiosity. It was rarely anything remarkable, but I would instinctively be aware of certain facts: like where and when they were going on holiday, and if there was going to be a surprise for them or a visit from relatives.

Maybe they thought I was good at guessing, but the phrase 'Ask Helen, she will know' was one which followed me throughout my youth. I suppose I was one of those children often described by adults as 'having an old head on young shoulders', as I often identified heavily with my teachers and got on well with grown-ups (with the exception of Mr Garner and Mrs Hough, of course).

I haven't mentioned my Nana Ada for a while, but she had continued to be a loving and supportive presence in my life. I loved her with all my heart. Having moved from their house on

Christleton Road, Nana and Granddad Joe now lived just minutes from our home. I would often go to their new flat when I had finished school. Without fail, she would always have a crumpet oozing with melted butter and a hot cup of tea waiting for me beside the fire as it blazed away. Granddad sometimes walked me home, especially on the dark winter nights, and I would quickly set to on my chores, to complete as much as I could before my mum and dad arrived home exhausted.

Sadly for me, I resented my mother for no longer being at home when I returned from school. All that anger eventually boiled over one day, triggered when she asked why I hadn't cleaned the bathroom. I remember answering that I had homework to do and it wasn't my job continually to keep the house clean. A catfight ensued and my mother screamed that she couldn't do everything. She was obviously stressed, but even though I was aware of this I answered back with a return volley of verbal abuse, smashing the pane of glass on the back door as I slammed it to behind me, and ran off to Nana's house. When I got there I told her I wasn't ever going back home. After a great deal of persuasion, Nana Ada arranged for me to be collected by my mother the following morning. I now know that my parents were just working hard to provide for our little family. However, as a child their absence was all I saw. Part of me was desperately trying to reach out to them, not for material gain but for them to accept my spiritual ability and give me the affection I craved.

It was during this difficult time that one particular day I felt something was desperately wrong with Nana. I couldn't wait for all my lessons to finish so that I could make sure everything and everyone was fine. No matter how hard I tried to push this feeling of danger out of my mind, I had an impending feeling of doom.

This was a new sensation for me, so I asked Sam why for no apparent reason I was having such a troublesome experience. He explained in simple terms that all of us have a spiritual alarm bell. We use it daily when we are introduced to new people or situations, and assess whether that person or situation might be a risk to us. He said that inner sense was our aura alerting us. For most of us it's not definitive, but it's a good general guide to keeping danger at bay. Well, I can tell you, the spiritual alarm bell inside me had been set off and was clanging out loud.

I was not supposed to leave during school hours, but as soon as the home-time bell rang, I ran as fast as I could to my nana's house. When I arrived, Granddad was in the flat on his own. Apparently Nana had gone out earlier that morning, to take the bus to Queensferry to see my Auntie Joan. Nana often took the bus to see friends and family, so at first it seemed feasible that my fears were about nothing. I went home and did my usual chores but my mind was constantly focused on Nana's welfare – I *knew* something was wrong.

Soon afterwards my granddad arrived at our house on foot, asking if we had heard from Nana as she was meant to be home by now on the evening bus. Mum explained it away by saying she had probably stayed the night at Joan's house, even though that wasn't a normal thing for her to do.

Immediately my spiritual alarm bell rang even louder and I pleaded with my mum, telling her that I felt something was wrong with Nana. In her typical off-hand manner, she passed my worries off as silly fussing. But in the end my granddad suggested my parents should telephone and leave a message about our concern at the British Legion Club or the Leprechaun pub for my Uncle Bob, who usually went for a pint there at night. (Auntie Joan and Uncle Bob didn't have a phone at that time.) Granddad said all this fuss was probably for nothing and went home in case Nana turned up there.

About 10 p.m. that evening our telephone rang. Although I

was in bed, I was so sure this was about Nana that I ran down to find out what was happening.

My mum was holding the receiver and her face had turned white. It didn't look like good news. She placed it down and almost collapsed, having to support herself against the hall wall. She lowered herself on to one of the bottom steps of the staircase. I sat down beside her.

'That was Uncle Bob. Auntie Joan put Nana on the five o'clock bus to come home. Apparently Nana wasn't feeling very well. She should have arrived back in Blacon for seven at the latest.'

Mum shouted to Dad, who was in the kitchen: 'There's something very wrong, Colin. You will have to go and fetch Dad and I will ring the police. Anything could have happened to her.'

At that moment I could see in my mind's eye Nana lying in what I could only describe as a ditch. She felt cold and almost lifeless, all alone in the dark.

I started to cry and my tears turned to sobs. Without thinking, I told my parents exactly what I could see. Mum put her arm around me and told me this wasn't the time to start talking about my spirit nonsense. I should go back to bed, as there was nothing I could do to help. I ran upstairs, absolutely furious, and slammed the bedroom door behind me. For a few seconds I stood there, holding in all my emotion, and then at breaking point threw myself on to my bed and cried. After a few minutes, I kneeled by my bedside and prayed for Nana's safety.

While I was praying, Sam stood over me and watched. On this occasion another four Guides joined him. After I had finished my prayer, he explained that they had come to send healing to my nana: their auras shone much brighter than Sam's, so I intuitively knew they were specialists in the administration of healing. I felt my prayers were being answered as I knew Nana needed all the help the spirit world could offer her.

About twenty minutes later I heard the key in the front door and then Granddad and Dad talking to my mum as they came in. I ran downstairs and threw my arms around my granddad and held him tightly. Before my parents could say a word about me being up, I told him that I could see Nana, all alone in the dark, lying in a ditch, cold and almost lifeless. 'You do believe me, don't you, Granddad? Because Nana needs us to find her.'

He nodded, not disapprovingly, but listening to me intently.

The doorbell chimed – it was the police arriving. I was sent upstairs out of the way, though Granddad promised to tell the police what I had said to him about Nana.

The police took statements and acted immediately by combing the area. After a couple of hours a constable came to the house to say they couldn't find her. Blacon was very dark at that time due to the area still being under development, especially with the low number of streetlights on the main road. They said that they were going to use a sniffer dog to help. The search went on throughout the night. Dad and Granddad armed themselves with torches to help while the police continued with their search. Mum sat waiting by the phone in case anybody rang, and I fell asleep on the settee under a blanket. I was determined to stay around, despite what Mum and Dad thought.

It wasn't until the following afternoon that the police found her, lying in a ditch, freezing cold and in a coma. She'd had a massive stroke, stumbled around during her attack and fallen unconscious into a large construction ditch along the side of the road. The trench was nearly six foot deep and quite wide as it was for large pipes and cables that were about to be laid. These days such work would have been conducted behind barriers but in those days construction sites were an obstacle course for the public. Fortunately, one of the sniffer dogs found Nana as no one could see her from the road.

She had broken her wrist, collarbone, a finger and two ribs in the fall, and was suffering from hypothermia as she had been out all night in the cold, but she was at least still alive. Under the circumstances that was a miracle.

The police informed us that she had been taken to Chester City Hospital. Nana had lost the use of her right side and her speech was impaired. She would have a long convalescence as she had suffered a major stroke.

That was when I started to cook alongside her and develop my own cooking skills. As Nana progressed with her physiotherapy and speech therapy, she gradually became able to do light chores around the house. However, she was never quite the same after the stroke. Granddad's favourite dish was her steak-and-kidney pie, but now she couldn't make much at all in the kitchen, so she would patiently teach me what to do, albeit very slowly as her speech was never fully restored. Eventually I too could make his favourite meal, which he lovingly praised as being as good as Nana's, though I am sure it never was.

Nana and I became even closer after that experience and she often said that if it wasn't for Sam and me, she would have been dead in that ditch before anybody found her. Nana fully accepted my spiritual empathy, and from then on insisted I come to her from school whenever I could to lay my hands on her for healing. To me, this was like being reborn as through her own illness she'd allowed me to develop my healing capabilities with her full belief and encouragement. So much happiness enfolded Nana and me, through so much suffering.

My Granddad Joe never said a word about it, but kissed me every time I visited and said he loved me. It was our little secret. After all, who else would believe me?

Around this time Dad announced plans to buy a semi-detached house, not far from where we were living on the council estate.

He said he wanted my mum and me to view the property that weekend. In his words, he had found 'the one'. It really surprised me that he could make such a big decision without asking us first if we even liked the property. I knew Dad had been showing an interest in moving, but not this seriously. If I'd been a little older maybe I would have noticed his eagerness and seen the signs coming. I had noticed that my mother had taken on more hours at work and so had he – it was obvious they were saving for something, and it had been made perfectly clear it wasn't a better education for me.

If they were to take on a new house, I worried about how they would pay for everything and if that meant they would have to work even longer hours. Would it mean I wouldn't see them at all? At eleven years of age, all there seemed to be in my life was school and coming home to an empty house. At weekends my parents would do extra work, gardening or visit my grandmother, so it was a rare occasion for them actually to give any time to me.

As planned, that weekend we viewed Dad's choice of our new home. Actually it was a lovely semi-detached house, built pre-war, with attractive bay windows fronting the road. It had a pretty front garden, and was situated in a quiet, tree-lined avenue full of impeccably kept properties. I did wonder if the house was a bit posh for us.

As we stood on the pavement outside, I could see from the corner of my eye a bright light radiating next to Sam, who was standing near the porch of what might become our new home.

We knocked on the door and, as we were expected, greeted very hospitably by a friendly middle-aged couple. Inside, the house was spick and span and felt cosy. In fact, I could not imagine having a home this comfortable as our house always smelled of stale cigarettes, an open chip pan and leftover coffee.

Pictures of a perfect family, complete with images of their

children doing homework at the table while the mother fussed over them, filled my imagination. As the man of the house showed us round each room, I couldn't take my eyes off his big moustache. It made me want to giggle as it curled up at the ends, like the ones you see on old pictures from the days of the British Raj. It took all my concentration to stop myself from laughing out loud, but of course in those days children were seen and not heard, according to my parents, so I didn't dare crack on that I found his appearance funny.

My father seemed to have made his mind up on the spot, so the man's wife made some tea and he invited us to sit and talk business – as he put it. We were going to have the house, it seemed, come what may. My mother tried attracting my father's attention by making a face when the owner was not looking and nodding her head, to suggest they should discuss things outside. I imagine she wanted to tell him that we should think about it properly and be in touch, or even that she wasn't sure she wanted to move there.

Dad ignored her. After a lot of boring chit-chat, it seemed he had eventually made an offer on the house. I could see by the expression on my mother's face that she wasn't too pleased at all. The couple politely said they would consider our offer and let my parents know in the next couple of days. Apparently they did have other people looking and as it was in the days of gazumping, there was a chance another buyer might make a better offer. Phew! I thought. Maybe Mum will get her wish after all, as she wanted to move to Wales.

As we were casually ending the viewing and getting ready to leave, Dad asked them if they had any children of their own.

'Yes, we have one son,' the lady replied . . . and a second later, without even thinking, I spouted out: 'I thought you had two sons? Though one has died recently – very suddenly.'

Uh-oh! Now I was in trouble, I realised, as my father gave me one of his glares of disapproval. However, irrespective of his condemnation of me for speaking up, I was right. The couple did have two sons. Yes, only one was living, but the one in spirit was still just as much their son as he had been when he was alive.

Sitting in the lounge, finishing my tea, I could see the young man quite clearly. He told me he had been suffering from depression and wished he had gone to talk to the medical profession or someone else about this problem. He explained to me that it was his fault not his parents' that he'd committed suicide.

This was a landmark spiritual communication in my life. Despite having messages from the spirit world given to me from my earliest recollection, this family reunion was probably my most profound experience to date. I was only eleven years old – and faced a major dilemma. On the one hand I had a grieving family who were perhaps unprepared to hear from their son. My personal predicament was that I had that son by my side, desperately wanting to communicate with his parents, while my disapproving father was ready to use his parental authority to silence me. It was a very tricky situation for a young girl to have to deal with.

There was also Sam standing by, offering his guidance and support. I felt an immense burden placed on my young shoulders. Nevertheless, despite my reluctance to communicate what I had seen and heard to this family, Sam explained that the couple needed to move on with their lives and that I was here to help them do just that.

Suddenly, the mother burst into floods of tears and rushed upstairs. We all looked at each other, not knowing what to say. I knew my dad wanted to yell blue murder at me for upsetting her and possibly destroying our chances of buying the house. I couldn't help but feel sad for her, as I knew her loss was still painful.

In one corner of the room I noticed a beautiful glowing violet light and a feeling of utter compassion radiating out and affecting everyone within it. Sam explained to me that this was the manifestation of a special Angel from a very high realm. He explained that it was a gift, not to help me, but the bereaved couple and their surviving son. He said that the son had committed suicide because he was depressed and the parents felt responsible for this, believing they could have done something more to prevent his death. It was the intention of the spirit world to take away their feeling of guilt.

'The warmth of this Angel's love will radiate into their hearts,' Sam told me. 'This will help them to come to terms with their grief and take away the guilt they feel. This is an Angel permitting freedom by granting benevolence to those in need and removing any fears for the future.'

I wondered whether I should share this fact right now, but my father was in no mood to be spoken to and I doubted the owner of the property was either as he was most concerned about his wife.

Sam and I held our mind connection and I heard him continue to speak in my thoughts. 'Do not worry, chile. You have done enough to help bring healing to this home. The energy from this Angel will do the rest.'

'Please excuse my wife,' the owner of the house told us. 'Yes, we did have two sons, but sadly our eldest committed suicide a little while ago and we are still coming to terms with his death. Please tell me, how could you possibly know this information? I asked the estate agent not to tell anybody.'

He then went on to say that their son had died away from this house in case we were worried it had happened there.

Although I remained silent, my father continued to scowl at me. I knew he was furious, but I also felt he knew I was right and that I could truly see spirit. The problem was, he did not *want* me to see spirit. Maybe in someone else it would have been acceptable to him, but it certainly wasn't so far as his daughter was concerned.

I proceeded to tell the owner of the house that from time to time I just came out with little messages. He looked dumbstruck, lost for words. To be honest, so was I. I was speaking out to a stranger when I knew my father didn't want me to. I don't know where the courage came from, but I blurted out that their son was safe in the spirit world and healing was being sent to his family so that they could recover and continue with their own lives.

At that my father nodded his head in agreement. I was astonished; I had never before seen him acknowledge that I had a spiritual voice. This was a first! However, in retrospect, I think it was easier for him to nod and agree rather than make a fuss and have a head-on confrontation with me in a stranger's house.

Silently the healing Angel moved his arms in an arc over his head. His body dripped with what looked like luminescent oil or shimmering lametta, but this was not tinsel or liquid but strands of pure energy which shone with a brightness that was hard to comprehend. His presence was so strong I was sure that other people in the room must be able to share my vision.

As his hands met above his head, there was a change in the whole energy of the room. I could see it bouncing off the walls with the same shimmering essence as it did from his body, and returning to him as though the energy itself was performing a cleansing and he was just the conduit. Then the Angel clapped his hands together. I saw tiny fragments of light almost like snow crystals falling to the ground, and an enormous feeling of well-being filled my body. Couldn't anyone else feel this? I wondered, as the energy continued to sprinkle down from his hands like snow.

Sam turned to me and announced he and the Angel were

about to leave. However, before they did there was one more task to accomplish. There was no further explanation given. In the hands of the Angel I saw a hangman's noose. The young man had hung himself. He was now standing next to the Angel and Sam as I saw the noose the Angel was holding disintegrate in front of me. Sam and the Angel then left, taking the young man in spirit with them. I was awestruck – I had now officially seen my first Angel!

The owner of the house shook my father's hand and said he would be in touch once he had considered the offer. My mother said goodbye to him. When the man came to me, he gently took my hand and looked into my eyes – absolutely speechless. No words were exchanged between us. I was just a child and yet I had understood and spoken to him about his traumatic loss. As I held his hand, I felt the healing energy flow from within me and travel into the man. Tears filled his eyes and I knew he had connected with me at that moment. For that second his guard was down and without a single word being said, *he knew* his boy was safe in spirit.

During the following week, every night my dad wanted to pick up the phone and ring the couple to ask for their answer. My mother stopped him. Secretly I think she was wishing they wouldn't contact us, as it was her dream to move to Wales. After a week had gone by with still no word from the couple, my parents thought that someone with more money had gazumped them.

Unexpectedly, while we were having tea one night, the phone rang. It was the house owner. He spoke to my dad for a while, then Dad rang off and yelled in excitement: 'We have it, we have it!' He sounded like an excited little boy. I could see by Mum's face that she was disappointed as her move to Wales was now on hold. Sam talked to me briefly as my dad beamed from ear to ear. His words were strange, almost chilling for me to hear: 'Your mother will go back to Wales when the time is right, Helen. But first your father needs this to happen for him to feel fulfilled in his short life – he will not see his fifty-first birthday.'

I knew my father's illness was severe, but now I knew he would die young. Sam had predicted a time of death. A wave of nausea hit my stomach as this shocking information filled my mind. Inside I was heartbroken, knowing my father's chilling destiny. However, despite this, his fifty-first birthday seemed a lifetime away, and a lot could happen before then. Maybe Sam had got it wrong. Or maybe I could after all cure my dad with the healing. Sam was always pressing me to heal my dad. On reflection, innocent doubt is a wonderful comfort afforded to children.

After Dad calmed down, he explained that the owner of the house was shocked by his experience with me. He had talked on the phone to Dad about how a girl of my age could possibly have known that they had lost their son. Both he and his wife had given it a lot of thought. They felt their home had many happy memories associated with it despite their son's tragic death, and that it should go to people with a growing family.

Even though the last few years had been tinged with great sadness for them, they believed that we had been sent to them and they could now start life anew by moving to a new house. I couldn't believe that telling them those few details could result in such a life-changing event for them, but it had. That and the visit from the Angel, of course.

Over the years I have discovered that our Guides, Higher Guides and Angels are always around when we need them. We may not all be able to see them, but their presence influences our lives and enriches them with whatever spiritual gift they need. For that poor couple, their grief was so immense they needed a fresh start. The Angel must have known that even a Higher Guide could not cleanse their home of such grief. In the face of their immense loss, it had to be an Angel's energy that granted them inner peace.

As it turned out the new house was always full of spirits, popping in and out. By the time I was twelve my Mum and Dad must have been exhausted by the number of times I told them that some-body was in my bedroom, or there were strangers standing in the garden, not to mention how often a woman I didn't know was standing in the kitchen peeling spuds! These days, however, I was not being told so peremptorily to shut up when I started to speak of my spirit visitors.

We hadn't been in the house long before Dad wanted to use his DIY skills. He knocked through the two downstairs rooms, separating the lounge and dining area with glass doors. It was very in vogue in the mid-seventies to have open-plan living areas. To me it was an inconvenience because every time I tried to practise on the clunky old piano standing against the dining-room wall, my father would complain about the noise because he was trying to watch TV in the lounge, with only the new glass double doors separating us.

What did he expect? I thought. It was he who opened up the rooms in the first place. Surely it wasn't my fault they were not sound-proofed?

On one particular Saturday my mother and I went on a rare shopping spree together. The day seemed pretty straightforward and uneventful until we returned home on the bus from Chester.

Walking up our driveway, we could hear a loud smashing noise and then a tinkling sound as though someone was crashing down on a keyboard. The nearer to the house we walked the louder the noise became, until eventually I caught sight of Dad tossing a piece of wood onto the ground near the front door.

It looked old with its lack-lustre polish but vaguely familiar . . .

though I did not at first connect the lump of mahogany veneer with my piano. Then the tinkling sounds hit my ears again, as the inside of the piano was gutted and thrown on the ground. I finally made the connection in my mind and realised what was happening. It was my beloved piano . . . my dad was chopping up *my* piano.

I dropped the bags in the drive, smashing the eggs we had just bought, and screamed 'Stop!', running up the rest of the drive as fast as I could. As I turned the corner to the back of the house the full impact hit me. The once-proud musical instrument lay scattered in pieces over the ground. It was defeated . . . its life taken . . . it was now dead.

Tears streamed down my face and Dad looked at me in disbelief. 'Don't be sad,' he said. 'It's a tatty old thing and it was taking up too much space anyway. You won't even miss it.'

Wouldn't miss it? I cried for days because I missed my piano so much. My dad never seemed to understand me. He never seemed to appreciate the strength of my feelings. From then on there was a distance between us. I will never stop loving my dad, he was a good man, but from that day forth I really didn't like him much.

It took me weeks to forgive him and finally speak to him again. Even when I did our conversations were stilted. I know this hurt him because he was an immensely proud man. I even think he secretly took pride in me, but he rarely showed it.

5

The Gift of Enlightenment

People often ask if I ever summon spirit. The answer to that is a definite no. I never summon any spirit, they just arrive of their own accord, and when they do, I decide whether I want to speak to them or not.

When I am approached by spirit, they do so in a friendly, kind and appealing way, rather like a friend asking for help. Nevertheless, there are times when no matter how pleasant the spirit world is to me, a sudden appearance can scare me half to death, whether Sam is around or not.

For a child of twelve, learning about the spirit world, did on occasion include an element of fear. One such occasion occurred during what Sam described as a specific turning point in my spiritual life. He said it was going to be when my true gift of enlightenment would show itself. I had no idea what he meant, but I was about to find out . . .

One night, I found myself waking up and becoming aware of a strange light hovering in front of my face. As I lay flat in my bed, the light seemed to change shape. At first it was no bigger or brighter than a candle flame. I knew this was no ordinary light, though, as it was about six inches from my nose and seemed to be slowly moving closer and closer to my eyes.

Even though I was learning very fast about spiritual matters, I still tried to apply the filter of logic to my experiences, just to retain my innate common sense. Trying to rationalise this situation, my first thought was that it was caused by the neighbour next-door. He often worked on his car until the early hours in his garage, so maybe he was pottering about late at night with bright lights illuminating his work. Or maybe there was a chink in the curtains, allowing a glimmer of light to come through. Where is Sam when I need him? I thought to myself.

I slid from under my bedcovers and looked out of my bedroom window; all I could see was a pitch-black night. Thick clouds were hiding the moon and there was definitely no sign of our neighbour tinkering around outside. I rearranged the curtains to make sure they were completely closed and turned around slowly, half-expecting that the light would be gone, only to find that the strange spot of brightness was still floating about right in front of me. It was as though Peter Pan had let Tinkerbell out of her cage! It seemed to have followed me to the window. As I turned around, there it was again, hovering in front of me. Could it be inquisitive about what I was doing?

Whatever it was, it was definitely inside the room with me, following my every move.

I asked quietly: 'What are you? Who are you?' I needed to know.

At that moment, as if in answer to my plea, it started spinning wildly around the room, gathering in brightness as it did so. Then in an instant it stopped dead, directly in front of my nose, before darting into each corner of the room in turn, illuminating the darkness until the whole room had taken on an eerie radiance.

I was speechless. My first impulse was to shout out and wake my parents from their sleep, but I didn't. I was marvelling at this amazing sight while inwardly aware that this was no ordinary light. It travelled smoothly towards me again, causing a wave of fear and awe within me. The light merged with my body, covering me with its luminescent glow, rather like a glowing overcoat. An amazing feeling filled my innermost soul: it was the most beautiful, inexpressible feeling of love and comfort. An experience I shall never be able to put into words as long as I live. The nearest I can come to explaining it would be to ask you to imagine a feeling of unconditional love and utter confidence; of being totally supported and totally comforted; and a feeling of total faith that you were safe – all at once!

I felt this glowing light was something very important. Something I somehow recognised but had forgotten. I had seen bright lights before around Sam but this was different. This was clinging to me like an extra skin. The inexplicable combined with the awe-inspiring caused me to tremble in reaction.

The light stayed with me for what felt like hours, but as I looked at my bedside alarm clock, I saw that only eight minutes had passed from first seeing it. My fingers and hands started to tingle with the sensations familiar to me when healing. They seemed to run through my body, only this time not aimed out towards others but all directed inward. The experience left me feeling tearful and humble.

The glow around my body dwindled and shrank back into an intense flame-like light, hovering in front of my face, where it had started. Then, without notice, it went – vanished into thin air. I realised with horror the enormity of what I had experienced and screamed out loud, more from shock than fear, until yet again my poor doubting father came running.

'What's going on?' he bellowed. I told him I had seen a bright light floating around the room. I explained exactly what I'd seen . . . and naturally he believed the moon and the curtains were playing tricks on me.

Why would he never take what I said at face value, but always tell me I was wrong and talking nonsense?

If I were to make a guess, I would say that was my first encounter with spirit in its truest sense. Such a pure form could only have come from the highest realms of the spirit world, and to be visited in such a way was a huge privilege for me.

As I grew spiritually and developed my empathetic abilities, I noticed that surges of positivity were often followed soon after by negativity; logical really when the laws of physics state that positive and negative have to remain in balance. Soon after this positive experience, I encountered something far darker.

It was a frosty but sunny morning, one of those chilly days when the sun shines through the glass and you feel as though it is warm enough to bathe in the sea . . . only to find that once you've set foot outside, the bitterness of the cold gnaws at your skin.

My routine at that time was always to walk my dog Gyp at 7.30 in the morning – like clockwork. It was a ritual he loved, mainly because he knew my parents and I were soon leaving the house for the day, and when we were out he would be locked in the kitchen until my return at 4.30 p.m. This walk was his leisure time and he loved it.

Gyp was a faithful old friend of a dog and we were inseparable. The bond between us was unshakable and I loved him to bits. He certainly never judged me for seeing Angels and spirit people!

This particular day seemed like any other. The nearer it got to 7.30, the more fidgety Gyp became. I swear he knew how to tell the time as he nuzzled up to me then sniffed the door, to give me a clue that he wanted a walk. From habit, I grabbed the lead – and as I did, I felt a chill travel right down my spine. My body prickled with goose bumps. Strange, I thought, it must be the cold.

Sam made his customary morning appearance as I prepared to leave the house. 'Be on your guard, Helen,' I heard him say in my mind.

I thought he was referring to crossing the road so took extra care to look both ways. Gyp and I trotted happily along, taking in our usual route as he sniffed at the trees and plants in his special doggy way.

I'd become oblivious to cars driving around at that time of the morning as everyone was either rushing to work or travelling to school. So one more going round and round, passing me a couple of times, failed to register with me as odd.

Then, without notice, a car pulled up beside me.

A man with greasy hair peered out of the window then wound down the glass on the driver's door to reveal his face. In those days you had to wind your window down by hand, and I remember hearing the screeching sound of the glass as it slowly descended, brushing past the bristles on the window frame.

'Excuse me . . . sorry to stop you but I am lost,' he politely explained. 'I have a map here. Can you show me where we are, and then direct me to Sealand Road? I know it's not far from here.'

I tried not to look at him as my parents had warned me about talking to strangers, but he continued to ask me in a calm, polite manner and to gesture towards the map he held in his hand.

I knew the place he wanted to be just a short distance away.

'Any idea where Sealand Road is, love?' he asked one more time.

Although he seemed pretty genuine in his request, I don't know what it was, as I looked at him, I suddenly felt a flash of fear fill my body.

I heard a voice in my head, loud and clear, saying: 'This man is dangerous. Let the dog lead go – run, run, run home!'

'Hey, love!' the man was saying as he started to climb out of the car. 'Just come over here and show me where it is on this map, will you?'

I stood frozen to the spot.

He started to reach one arm towards me, with the map in his hand. 'It will only take you a second to show me . . .'

I found I couldn't move and the man was nearing me. 'Go away or I'll let the dog go!' I threatened.

Sam appeared right beside the stranger's car and yelled to me in a loud voice: 'Run now, Helen . . . Run, Helen . . . Run home!'

Without hesitation I turned to run away. The man recognised my fear and lunged for me. 'That mutt won't hurt anyone,' he sniggered, and started to run after me, almost succeeding in catching my arm. I dropped the dog lead. Gyp stood firm, sensing the danger. He had never growled or snarled at anyone before, but now he was showing all his teeth and starting to pounce at the man's feet, trying to bite him. Gyp meant business. The man realised he would be attacked if he persisted. He turned tail and climbed back into his car, slammed the door and revved the engine into life.

I didn't look behind me as I ran. The horror of what was happening overwhelmed me. I'll never make it, I thought. It's too far for me to run home . . . he's in a car . . . he will reach me faster than I can get to safety.

Gyp and I would walk in a large square along four different main roads with a couple of side turnings leading off them. I was then down the second road so the same distance from home whichever way I decided to go. It would take me five or six minutes to run home at full speed. I won't make it, I can't make it, was my only thought.

I had been running for a few minutes when I turned a corner and started along the final stretch towards our house, which stood at the centre of the street. I had no idea where Gyp had gone, I was on my own. The house was close now. I could see the outline of Dad's car in the road outside our gate . . .

My chest was pounding and I could hardly breathe. The cold air in my lungs was making me gasp for every breath. It felt as if I had run miles, and all the time I knew the man in the car was after me and about to do something very bad once he caught me.

Like a cliché-ed scene from a movie, I realised I could see the car heading towards me. The man had taken the opposite way from me and was trying to head me off. Was I going to make it? I was so near my home and safety . . . Why didn't a neighbour come out? Why couldn't they see me running? I tried to yell but no one seemed to hear and I needed all my strength to run.

The car was closing in when Sam appeared, gesticulating with his hand towards a neighbour's path and garden. That would be suicide, I thought. I'd be trapped. Home was only about ten houses away now, but it might as well have been miles as the car was upon me. Placing my ultimate trust in Sam, however, I followed his directions down a neighbouring driveway and hid behind a garden wall as the car crawled slowly past the drive.

What if he got out of the car?

Just another hundred yards or so and I will be home, I thought to myself. I could tell by the engine noise that the predator had driven past the gate but could hear him negotiating the gearbox. He reversed at speed to come and take another look for me. Although I couldn't see the gate, I could hear the sound of his engine fading a little as he reversed again.

Frantically I banged on the back door of a stranger's house – but no one came. Where was everyone?

Although I couldn't see Sam, his voice was crystal clear in my mind: 'Use the field!' Luckily all the gardens on this side of the street backed on to grassy fields. It seemed Sam was suggesting the safest route was to run to the very end of the garden and climb over into the field. The car couldn't drive there and the man wouldn't know I had climbed the fence. I kept low and scampered to it, quickly climbed over and ran until I saw the familiar sight of the poplar trees at the end of our garden. I had made it back to my own territory! I ran straight in at the back door of our house, screaming out to my parents as I went to hide upstairs. My mother panicked and followed me into my bedroom, asking what was wrong and why was I so muddy?

Through sobs, barely able to speak, I told her about the man and she darted over to look out of the front window. 'Can you see him now?' she shouted. I peeped out at the side of the curtain, scared that he might see me again if he was patrolling the street. I couldn't believe my eyes. There he was! I spotted his car, idling along the street below as though nothing was wrong. 'That's him!' I screamed, pointing to it as I ducked down out of sight under the windowsill. My mother tried to see his number plate as the car disappeared around the corner. 'The nerve of him!' she screamed.

Still sobbing, I explained what had happened and Mum immediately rang the police.

During the wait for them to arrive, Sam joined me, which made me feel more secure. In my mind I thanked him for saving me. I nearly told my mother about him telling me to run, but if I had, I feared she might not believe that the man had been chasing me. After all, I might have imagined that too!

Mum and Dad joined me in a restorative cup of tea. Neither of them said much but they looked relieved and smiled at me tenderly. Some time later I gave a description of the man to the police while they put together an Identikit picture of the predator.

Apart from feeling very shaken up, I was also upset because Gyp was still missing and I had visions of him being run over or lost. Fortunately, as the police were leaving a panting Gyp ran in through the kitchen door. That day he got the best doggie treats ever.

Weeks later the police informed us they had caught a man from the description I had given. Unfortunately they could only caution him because he had not actually committed any crime. We found out that he was indeed a paedophile, living in the area, and the police already knew him well.

I knew I had had a very lucky escape from the clutches of this evil predator. Thanks to Sam's quick thinking I had managed to escape with my life, but the fact that this creature still prowled the streets in his car sent shudders through my mind and body, and I couldn't stop thoughts of what might happen if he ever managed to snatch another unsuspecting child from going round in my mind.

A couple of months later, my beloved Nana Ada became very ill and was admitted into hospital. She had cancer of the throat, though in those days the disease itself was rarely mentioned. Everyone spoke in hushed tones if the word ever had to be used.

During my hospital visits to her, Sam would tell me to try and hold her hand or to touch her head, as that way I could pass valuable healing energy into poor Nana. When I saw her on these visits, I was heartbroken to see my dear grandmother looking so ill. My parents said she would be bed-bound for some time and doubted she would be allowed out until another bout of treatment had been successfully completed.

Throat cancer is a cruel illness. These days, medical science has progressed in its treatment of the disease. Unfortunately, much of the modern treatment we take for granted today was not available in 1971. My nana's lifestyle – she smoked Woodbine and John Player cigarettes all her life – had metastasised her cancer, which had now spread to different parts of her body via her lymphatic system.

Sam tried to comfort me as I entered Nana's side room from the main ward. As I looked into his eyes I could see he was trying to give me strength. He put words into my mind: 'You must try and hold your nana's hand to pass on valuable healing to her.'

A few weeks earlier she had been allowed out of hospital to go to my cousin Peter's wedding, and although she was in a wheel-chair, looking frail and unwell, she did seem to have a wonderful day. She had been looking forward to that occasion for a long time. Despite being very ill, she had looked much stronger then than she did today.

To say I was shocked when I saw her is an understatement. I felt physically shaken by her appearance. Nana was wired up with all types of gadgetry and tubes, including a drip feed because she could not swallow. My mother told me to sit down quietly next to her while she spoke to the ward sister who had followed us into the room. I heard the nurse say that my nana was doing quite well and may even be allowed home if we could cope with nursing her.

Although Nana was a small lady, she had always been a naturally strong character, weakened only by her stroke. Today, lying here so helpless, she looked weak and fragile, no longer the little power pack who had mothered me over the years.

My nana opened her eyes, saw me sitting next to her and reached out to touch my hand. She was too ill to speak but her eyes filled with love when she saw me. I reached out and held her hand, trying to allow precious healing energy to escape from me into her, just as Sam wanted me to do. By now he had walked over to be with us as my parents and granddad stood in the far corner, discussing Nana's condition in whispers.

She and I knew they were talking about her and I could feel her distress at not being able to join in the conversation.

I could feel her respond as I delicately touched her hand. Our joint energies bound us together. She could not talk and tried to whisper huskily to me, but I could not understand. As I bent nearer to her, I heard her ask me for a glass of water. Such a simple act as sipping water was potentially traumatic for her as the cancer had spread down her gullet and into her stomach.

The nurse and my parents were still engrossed in conversation and ignoring me as I continued to channel healing into my dear nana. Again she whispered weakly, 'Please, darling, let me have a drink of water.'

I felt a sensation of warmth travel from my hands into her frail body. The healing just flooded from me as if Nana was a dry sponge absorbing liquid.

What happened next seemed to stun everyone. They turned and looked at us in absolute shock as I reached for a glass and filled it with some water from a jug by her bedside. I cradled her head with one hand and held the glass with the other, raising it to Nana's lips so that she could drink.

The nurse and my parents watched in disbelief as Nana drank a whole glass of water for the first time in over a week.

Visibly shocked, the nurse said: 'That's marvellous, but how can it be possible? Ada has not been able to swallow for days.'

The onlookers saw my nana drinking but did not see the miracle of healing happening in front of their very eyes. Sam smiled. He was familiar with miracles, however small and barely noticeable.

My nana loved me being with her. She had always been there for me in my times of need and now I believed there was something I could do for her. Nana had been like a second mum to me, looking after me when I came home from school. I loved her to bits, and the thought of her suffering this cruel illness filled me with heartache. Anyone who has had to watch someone they love suffering, feels similarly helpless and lost. The pain I felt then was deep in the core of me.

However, my parents insisted they had spoken to the nurse and Nana would get well soon, especially now she was able to swallow. My inner self knew that Nana would never be well; she would never again be the person I had known. The nurse's prognosis was either patronising or delusional.

As I sat at Nana's bedside I continued to pass the healing energy through to her, by holding her hand and stroking her thin grey hair. It shocked me how sparse the hair had become on her scalp: I realised how old and frail she had become. My arms tingled with spiritual energy; the palms of my hands were red from the heat they were administering. Although I was still very young, I became aware that I was a conduit for my healing Guides. I was passing on the gift of healing on their behalf: their little helper.

Four pillows were behind Nana's back so she was fully supported as she sat up in bed. What I saw next was truly shocking to me as a child, although it is a phenomenon I have since witnessed many times as a professional healer in my adult life. Seemingly coming from Nana's nose, I saw thick silvery smoke float upwards and gather a couple of feet above her head. The smoke-like substance was plentiful around the nose but thinned out to a wisp at the highest point, vaguely resembling an upside-down funnel placed over Nana's face. However, rather than dispersing into the surrounding air, the smoke thickened and coiled around itself, creating something that was more dense, giving the illusion of being solid. I was amazed that the adults in the room were oblivious to what was happening. It took all my self-restraint to stop myself from shouting out and pointing, so that they would see what I could see around Nana's head. In my mind I called it a 'silver-cord'.

Surprisingly, I kept my cool and sat quiet and still at the bedside like a good child. I looked to Sam for guidance, but he merely stood in the corner of the room, smiling and nodding his head in approval of my actions. Intuitively, I placed the palm of my left hand on the crown of Nana's head while I continued to hold her right hand in mine. After a few moments, the smoke-like substance seemed to recede back into her body. I didn't know what it was for or why this was happening. Everyone else was still so intent on their conversation they never seemed to notice me looking incredulously at her nose!

It was Sam who sat beside me on Nana's hospital bed and explained what I'd seen and why it had shown itself now. He told me that I was helping Nana by charging her body with much-needed energy. However, he continued to explain, Nana was so ill her body was preparing itself to die. My eyes welled up instantly and in my mind I screamed at him that under no circumstances was I going to let my nana die. I held on to her limp hand with both of mine, as if her life depended upon it.

Ignoring my defiance, Sam went on to explain in simple words: 'Helen, what you saw coming from your nana's face is part of her spiritual body. The healing energy you passed on to her has given her enough strength to carry on for a little while longer. As Nana held on to life so desperately, her spiritual body responded by returning to the living one.'

Although I felt I understood what he was trying to say, I must have looked a little puzzled. In response, his mood shifted and I sensed he wanted to be more serious. His manner became more teacherly. 'Such a sight as you have just experienced will soon be commonplace for you. What you have just seen over your nana's face, and named a silver-cord, appears whenever a person's spirit is ready to pass over into the spirit world.'

Death had not touched my life until now, so this lesson was

hard for me to grasp. However, I knew at that moment, from the very depths of my soul, that saving lives was part of my destiny.

He continued to explain to me that once the silver-cord had been exposed, I could cut it to facilitate a quick passing over for the spirit into the spirit world. My child's mind went into overdrive at this revelation and I asked him accordingly: 'Are you saying I can kill people by cutting their silver-cord?'

He replied: 'Of course not! What I am saying is this. If the body has reached its time to die, the silver-cord will expose itself. Without intervention, it may take quite a while for the spirit to leave the body as it will fight for life as long as possible. By cutting the silver-cord you facilitate a quick passing over for the spirit. Death was taking place anyway, with or without your involvement. Helen, you could have cut your nana's silver-cord then and she would have passed over into the spirit world within the hour. Nana would have been able to die peacefully with you all around her.'

I couldn't believe Sam telling me this. Why would I even consider such a murderous act? I wanted to make Nana well, not end her life. A lonesome tear rolled down my face.

He gave me a compassionate look. 'I know this is very hard for you to understand. With your healing energy and your nana's desire to live, her life will now continue for a little while.'

I was still confused, upset and angry: how could he even consider that my nan would want to leave us? He smiled, knowing what I was thinking, and said, 'She doesn't want to leave you, my dear, but neither does she want to stay living like this. Sometimes the greatest gift is to let those we love go free to follow their own path.

'She has fought to live with the healing energy you are administering now. That's why people often die alone . . . because energy from those they love anchors them here. Without it, they let go. Soon though, dear, your nan will be healed.'

I was more confused. Did Sam mean Nana would be cured?

My mother then came over and asked me to move so that she could kiss Nana and hold her hand. This was her mother, after all, and her heart was breaking too.

Apparently the nurse had told my parents that the doctors said Nana was going to have some more radium treatment in the next few days, and that afterwards she could come home if we could cope. Well, this seemed like good news, I thought. If the doctors said she would be well enough to come home – it must be true!

Nana seemed tired but happy. She was even smiling, and said she felt better than she had for ages, in her tiny, weak, whispering voice.

In those days a Matron ruled the ward with a rod of iron, and when she appeared and asked us all to leave, saying that Nana was tired and needed rest, no one argued. Matron's voice of authority convinced my parents and Granddad that they should go home immediately, with everyone promising to see Nana the next day.

My mother collected Nana's washing together in a bag and kissed her tenderly on the cheek. When I bent down to kiss her she looked at me, held my hand and said, 'Thank you, darling. I really wanted that drink.' Her eyes smiled at me.

We drove home in the car and the conversation about Nana was quite upbeat. Mum and Dad were talking about having her at our house after the next bout of treatment, so she could be looked after. Having Nana living with me was a dream come true. So I went to bed that night feeling optimistic about her welfare.

After sleeping for what felt like an hour or so, I woke to find Nana sitting by my bedside. I was happy and surprised to see her, and joyful that she was now out of hospital, seemingly much stronger . . . and so soon. Maybe she didn't need that extra treatment after all. In fact, she even looked younger as her face was no longer drawn and pale.

'Hello, Helen, my love,' Nana said in a tender voice.

'Oh, Nan! You're out of hospital . . . are you better?' I said, thinking that she must have come home that evening with my parents after I had gone to sleep.

'Oh, yes, my love. I am much better now. I have come to see you, specially.' She said. 'I want to tell you something, my love, and I want you to be very grown-up about this. You need to know that you are not going to be seeing me very often any more, and in the morning I want you to tell your mum that she is not to worry about me and that I love you all. Tell her that I am all right, but I am going away.'

By this time my eyes had filled with tears at the prospect of my beloved nana moving away from us all. How could she even think of doing such a thing when we all loved her so much? I'd thought she was going to live with us for a while. I wanted to turn on the light and shout to my mum there and then, but as though to pre-empt me, she said, 'Don't turn on the light, love, it will soon be light enough.'

'What do you mean, Nana? Where are you going?' I asked in desperation, tears streaming down my cheeks.

'I am going on a special trip.'

'Oh, Nan, can I come?' I said, thinking that she was off on some sort of long holiday.

'No, darling, you can't,' she told me gently. 'Now, I want you to go back to sleep, and tell your mum my message when you wake in the morning. Tell her that I have been to see you. Don't worry, Helen, I will see you again, sweetheart, don't worry yourself. Try and sleep my love.' And with that, as I lay back down in my bed, she bent over and gave me a wisp of a kiss on my forehead.

Strange, I thought – not like the usual hug and kiss Nana gives me. But I thought no more about it.

'Are you sure I can't come, Nan? I will be good,' I murmured.

'Darling, you are always good. It's just that I have to do this on my own. You know how much I love you so please trust me. Rest assured, I will always be alongside you. I will let you know once I have arrived safely. Now don't you worry, you will see me again soon. Go back to sleep.'

I decided that she must be going to see my Auntie Joan and Uncle Bob. Nana often took trips on the bus to visit them, though it was a little dark for that now. Still, I trusted my nana so much that I was happy to listen to her, even though it didn't seem very logical for her to go off at night-time.

The last I saw of her was when she blew me a kiss, standing by my bedroom door. Then she was gone. I looked at my clock. It was 4 a.m.

When I awoke to my alarm clock's ringing, I was surprised to find Sam sitting on the edge of my bed, waiting. 'You need to tell your parents that your nana was here last night.' I felt there was something different in his tone today. He didn't sound like his normal chirpy self.

The alarm clocks in the house all rang together at 7 a.m. We had to get up at that time because Dad had to go to work early and I had to get to school by 8.15. I had been tossing and turning, drifting in and out of sleep for a while, waiting for the alarm to go off so I could tell my parents about Nana's visit.

Prompted by Sam, I couldn't contain myself any longer and burst into my parents' bedroom as if it was Christmas Day. My father complained, saying I should knock first as he could have been naked.

'Why didn't you tell me Nana was going away?' I demanded of my parents.

They both looked at me, confused. 'What do you mean?' Mum replied.

I told them what had taken place and they immediately dismissed it as some sort of vivid dream. 'Nana couldn't have left hospital, we only came from there late last night,' Mum explained. 'She was still there then. You can be such a silly girl!'

We all went downstairs for breakfast. As we were eating it around the kitchen table the phone rang . . .

It was the hospital.

My mother was ashen-faced as she listened to the nurse's message. She then shouted to Dad to come to the phone, leaving it hanging from its cable as she stumbled into the kitchen and sat down in a daze. My dad continued to take the call and I heard him saying 'oh, dear' and 'OK, yes'. Then he came in to explain. My nan had died in the early hours of the night – at 4 a.m. The hospital had decided it was no use my mother and father returning until the morning, as Nana had already passed when they attended her. She had died on her own. The hospital staff had decided to wait until now to call and tell us of her death.

What a way to break the news, I thought. My poor nana was by herself when she died . . . or was she?

Sure enough Nana had gone on a special trip, like she'd told me. At the age of sixty-six, Ada Elizabeth Smith had finally given up her struggle with this life and passed into the next . . . at exactly the time I had received a visit from her in my bedroom!

'Happy holidays, Nan,' I said as I blew a kiss into the air.

6

Teens, Teens, Glorious Teens

They say that with age comes a certain amount of wisdom and experience, but in my teachers' opinion, I was always 'an old head on young shoulders'.

I suppose my 'old head' is why I can empathise with the people I meet and, when necessary, introduce them to the gift of healing. Healing and healing messages have always played a prominent part in my life, and by using my abilities on a day-to-day basis I have been able to develop them as would, let's say, a musician who practises daily. Having said that, it doesn't matter what we do in life: it is from early seeds that greatness grows.

Although my gift was recognised from an early age, unfortunately it was by an audience of one: my nana. As I entered my teens, I was beginning to understand what might lie ahead of me in the future. I could see myself reaching out with the message of healing, hope and comfort, my hands and voice being the conduit for those in the spirit world. In my adult life, an undercurrent of people has duly sought out these healing abilities, a faithful network of supporters. However, as a child it was impossible for me to receive understanding and support from those closest to me.

Sam had always explained to me that the work I was going to achieve would be important, but in my teens I suppressed any thought of this. It seemed hard enough to me to get through the normal adolescent problems on a day-to-day basis, let alone think about a future as a spiritual empathist. How could I possibly do it, I thought, when my own parents, the very people who loved me the most, blocked out my spiritual gifts? What chance could there ever be of achieving this bright, fulfilled future Sam was talking about?

Every time I questioned him, Sam gave me one of his knowing smiles: 'All in good time, chile. Everything has to be done in its own good time. You will see.'

It was certainly a pretty daunting prospect, especially as I didn't have a clue what career I might take up once I became an adult.

On reflection, having to explain to my parents about my nana's visit to me after she had died in her hospital bed was another landmark experience for me. I believe that though my mother initially resisted my account of what had happened, part of her capitulated as she admitted just the chink of a possibility that I was indeed someone of extraordinary abilities. I began to realise that it wasn't necessarily spirituality that they didn't believe in, but rather that their child could be spiritually gifted to deliver its message and healing hope. They couldn't believe that a child of theirs could possess such a gift. In retrospect, I think this was their dilemma.

A few days passed and the visitation was conveniently not spoken about (although I doubt it had been forgotten). The time came for Nana's funeral. Even though I had pleaded to attend the service, my parents decided it was best for me to stay away as I would be too upset. However, I did attend a private Communion with only close family in church the night before and said prayers for my nana, so I think my mother felt that would be enough. I was devastated to lose my dear grandmother, but my mother somehow assumed it was only adults who truly felt grief and that a child could not share the same depth of emotion. How wrong can a parent be?

Nowadays if my own children asked such a thing of me, I would of course allow them to grieve in any way they felt they had to. In the early 1970s, children were treated differently.

On the day of the funeral, as all the guests arrived back at the house for the wake, I remember standing with my mother in the kitchen, making cups of tea. I felt it would be the ideal occasion for me to explain my feelings and speak my mind about the way my parents had dismissed my grief and kept me away from the funeral . . . WRONG!

As I started to make the tea it reminded me of how my nan would always have crumpets or cake ready for me every afternoon when I came home from school. I tried to explain to my mother and Auntie Joan who was with us in the kitchen how sad I was at losing Nana, and how I'd felt she was like a second mother to me. I started to cry and my mother told me to go to my room as I was upsetting her too much. Maybe I had hurt her with that last statement and she had never before realised I thought of Nana in such a way.

I sat alone in my bedroom and sobbed. Sam soon joined me. He has this uncanny knack of knowing when I need him. He sat on the edge of the bed beside me. At that second my Auntie Joan and my mother came in and walked over to me, and the three of us shared a loving cuddle. It seemed strange to me that they couldn't see Sam as he was sitting on the bed, very large and black. He even stood up to allow the ladies to sit down: unnecessary, but visually polite.

Through my tears, I tried to explain to my mother all the pent-up emotions inside me; why I'd felt that my nana was like a mother to me – always being there when Mum couldn't be, believing in me when she wouldn't, and giving me comfort when she didn't. I explained it wasn't that I felt my mum didn't love me – I knew she loved me more than anything, especially as I was her only daughter – but I was angry with her for always disregarding me when I spoke about my spirit visitors. Nana, of course, never did that. I had bottled up my feelings for too long. Now they boiled over in a deluge of words, cuttingly delivered with frustrated rage which shocked my mother into more tears. I know my words hurt her – that was my intention.

She didn't know how to respond, I had wounded her so deeply. My father came up then to see what all the fuss was about and found the argument in full flow. The women asked him to hold the fort downstairs as I was very upset and needed their company for a little while. For the first time I saw a chink of sadness in my dad's armour of stoicism.

After a while I insisted I was OK so my aunt went back down to the adults gathered below and my mum stayed behind to settle me down.

She spoke softly to me, saying that Nana was in a better place and that she would miss her too.

A better place! She knew there was a better place? Why, then, did she never listen to me when I tried to talk about the spirit world? Why wouldn't she understand that I could talk to people from this *better place*? I kept telling her I knew all about this *better place* as they came from there to talk to me in spirit. Again she dismissed this as pure imagination. My anger continued to seethe. I desperately needed her to understand, at the very least to acknowledge my words. No matter how hard I tried to tell her about Sam talking to me, she always seemed to dismiss what I had to say. I needed to prove to her that I could see them! Sam's voice rang inside my head, unheard by my mother, suggesting I had said enough. In fact, I could see him shaking his head, as if to say 'Don't say any more'. My mind was still bursting with anger and my whole body aching with grief!

I still so much wanted my mum to believe in me that I blasted her with something I had known about for years. It was a spiritual message I had been trying to spare her from before this as it was devastatingly hurtful. I told her what Sam my Guide had said to me some time ago about my father's health: he was going to suffer and die at fifty years of age.

This was a devastating moment for my mother. She was visibly shocked as I spoke the words. She had just buried her mother and now I was telling her of another death – that of her husband.

She screamed at the top of her voice, yelling at me never to mention this again. 'What you are saying is very cruel and hurtful, Helen,' she told me. 'You are only saying this because you feel I don't understand you!'

I continued with my onslaught, claiming that no matter how my dad and she kept denying I could see people in spirit, the fact remained I COULD! I could see loving Angels bursting with light; my Sam and other teaching Guides who would glow brightly with energy; spirit family, friends of family, and countless spirit animals around me all the time. Not only could I see these spirit people, they talked to me and spoke about the lives of others and how I could help them. Why couldn't my parents just accept that I had this ability, instead of constantly denying its existence? I cried out that I was sick of them always pretending I was telling some sort of story.

A world they could not see actually existed and I had to live with it, whether they liked it or not. I explained that by not accepting my gift, my parents were turning their backs on me. I continued raging at her until my mother looked defeated and worn out by the verbal onslaught.

Then she cried inconsolably and I felt tremendous guilt. My words had been harsh and delivered with venom. But at least my feelings were out in the open now.

My mum had had enough. She couldn't cope with me any more, not today of all days. She left the room. I lay on my bed and sobbed some more. A mixture of teenage hormones, grief and the desperate need to be heard by my parents had had the combined effect of turning me into, at least for that day, a confrontational little monster.

Without invitation, Sam once again joined me and sat on my bed. He jolted me out of my sobbing.

Why was he looking so sad? I sat up and huddled myself next to him. 'What's up, Sam?' I asked.

'Helen, do you not believe your Nana Ada loves you?' he replied.

I nodded affirmatively.

'Are you not happy that your nana is free from all her illness and out of pain?'

I nodded again.

'Are you not happy she is now laughing with her own mother and father?'

I nodded.

'Do you not remember Nana saying that she will see you again?'

Once again, I nodded.

Sam gave me a beaming smile. 'Good, chile! Then you have no need to cry, do you? My dear, it is good to cry a little. Tears show

how much you care that your nana is not with you physically. But then you need to let go and allow her to go forward with her life. When you continually cry, it is as though you do not believe that Nana is well and happy in the spirit world. If you keep crying, you will make it difficult for her to settle down and be happy with her parents.'

I sat and thought for a moment. He was right. My nana was safe, and had come to tell me she was going on holiday as she went into the spirit world. I dried my tears. 'Why don't my parents believe me when I speak about you or my other spirit visitors, Sam? Why?'

He thought for a moment. 'They want to believe you. In fact, your mother does have faith and belief in you. Your father still has doubts because he has inner fears. He is afraid of what you will say if he asks, for he knows you know the answers.

'They love you with every bone in their bodies, but they cannot reach out in the way that you touch people's hearts. You have a special and unique gift. They are scared for you, Helen. By not mentioning your gift to anyone, they feel they are somehow protecting you. To a certain degree, I understand that. One day, you will be inundated with people demanding to talk to you, my dear. They already know this. They feel it. They don't doubt you, they simply prefer to look the other way. I know you cannot do that, but Helen, before they leave this earth they will tell you that they can see. One day they too will catch a glimpse of what you can see. Only then will they begin to understand the vastness of your ability. It is frightening, Helen, I understand this as your Guide. But you, dear child, see their fear as rejection, when really all they are showing is misguided love.'

The following month was very strained at home. I barely spoke to my parents, not even at the dinner table. At weekends I locked myself in my bedroom, listening to my little transistor radio or doing homework, just to be out of their sight.

Eventually I decided enough was enough and that I needed to talk to my mother to clear up any bad feeling. Mum was alone, ironing in the kitchen, when I decided this was a suitable time to tackle her.

'I am sorry, Mum, that I shouted at you on the day of Nana's funeral,' I said with genuine contrition.

My mum answered me in a whisper as Dad was asleep on the couch in the lounge.

'Why would you say such a thing about your dad, Helen? That was wicked talk!'

As usual in my time of need, Sam came to the rescue. 'Tell your mother that the prediction was not made to frighten her but so as to warn her, for the good of the whole family. Your father is going to become gravely ill unless he changes his ways. His weak chest can only stand any chance of recovery if he stops smoking.'

Sam went on, 'It is easy to listen to happy predictions, but to hear of impending sadness requires great love and a leap of faith. Tell your mother these words and ask her to listen to you.'

My mother's face paled and she was noticeably shocked on hearing me say this. The iron was slammed down on to a blouse and hissed as if it too had the ability to be angry.

Composing herself, my mother looked hard at me. I don't know if she liked me much at that particular moment in time as I could see the heartache and despair in her eyes. She walked over to the kitchen sink. Her head drooped like a wilting tulip and tears rolled down her face into the metal bowl beneath.

Sam stood near her and held one comforting arm around her shoulders, but he was invisible to her and she could not see this tender outreach of love and compassion.

Through my tears I pleaded with her, saying I was sorry to

have to give her these messages. I told her I trusted my Guide Sam and did not want anyone else whom I loved to die.

My mother replied quietly, still not wanting to wake Dad. She said that she *had* listened, but she did not want me ever to repeat this to Dad, and I was never, ever to mention it to her again. Not quite the response I was looking for, especially as I was trying to help my dad improve his chances of living.

So from that day forward, I knew where I stood. My predictions were not to be spoken about in my own household. My nana had been the only person with whom I could be my true self, but she was gone.

Who could I talk to now?

But life continued, as it does. I was then thirteen years of age.

Laughter started to return to the house and my parents were happier than ever about their decision to buy their first home in this beautiful leafy avenue.

Word had spread around the neighbourhood of my near-abduction, so everyone I met in the street wanted to talk to me about it and they were all kind to me when they did.

I had already made friends with Bernard Rameson, the owner of the house next door when I had talked to him over the hedge a few months earlier. Mr Rameson didn't quite know what to say to me at first. However, the ice between us was broken when, as he tugged away at the dense foliage, he fell over backwards with a handful of greenery in his hands, like some sort of slapstick comedy sketch, and we both started to laugh.

He was regularly in the garden, working hard, so with the odd conversation we struck up, over time we had established a neighbourly rapport. On one occasion he looked particularly sad as he cut away at a border of red hot pokers lining the garden path. I couldn't help but notice his jaded aura. It seemed tired and lustreless, almost as if it hurt him to breathe in and out.

He chopped away with the shears with such gusto, I swear he was waging a vendetta against those poor plants as he fought his way through them. It was as though he was taking out some deep-rooted aggression on them. But even though he was determined to fight the battle, I doubted he was going to win the war.

He was a tall thin man with a tight bristling beard, grey like his hair. He had a kind face and a soft pleasant voice. I suppose he would have been in his late forties or early fifties then, which at the time I thought was ancient. As I gazed at him, something inside made me feel compassionate towards him.

I knew I would be in trouble with my parents for speaking about my spiritual messages, but I just couldn't help myself: Mr Rameson seemed to be in great need. I don't know why, but I started to talk to him about the spirit world: its beauty, the inhabitants, and the full glory of life over there.

In fact, it was Mr Rameson's Guide who was urging me to talk to him. The Guide said there was something he needed to hear. I never questioned why, just proceeded to give. I had learned from an early age that our Guides and well-wishing family relatives often have something very important to say to us, and those in need always deserve an answer or some help. Nevertheless, Mr Rameson looked quite surprised that our conversation was of such a spiritual nature.

'There is no need to be scared,' I told him.

'Scared of what?' he replied

'Why, the spirit world, of course! There are so many people who can help us over there, and no suffering or sickness. When we die our spiritual body is intact and we feel no pain, no matter what illness or sad situation we have had to endure.'

Despite his obvious shock and puzzled expression, probably

wondering why a young girl would say such a thing, he enquired about this further, asking me questions and quizzing me as to how I knew so much. Surely a young girl doesn't know about such things? he commented. We'd had quite a tête-à-tête by the time I had finished with him, and as I walked back into the house, satisfied that I had done what his Guide had asked, I bade him goodbye with a wave and a smile. I looked back over my shoulder and could see him in silhouette, stunned into immobility, clippers still in his hands, as I disappeared inside.

A few hours later the doorbell chimed. It was Mr Rameson.

As soon as I saw his face peering at me through the glazed front door, I wondered why he had come round so quickly after our chat. Was I in trouble again?

Before I could reach the door, Dad had opened it and our neighbour relayed to him all that I had said in the garden earlier. I was mortified as I stood in the hall, first looking at Dad's face then Mr Rameson's. Yes, I must be in trouble, I decided.

My father looked at me scornfully. And as though Mr Rameson read his facial expression, and realised that he had dropped me in it, he intervened, saying, 'Please don't shout at Helen. I have only come across to thank her for our conversation.'

My father invited him into the kitchen for a cup of tea but Mr Rameson refused, saying he was in a rush but had wanted to pop round before he went out.

'I know we don't talk very often,' he said, staring Dad straight in the eye, 'but you have no idea how interested I was in what Helen had to say. My wife and I are Catholics, and when Helen spoke of her Guardian Guides and Angels it gave great comfort to us, especially when she explained that there is no suffering in spirit. In fact, it gave us both a feeling of great strength.'

Our neighbour continued: 'You see, my wife is very ill. She has kidney disease and needs a transplant to survive. She is on a waiting list for a donor organ but meanwhile has to have permanent dialysis and is often in hospital, sometimes for lengthy stays.'

My father seemed puzzled as to why he was being told this. Our neighbour continued: 'We have a daughter called Catherine who still lives at home with us. She is twenty. That's who you will have seen, pottering about in the kitchen or the house. I felt you needed to know, just in case you thought I have a young bride!'

My father laughed with him, nervously.

'The thing is – did the neighbours tell you about my wife and her health problems? It's just that Helen spoke as though she knew our family had been through a considerable amount of suffering.'

My dad seemed speechless. I could see he was struggling to think of an appropriate answer as he turned and looked straight at me. Finally, he answered truthfully: 'No, sorry, they didn't. But please wish your wife well from us all, we had no idea she was so ill.'

I think my dad was mainly relieved that our neighbour was not upset with me, and his voice reflected this relief. 'I am sorry if Helen has upset you. Things often pop out of her mouth . . . she doesn't always know what she is saying.'

I smiled; it was lovely for me to find someone who had actually listened to what I had to say. Mr Rameson glanced over at me and gave me a smile: 'Please pop around any time, Helen, you would be more than welcome.'

'Are you sure you won't come in and have a cup of tea?' my dad asked politely as Mr Rameson turned to leave.

'It's kind of you to offer but I can't, sorry, I have to take my wife to the clinic. Anyway, nice meeting you again, Mr Sparrow. Hope we get to chat again soon.'

As an afterthought, Mr Rameson turned back to face me and

looked me in the eye. 'And thank you, Helen – you are a real little Angel.'

From then on I would pop in to see Catherine next door for a chat when she came home from college or was out in the garden. During my visits I could see that her mum was extremely frail and ill. Each time I called in an enormously tall man, beautiful in appearance and illuminating everything around him with his brightness, stood like a guard beside her. Waves of compassion and healing love emanated from him, comforting all of us present even though the others were not aware of it. He often crouched down beside me and gazed into my eyes as I talked to Catherine, smiling tenderly in affirmation of what I said about the spirit world. He never spoke, just watched, but I felt as though his presence was important. His clothes were draped in folds and folds of material that looked voluptuous and cosy like heavy velvet but shimmering with life and energy. He had a book in one of his hands that he would occasionally get out as if to read, though he never wrote in it. I was shocked when Sam popped in one day and explained that this was an Angel of Death.

I always imagined that such an Angel would be fearful and black, full of grim thoughts, but instead he was full of grace and gentleness, exuding care and compassion. It never felt as though he wanted to take anyone, in fact I felt the opposite, as though he only wanted to help and would patiently try to offer healing to the suffering.

On one of my visits to their house, Catherine's mum was confined to bed, too poorly to even walk and, when I went into the bedroom to say hello, I could see him kneeling by her bedside gently holding her hand, even though she was totally unaware of his presence.

I asked Sam if the Angel always looked so handsome, because with his strikingly good looks and dark hair he would make a woman's head turn. Sam replied that an Angel of Death is always a beautiful soul and appears to people in many different forms but the energy is always that of compassion towards those who are about to pass. That energy was to help nurture the passing and assist the journey of the newly departed. I knew now that Catherine's mum would soon be entering into spirit, but how could I tell my friend?

Sadly I didn't have to, Catherine's mother died a few days afterwards.

Before she did, as a parting gift, Mrs Rameson had arranged for Russ Abbott to attend Catherine's twenty-first birthday party. Russ Abbott, his wife Trisha and their children were the Rameson's other next-door neighbours. Russ was then fast climbing the steps to comedy stardom and had just started to make regular appearances on television. I first met him when we were fellow party guests.

Thanks to him we certainly had a night to remember. None of us had ever laughed so much in our lives. Russ is a naturally funny man. Needless to say, the whole evening was a great success. Not long after that, towards the end of the year, after Trisha had given birth to a baby daughter, Russ was offered a huge television contract. They moved from our road to a larger house in Cheshire and unfortunately our paths have not crossed since.

I often see him on TV, though, and think of him, especially as my mother adopted their black-and-white cat, which we called Sooty. They couldn't take the cat so she offered it a home. I can honestly say that that animal was loved by everyone and led a pampered existence, living to a very ripe old age.

At nearly thirteen years old I was far too young to consider boys as anything other than friends. In my small close circle of girl-friends, we didn't really see the necessity of mixing much with them at all. Our hormones were not as active as they seem to be in young teens today, and we were content in our self-appointed role of good girls.

School-time, however, was about to change all that. Our mornings were spent at Blacon at Charles Kingsley, and afternoons at the other side of town at Bishop's School. The next week it would be vice versa. An educational fiasco, in my opinion . . . but children should be seen and not heard.

This was during a period when the government thought that a school with a good reputation could help boost the efficacy of a failing one by amalgamation. They were so wrong! All-girls Charles Kingsley School was the one with the good reputation. Now it was all change to accommodate the political diktat of the day and we had to merge with co-ed Bishop's . . . beginning the slippery slope to our educational and moral downfall!

Once the new term started, the battlelines extended far beyond the playground. There were clear divisions between both sets of staff, both sets of pupils. It was like mixing oil and water, or rather trying to. On the one side we had my all-female school with its primly dressed and polite girls, having to morph with the co-ed mixture of budding hooligans and naturally troublesome kids on the other.

The playground became a warzone between 'us and them', and certainly not the level playing field of equal opportunity that our political masters had imagined. It wasn't long before bright girls found it acceptable to become mediocre or worse, as they succumbed to the lowest common denominator in order to win acceptance by their peers.

Pregnancies became rife and violence ruled what was formerly a peaceful playground. Where previously we had jumped to attention when a teacher raised their voice, within a term or so the teachers found themselves battling to keep the larger classes under any form of control.

I felt inwardly demoralised by my parents' choice of school for me. I couldn't understand why they hadn't wanted me to excel at a better one when I was given the opportunity. There they were, two hard-working people obviously aspiring to do better by earning more money for luxuries, yet they wouldn't invest in my education.

They say that your school years are both the happiest and the worst of all your years . . . In my case, what started as the best of my teenage years ended in yet more tears.

Once the girls of Charles Kingsley had settled into the new regime of smelly socks in the changing rooms, football in the playground and catcalls in the classroom, both pupils and teachers alike tried to adapt to a co-ed campus.

There was no longer a gaggle of girls huddled in a corner looking at the latest copy of *Jackie* magazine during break: instead they were leering at the boys they fancied, parading around with newly painted faces and regularly brushed hair, hoping to catch some male attention.

The vanity mirror became just as important to them as the fountain pen. The boys, knowing the girls' eyes were upon them, strutted about like peacocks, aggressively kicking their footballs in the hope of making an impression. Blouses grew tighter and skirts soared higher, along with the faint whiff of testosterone mixed with cheap perfume.

For the older girls this was a massive change. It was one that won mixed reviews from parents, teachers and pupils alike. The more liberal-minded liked the idea of a co-ed environment; others hated it. After nearly two peaceful years in an all-girl environment, I saw the change as more of an inconvenience than anything else.

The school itself was changing at an alarming rate, mainly due to the fact that Charles Kingsley had more than quadrupled its intake overnight, which meant that the existing classrooms could not house the vast numbers of new pupils. Our once-beautiful school grounds were being carved up by new construction works, as builders transported diggers and building materials around them. It was as if a wicked witch had cast a spell and was going to transform our school into something much bigger and more sinister. Granted we were to have new halls, classrooms and special equipment, which I can only assume were paid for by the government as there was no way the local authority could have funded a project of this magnitude.

We went from a school of 800 pupils to one with over 3,000, in a flash. To try and cope with the merger, the first- and second-year students had to travel by bus ten miles to the other side of town where Bishop's School was situated. It meant that we had to catch buses at 7.30 in the morning to beat the rush-hour traffic through the city, and then we were transported like cattle back to Charles Kingsley in the afternoon, to catch the end of the lunch break and resume lessons there.

Those bus trips were a nightmare. The prim girls of Charles Kingsley found themselves shut in with the hooligans from the other school, which started a new wave of different kinds of bullying. Although I had not yet ended my third year of secondary education, I knew it was going to be a rough ride if those bus journeys were anything to go by.

While I was at Charles Kingsley, I became friends with a girl – let's call her Janet. She lived in the station house near the railway track, with her parents and many siblings. My relationship with her was a strange one because we had so little to do with each other in school. This was mainly because she was in a lower set than I was, and my lessons never overlapped with hers. Her mum worked similar hours to mine in the city, so we palled up one day as we walked the same route to school, taking the short cut through the council estate. From then on we literally became walking buddies and would chat about this and that on our way to and from school. Sometimes we would go to my house to do homework together. We never went to hers after school because her home was very busy with so many siblings, and her mum didn't seem to like her friends going back to the house.

I always suspected that Janet felt safe with me at my house. Once I even asked her if everything was OK at home because her mother had remarried and Janet hated the man she now lived with. She wouldn't call him Dad; in fact, she refused even to speak about him unless she was calling him bad names. I had the overwhelming feeling that she was so unhappy that she would either run away from home or else be hurt there in some way for speaking out.

One day as she spoke to me I had a spiritual picture of her being hit. I felt sick to the pit of my stomach, sure something awful would happen to her. I told her she could always come to me at my house if she was scared. When I shared these facts with my mum and dad, they became alarmed and said that we should not get involved in family disputes. If there was domestic violence, they said it was up to the police and Social Services to sort it out, and was definitely not something I should be talking to my friend about. I got the impression that my parents wanted me to distance myself from Janet once they found that her background was so unstable. She was my friend – so I didn't.

After Janet had not attended school for a couple of days, I thought she must be ill at home with a cold or some other illness. She had left a couple of schoolbooks at my house on her last visit so I asked my mum if we could take them round to her one evening. After my scare with the sexual predator some time back,

Mum never let me walk out at night or in the early mornings alone. So she agreed to come with me and walk over to my friend's house, to see why Janet had not been to school.

Their house was difficult to reach as it had to be approached down a long concrete staircase from the main road. The house lay parallel to the train tracks. After you reached it, there was a row of lock-up garages used by nearby residents.

There were police patrolling along the road as we approached and they stopped to ask us why we were going down to Janet's house. My mother explained that I was a schoolfriend of hers and said that Janet had been off school for a while. She showed him the schoolbooks and said I was worried that she might need them for her homework.

The police officer looked at us both gravely: 'I am afraid you cannot go to the house. The family is not at home. There has been an incident and there are ongoing police enquiries. No one may enter beyond this point.'

My mother was puzzled. She told the police officer again we were only going to drop off some books.

The officer caught my mother's sleeve and turned her away from me, whispering into her ear so that I could not hear what he was saying. My mother nodded back to him and turned back to me, saying that we should go straight home and once we were there she would explain everything.

As if some invisible bell had summoned him, Sam appeared beside the police officer.

Needless to say teenagers don't let things rest . . . all the way home I quizzed my mother about why she looked so stressed and upset. What had the police officer said to her? What was wrong? Why couldn't we go to the house to see Janet? Had something happened to her mum or dad?

As we approached our home, Mum cried. She explained that

her stepfather had murdered Janet. They had found him hanging in a lock-up garage after he had apparently murdered her.

I was devastated to hear this and felt guilty that I had not said enough to Janet or anyone else about my worries for her. Why didn't I ask her more questions when I felt she was unhappy in her home life?

My own youth blanketed my better judgement and stopped me from asking the spiritual questions my Guides had prompted me to ask. Why hadn't I listened to them? Why hadn't I paid more attention to what the spirit world had wanted to say about Janet? I was so sad, and felt very guilty.

That night Sam visited my room and sat beside me as he had done many times before. 'It is not your fault, my chile. You did what you could. You were a good friend: that is all anyone can be. Now Janet is safe and loved in the spirit world, and no more harm will come to her.' He sat quietly beside me as I cried for the loss of my friend, and spoke more words of wisdom to me: 'We cry for those we have lost when in fact they have just been found.'

Some time later I learned that Janet had been sexually abused and brutally beaten to death by her stepfather who then killed himself. Where was the justice? I wondered. On reflection, I was still too young to take in the full extent of what had happened to my friend, and since that time I have blanked my mind to any further information about how she died.

My experiences throughout life have taught me that the spirit world always introduces people to me for a reason. When I was younger I didn't always understand what that was. In Janet's case, perhaps I was meant to warn her about the murder or offer her sanctuary, but I had been too young to understand the scale of the danger she faced.

After that I felt angry with Sam and any Angel that happened to be listening. I wanted to know why my friend had had to die.

Janet's death opened the door to me thinking all sorts of dark thoughts. For the life of me, I just couldn't understand why this had had to happen to her, or why there were even murderers out there in our world. It all seemed senseless to me. Where did such evil souls go when they died? I certainly didn't want them to share the same space as myself, and when they died would they be with my friend who was now in spirit? These questions kept filling my head, so the next time Sam joined me for a nightly chat, I decided I was going to confront him and tackle the subject, whether he wanted to talk about it or not.

I was not only maturing in years but also in spiritual experience, and my teenage inquisitiveness was not going to rest easily unless I received some answers, especially as films about demonic subjects like *The Exorcist* were now being shown at the cinema. I needed to know so much. For starters, were films like these a true depiction of Satan's work? Was there really such evil in this world and the next? I needed to know more about its inhabitants, here and in spirit. I now knew that evil could lurk in our world: I wanted to know if it existed in the next. I felt a thirst to know if the inhabitants of hell were capable of affecting our world. Was it possible for malevolent spirits to stray outside their own black inner sanctuary of hell?

Sam may have spoken to me a little about good and bad situations in life, but he had never mentioned whether there were beings living in some sort of hellish purgatory. Was he just avoiding my requests because the place actually existed, or was it pure myth and he was trying not to be distracted by irrelevancies?

Why is it we all feel a desire to know more about the things that do not and should not concern us? Is it sheer morbid curiosity or a useful way of arming ourselves against the depravity that exists, in this world and the next?

Most living human beings show little sign of the depths of evil that my friend had to contend with on the fateful day of her murder. In fact, most people are like me, content to live out their lives in peace, offering only kindness towards others. But as tranquil as we may appear to the world, we still have our occasional flare-ups of emotion or temper within our own family and network of friends, so there is a negative side within all of us, to some extent. As Sam had previously explained to me, life is all about balance.

Though it scared me to contemplate the answers to my questions, I felt I did need to know more in order that I might be able to protect myself and others from evil energies. Despite the fact that Sam was reluctant to tell me more about the subject, he eventually gave in and proceeded.

'Are you sure you want to know this, Helen? Once you do, then there is no going back! As I have explained to you on many occasions, ignorance can protect you to a certain degree. Once that is gone, you are confronted with the unadorned truth. For every question you ask of me, my answer will evoke ten further questions. The thirst cannot be quenched. Trying to understand all there is to know is an endless journey.'

I gulped, but the Leo in my star sign made me reply hastily, 'Yes, I need to know more, Sam. I need to know as much as you can tell me. I feel that only then can I begin to shield and guard myself against such evil should these entities try to camouflage themselves spiritually when they visit me. They could well try to penetrate my daily life. Anything you tell me has to have a positive aspect. I need to know how I can deal with these evil entities and defend myself against them.'

He stroked his chin thoughtfully and I could see that he was pondering how much detail I could take – especially at my young age. 'Look, Helen, if I start to tell you everything I know about the depths of depravity within the spirit world, you will not thank me.

I will, however, give you some detail: specifics that I think might help you. You should then be able to distinguish any "evil" energy, when it comes close to you or others around you. You see, evil deeds proceed from various different avenues, invading both your living earthly world and indeed your own personal and spiritual life.'

As he spoke, I wondered if I was going to be able to cope with what he would say next.

'So do evil beings come from spirit into our living world?'

Sam paused for a moment then told me, 'Yes, Helen. From time to time they do try to dominate your earthly world.'

I thought about this. Perhaps Sam was right; to be in ignorance is sometimes to be in a better place. I was starting to have second thoughts about pressing him to tell me more, though some day I was sure I would need to know about hell's inhabitants.

'My dear.' Sam smiled at me. 'You are young. Enjoy your youth and innocence – the evils of the world you will know about soon enough. You and I will have many future conversations about the evil side. For now rest easy and know that good always supersedes evil. There are many who protect not only you but all people on earth. One day I will explain so much more.'

7

Dogs Are Man's Best Friend

My Granddad Joe was lost after Nana Ada died. They had been married for nearly fifty years. After spending all that time together, even though it had had its ups and downs, it was naturally a major loss for him. When he started to live alone, it became apparent that not only had my nana provided emotional support, she had also handled all the practical side of their life together as Granddad's housekeeping and cookery skills were limited. He started to look thinner as he was eating sandwiches for all his meals; they were the only things he could make. My mother was worried about him being on his own and suggested that he came to live with us.

We only had a three-bedroomed house and the spare room was quite small, but Granddad must have been so glad of the company he gratefully accepted straight away. Besides, it meant that someone was now home when I arrived back from school. Even Gyp must have thought his ship had come in, as rather than being locked in the kitchen all day he now had company to fuss over him.

He loved the fact that Granddad now took him out for walks during the day and that he didn't have to sit cross-legged waiting for me to arrive home to take him out. In fact, on reflection, looking after Gyp became mutual therapy for Granddad and me after the loss of Nana. I loved having Granddad with us as he always sat me down with a cup of tea when I arrived home and asked me to talk about my day. The potatoes were peeled and the house was a little tidier without my labours being necessary. And I could share my feelings about the spirit world with a real living adult – these were happier times for me.

After I had seen Nana at the bottom of the deep ditch when she'd had her massive stroke, Granddad had never doubted my gift. Although he had not talked openly about my spirituality, especially with my parents, he had always been there listening to my stories about Sam when I spoke to Nana. On reflection, I suppose I would always natter on, deep in conversation, not even noticing whether he was listening or not. He was usually in the background, watching TV or reading his newspaper, and I thought that Nana must have talked to him about me later on when I had left their house to go home. As it happened, Granddad was now telling me he *had* listened and he *did* believe when I enthusiastically talked about Sam and the spirit world.

I was very surprised one day when he stood up, walked around to my side of the table and hugged me, saying: 'It's OK, my love, you have nothing to hide any more. I am a firm believer in what you can see and hear from the spirit world. Helen, my love, you can tell me anything.'

I was ecstatic upon hearing that and inside felt an impulse of joyous love. At last a member of my own family, other than my nana, believed in me. It was a wonderful feeling.

So after school Granddad would not only listen to me, but we had fabulous conversations about some of the spiritual experiences he himself had had when he was younger. Granddad had been in the Navy, serving with Lord Mountbatten during his early command. Mountbatten had sailed to Singapore in a new destroyer which he was to exchange for an older ship. That was where my granddad joined the service. Mountbatten was appointed Commander-in-chief of the Mediterranean fleet, and serving under him Granddad visited most ports there. He liked to talk about Istanbul and Gibraltar, but his fighting experiences he largely preferred not to mention.

Sam was also happy to have my granddad at home and there were even times when I thought my granddad could sense him. He sometimes said he saw someone in his bedroom. Sam often sat cross-legged by Granddad's side while he sat on the deckchair outside in the sun reading his newspaper. Sam always said that my granddad had a deep spirituality, although he never expressed it openly.

During the fighting Granddad Joe had seen his friend killed in an explosion, and said he would never forget having a spiritual visit from him one night when his friend came back to talk to him. He asked my granddad if he would contact his family when he got back to Britain, after his naval service had finished. The dead friend's wife was pregnant and he was going to have a son he would never be able to hold, but would always watch over. After the war my granddad did visit his friend's wife to share this story, and she did have a little boy exactly as predicted. The reason she was so shocked to hear about her husband's words was because at the time of his death he'd had no knowledge he was even going to be a father.

The school term after Granddad came to live with us, my class was joined by a new girl who came from a prestigious private girls' school. She was being ribbed by the other children because they all said she was posh. Actually, I liked her and felt she was being treated unfairly. I understood how it felt to be different, and kept out of the mainstream mayhem of my other classmates. In the new girl's case she was being singled out because she came from a good family. I quickly made friends with her when no one else seemed to want to.

The new girl's name was Denise and she fast became one of my best friends. I learned she lived on the other side of Chester, in the posh area known as Queen's Park, which was situated by the banks of the River Dee.

Denise's father had recently died of cancer. She and her sister had to adjust not only to a new life without him, but also a new school – and a state school at that. Their mother had to take charge of the finances and make some very tough decisions in order to keep the family solvent. Even though in many adults' eyes Denise had come to terms with her immense loss, I could spiritually see and feel her pain. On occasion, in school breaks, we would talk about him and I noticed she found it difficult to cry, mainly because she had buried the pain so deep inside her.

On reflection, I believe her Guardian Guide and Angels wanted me to be with her, to help her to adjust to her loss and understand that her father lived on in an afterlife.

You see, we all have a Guardian Guide and Guardian Angel, no matter who we are. Despite what other people may say, when I have seen Angels, although they watch over us, they do so in an entirely different way from our Guardian Guides. When Angels arrive in our presence, it is a wondrous and special gift bestowed upon us as they have magnificent abilities. While it's fair to say our Guardian Guides are amazing helpers and teachers, an Angel's gifts go way beyond that. To sum up the difference in one simple sentence: a Guide teaches and helps you make choices; an Angel bestows whatever is in their gift.

For example, if healing is needed then that will be what they bestow. Or maybe communication, patience or understanding. Whatever their particular gift, that is what they bring when they visit. What has to be remembered is that Angels choose when and where they wish to visit. Our Guardian Guides are with us always: following us, living with us, teaching us. For the uninitiated, our Guardian Guides may even be viewed as Angels of a sort – but they are not. If you are lucky enough ever to see an Angel, trust me, the difference between them and Guardian Guides is clear and distinct.

Denise and I became so close that soon I was staying at her house for sleepovers. Also her mum thought I was good company for her as our friendship seemed to have brought her out of her former depression. Denise's mum was different from my mum and dad; her views about life were the opposite of those of my parents. Her policy was always to encourage her daughters to succeed in life, and she wanted her girls to achieve a university education. I envied this level of parental aspiration.

Her house was gorgeous, with huge picture windows extending the full length of one wall of the lounge, letting in all the sunlight and warmth on offer. The house was split-level and the upper lounge area gave a view over the surrounding fields, stretching down to the river. It was genuinely beautiful, and on a sunny day the countryside views and the golden sunshine seemed to fill up the whole house with positive energy. For me, it was an awesome experience just to be there.

Beneath the lounge Denise had her own apartment area that she shared with her elder sister, Helen. This we called the 'den', and because it had its own TV in the lounge area as well as a small kitchen, the girls were able to feel totally independent when really their mother was on the floor above. It was every teenager's dream, independence with security. I loved it and dreamed that my mum and dad would one day buy a house as beautiful.

I would stay at Denise's house regularly during weekends or school holidays and we would have great fun in the city, shopping or watching the lads row on the river. I never considered Denise posh or different from anyone else; to me she was just my friend – a girl I got on well with. It was when she rolled back the garage doors that I truly appreciated the financial disparity between our lives. When those doors opened, the garage was seen to contain not one but two cars, one of them being a magnificent Silver Cloud Rolls-Royce and the other a very expensive luxury saloon car. Despite the Silver Cloud's age, it oozed class from a bygone era, and inside smelled of fine leather. It wasn't a beast, it was a rare, refined beauty. I thought all of Denise's life was beautiful, and destined for further privilege, but rather than think her lucky because of that, I thought how sad it was she was bereft of the one thing she really craved: her father.

'Mum hardly ever uses it,' Denise said sadly as we looked at the elegant automobile. 'It was Dad's, he loved old cars. Mum won't sell it and I don't want to go out in it. She sometimes drives us into town to give it a spin, but I crouch down on the floor so people won't see me.'

Poor Denise was in a similar situation to me; she was different from the other kids and therefore open to bullying. I could see tears welling up in her eyes as she desperately tried to swallow down her distress. She was crying not just because of the loss of her dad but because she felt guilty for the way her family lived.

Her arriving by Rolls-Royce and living in a luxury house did not go down well with the council-house kids at school. Her world had been shattered by the loss of her dad, and the privileges the family had once taken for granted had certainly been curtailed. I knew that if her father had been alive she would still have been in her private school.

Her mother was oblivious to the daily abuse she had to face at school as Denise shielded her from the truth. Despite the brave faces they all put on, the family were all suffering in their own particular ways. As her friend, I was the only one Denise confided in. This was important to me because as far as friends were concerned I had only two or three to whom I became close during my childhood. I was also careful to keep well away from the ones I felt might prove fickle and turn on me if I shared myself with them, so I suppose mine was a self-inflicted loneliness. Denise understood my attitude as she had experienced grief and was open to a more spiritual acceptance, if only as a way to rationalise her father's death.

Despite Denise being a great friend, each time I tried to talk to her about the subject of life after death, it naturally evoked strong emotions in her because of her father. I decided my ability to see spirit and communicate was a subject I had to broach with her. I didn't want to distance my friend, after all I only had a few, and I loved Denise. But she was still angry to think that if there was a God and this wonderful system of Guardians was in place, then why had her father been taken? To be perfectly honest, as a young girl I didn't have the vocabulary or experience to deal with that level of grief. However, I did explain to her that her Guardian Guide watched over her, and that anger was an emotion her father would not want her to feel. He would want her to find happiness, despite his earthly absence, so she needed to do this *for him* otherwise he too might be very sad.

Strangely she never doubted my spiritual awareness; in fact, over breakfast together one day at their house, her mother remarked on the way my presence there actually helped Denise as sometimes as a family they failed to talk about their grief to each other. Even at my young age I knew that recovering from grief could take time. I was still recovering after Nana's death.

To travel to Denise's house for a weekend stay we often used the school bus across the city on a Friday night, stopping at the River Dee and walking across the suspension bridge into the Queen's Park area. During the weekend we would enjoy taking her pet Alsatian dog out for walks and watching films on TV. Life was pretty simple then. There were no PlayStations or Nintendo to keep us amused, just girlie laughter and school chit-chat. Even so, I think this was one of the happiest periods of my childhood.

Denise's dog, Sheba, loved going for walks with us, sometimes swimming in the river, and we would spend hours being entertained by the Alsatian. Denise would toss the ball into the water and the dog would dive in excitedly to retrieve the toy. It was a favourite pastime of hers and we laughed afterwards as she sprayed us with smelly river water, soaking us as she shook her own coat dry.

On one of my many visits to Denise's, we were out walking one day with the dog when I had a blinding premonition. A searing light entered my eyes like a camera flash and I knew by the feelings associated with the pictures in my head that I was seeing something dire that was about to happen.

Denise was walking ahead with the dog, oblivious to my trance-like state as I stood there riveted to the spot. A few moments passed. She shouted for me to catch up, jolting me out of the vision I had just experienced.

But, like a slow-motion video playing in front of my eyes, I could still see the dog jumping into the water and being sucked under by a strong current, to a slow death by drowning. How could I tell Denise what I had just seen? Would she understand about my premonitions? Could I afford *not* to tell her even though I knew it might alienate her? I didn't want to risk losing such a good friend. All these different thoughts were competing in my mind.

Although my few friends knew I had some sort of spiritual sight and I often talked about seeing my Guide Sam, I never really opened up fully about the true extent of my visions or spirit visitors. After my parents denied my ability and seemed more at ease thinking of me as a fanciful storyteller, I was always in fear of my friends ridiculing me or, worse still, abandoning me. The thought of having no friends at all was a daunting prospect for a child.

To them, my ability to know where they were about to take a holiday was enough of a surprise; it would have been unbelievable – freaky in a child's eyes – for me to be able to predict a death. Normally with my friends I discussed nothing more than trivia.

So how could I tell my best friend that her beloved companion was about to meet a watery end? Most of the chats we'd shared about the spirit world would make her cry. It wasn't that Denise didn't believe, it was simply too painful for her to talk about the death of her dear dad. Making the decision to censor the truth is difficult enough for an adult to do; deciding on it as a child was traumatic for me as Denise was my best friend. Even so I couldn't let it rest as thoughts of my friend Janet came into my mind. I always feel an overwhelming compulsion to protect people, but sometimes doing so involves using words they really don't want to hear.

After careful thought I decided that it was best just to stress to her that she should be careful when out with the dog, especially near water.

I asked her not to throw the ball into the river, saying I was nervous that the dog might be hurt or have an accident. Denise dismissed my comment, saying that Sheba was a strong swimmer and loved the water so much, it was doubtful she would get herself in any danger. Other than telling her again to keep Sheba out of the water from now on, I did not elaborate my warning any further, fearing it might harm our relationship.

The next day, before I set off back home, the vision repeated itself. This one was even more startling . . . I could physically feel myself gasping for breath as once again I witnessed the dog drowning.

What should I do?

I decided to warn Denise again to take care when she took the dog for walks. Surely that would be enough? I thought.

The year was passing by fast. It was the early spring of 1973 and Denise and I were busy revising for our exams. We would often revise in Chester's City Library, afterwards talking and laughing together as we walked around town. My trips to Denise's house at the weekend became limited, as her mum felt she needed to revise more.

Although I worried for Sheba, I have to be honest and say it was nothing compared to the worry I felt for my own beloved canine companion, Gyp. Now entering his sixteenth year, his aged bones were starting to creak and seize up with rheumatism. When I took him for his daily walks I noticed the agility of youth was gone, but he still looked the same to me, always with a cheery expression and steadfast by my side. As children we rarely think of those we love getting older, we just assume that they will continue the same – no matter what . . . forever.

He loved to walk along the sand, chasing seagulls, so my parents often drove to the beaches of Rhyl, Prestatyn, Rhos or Llandudno from Chester, just to let Gyp run in the wind along the sandy shores. I think they felt guilty because he'd been locked up all day prior to Granddad joining us, when they were out at work and I was at school. These outings were a wonderful treat for him. When we invited him into the car, the old-timer would sit quietly until we were all inside, as good as gold, with – I swear – a massive smile on his hairy face. This was his chance for some real exercise and freedom, a privilege well deserved in his old age. We all loved him . . . especially me.

One Saturday morning we travelled down to visit the beautiful one-mile beach promenade at Rhos-on-Sea and Colwyn Bay on the North Wales coast. It started out just as a normal walk on the promenade in the vicinity of the pier, one that we had done many times before. I carried Gyp's lead in my hand; there was no need to attach it to his collar as the promenade walkway was extremely wide and very dog-friendly. If dogs happened upon each other, which they often did, there were no territory fights. They just had a little smell of each other and walked on quite happy. All very civilised in the canine way.

Then without any warning a ball bounced in front of us. Just up ahead were two children, standing still with tennis racquets, watching their ball bounce past us at speed. Not a strange sight in context, as many people played games at the seaside. Now it was Gyp's turn to join in the fun and, despite his ageing bones, he did a flying spin and bounded off after the ball. From this point onward, life went into ultra-slow motion for me. First the ball bounced off the edge of the promenade, which was fenced off only by metal railings; then, without hesitation, my Gyp followed in playful pursuit right off the edge. He had inadvertently jumped off a very high section of promenade and plummeted to the rocks below.

For a split second I froze while I watched. There was nothing I could do. Nothing any of us could have done. I ran over to the railings, beside myself with shock when I saw the immense drop below and that Gyp had landed on his back on the jagged rocks.

The fall had hurt him so badly that he seemed unable to find his feet and stand upright. He whimpered in pain and I screamed for my dad to help. I was frantic.

Fortunately about thirty metres down the prom a set of concrete stairs led to the beach. The tide was out, so the three of us ran down on to the sand and hurried over to the rocks where Gyp had landed. My father scrambled across the slippery rocks to rescue him. After many stumbles Dad eventually reached Gyp, carried him back along the beach and to safety in the car. Had the tide been in, I really don't know what we would have done.

Rushing back to Chester, we took him straight to Mr Lambert, our family vet. His surgery was just a few yards round the corner from Dr Cornforth's old surgery, right in the heart of Chester.

Poor Gyp never fully recovered from his ordeal and very soon afterwards developed a growth on his spine, possibly aggravated by the accident. After tests, the vet sadly diagnosed a malignant tumour and suggested that the kindest thing was to put him down. He left us alone for a moment to consider his suggestion.

My father and I stood in the surgery, looking at Gyp who lay flat and motionless on his blanket, seemingly in too much pain even to want to move. I couldn't bear the thought of my Gyp dying. Maybe I could give him healing like I had when Nana Ada was ill in hospital. I thought it might keep him alive for a little longer . . . the tumour might disappear. I told my father I didn't care what he thought or said, I was going to give Gyp some healing now – here in the vet's! Standing right next to me, Sam had arrived to offer his support, his outstretched hand on my shoulder. Intuitively I positioned my hands for the healing ritual, one on Gyp's head and the other on his body, close to his heart. I could see his silver-cord exposing itself from his nose area and, knowing what this meant, desperately wanted it to return into his body.

Sam crouched down too as I kneeled beside Gyp, lying on the floor. 'He is so ill, my chile,' Sam said compassionately. 'This is a time when your healing can only help to ensure your Gyp passes safely into spirit.'

I wasn't listening to Sam's advice, but his tender tone reached me. 'Dearest chile, you need to let him go.' I started to cry then and told my disbelieving father what Sam had said. My father said he needed a cigarette and walked outside, leaving me alone with Gyp.

Sam continued: 'I know how painful it is to witness any suffering. That is why it is kinder to allow Gyp to come to the spirit world, where he will be free from pain. He has given you much love during his life. Now it is time for you to allow him to leave.'

My father walked back into the room then with the vet who asked if we had made a decision. I could see that my father too had tears in his eyes. After all, Gyp had been part of the family for sixteen years.

I was nearing my fifteenth birthday. My dearest friend looked into my tear-stained eyes and, seeing the expression on his hairy face, I knew he had said his last goodbye to me. Sam said he would stay with Gyp to make sure he passed safely into spirit where he would take him to my relatives. I couldn't even answer him in my mind as I was emotionally spent. Grief had drained every ounce of my energy. I was inconsolable.

Dad stayed with Gyp while I waited outside as the vet gave him a lethal injection, euthanising him out of pain. I couldn't bear to watch.

I sat on the vet's doorstep with the dog lead in my hand. It broke my heart and I sobbed uncontrollably. Gyp was more than my best friend, he had been there as long as I could recall. Not one day of my life had I not had him with me. I loved him more than words could ever say. What was I going to do without him?

Some people think it's crazy to grieve so badly after the death of a pet. Nevertheless, like friends or family, they are an important part of our lives and we should give due respect when death arrives for them. They bring us joy, fun, companionship, loyalty, and, most of all, unconditional love when they share our lives. So it is only fitting we should feel grief when they are gone.

Don't you think the animals we look on as pets would be better called companions? To call them a 'pet' implies an inferior role, when in fact to many of us our animals are constant, caring companions and can be as close as any relative. Research has shown many people are emotionally dependent on their animals; I know I was dependent on Gyp in my early years, and the bond I shared with him ran deep. Our faithful companions might not speak openly to us, but they certainly do convey their feelings. I swear Gyp understood every word I said to him.

The house felt empty without him in it. My mother was upset for days. My granddad was devastated: he too loved Gyp and missed his daily jaunt with him. It was a sad loss for all of us.

Sam would continually offer kind words of comfort, telling me that Gyp was in spirit with my Nana Ada and that she was now looking after him for me. It did ease the pain a little, but I missed them both so much. They had loved me unconditionally for what I truly was.

Life continued as usual at school, with the added distraction of huge cranes delivering massive concrete blocks to build the new extensions. It was hell as far as I was concerned. I still had to bus across town between Bishop's and Charles Kingsley. Thank goodness for Denise, who kept me sane throughout the drudgery.

The emptiness at home reminded me of when I'd lost Nana.

I was so unhappy. Denise seemed to be the only person able to understand my grief. I felt embarrassed to express such a depth of emotion to other people over what they saw as *just a dog*. Denise had lost her dad, after all. I knew it wasn't the same kind of loss, but to me Gyp had been a good friend. Like a sister, Denise totally understood my sorrow and somehow talked me out of my black mood.

About three weeks after Gyp's passing, I noticed that she was not in school one day, so I decided to give her a phone call once I'd arrived home. The news I received was shocking. Her mother answered the phone and told me that Denise could not speak to me because she was too upset. She explained how Denise had been walking the dog that morning before school and had thrown the ball into the river.

My heart raced and I froze where I stood as I knew instinctively what had happened.

Workmen had been repairing the underwater grids in the River Dee. They are there to collect debris by the weir before the bridge leading into Handbridge. A strong underwater current there had caught the dog unawares as it swam out to retrieve its toy. Unfortunately the suction from the grid was so strong it dragged Sheba to the bottom of the riverbed where she became entangled in wire the workmen had left submerged there. Unable to get free, Sheba had drowned.

All alone by the waterside, Denise was beside herself with fear as she screamed for help. It took all the strength of a passer-by to restrain her from jumping into the river herself to try and rescue her dog. If she had attempted it, the result might well have been her drowning herself as the currents were so strong on that occasion. Someone phoned for the fire brigade and frogmen had to rescue the dog. Unfortunately it took hours to recover Sheba from her watery grave.

Denise's beloved companion was dead.

Her mum explained that Denise felt doubly guilty because Sheba was originally her dad's. Before he died, he'd asked her to take good care of his dog. Sheba was the strongest connection she had left to him, and now even that was gone.

It took Denise months to come to terms with losing Sheba and we did not talk about the subject for a good while. Then one day, out of the blue at school, she quizzed me about what I had said to her that day I had my premonition. I think she was feeling very guilty for not listening to my warning.

No matter how much guilt she felt, I explained it would not bring Sheba back into her life. I told her I felt the same way about Gyp. Sheba knew that she was loved and that Denise didn't intentionally set out to hurt her in any way. We cried together as I explained that the entire spirit world can only give us warning of impending problems or disasters. The rest is up to us. We have to decide whether we act upon that advice or not. In hindsight, of course, it's easy to see that we should have listened more carefully. But maybe some things are not meant to be changed.

As we continued with our chat, I described the roles animals have in spirit and how they stick with human beings over there when they have known real love. Animals are living beings with souls just like us, and when they enter the spirit world they too live a new life, free from pain. They have a choice whether to live in a separate animal kingdom or alongside the families they have loved or want to love. This is a choice they make freely for themselves.

Soon after Sheba's accident, one weekend while I was staying with Denise, a bright light appeared in the corner of the room and I could see her dad standing beside both of us. He was holding Sheba's lead and the dog was sitting patiently by his side. I described what I saw to Denise: this was the first time I had seen her father so clearly. We cried together as she remembered Sheba and her dad, and I remembered Gyp and Nana. We both found solace in the knowledge that our dear companions have a continuing life with love when we are not there to give it.

As I finished speaking, Denise's father and Sheba faded away. Unfortunately, Denise could not see what I could. However, she knew by the look on my face and the emotion she was experiencing that spirit was with us. We looked at each other and hugged, happy in the knowledge that those we loved were still with us.

It wasn't until about two months later, after much praying by my bedside, that I received a visitation from my own dog. Gyp came bounding to my side, accompanied by Granddad Stanley who was formally dressed in Army uniform. Actually I had been praying for Nana to bring him, as I desperately wanted to see her once more and she had promised to come and see me.

It all happened very quickly. Within seconds they were gone again, almost as though a firework had exploded only to disappear and fade into nothingness once it had shown its glory. I cried because I had seen Gyp again, and cried some more because he had gone. I cried for my ever-faithful friend who throughout his life had defended me from danger when I needed him, and loved me when there was no one else to turn to.

I was happy, though, that my companion had found his way into the spirit world, with family we loved and who loved us. I was content to know that my faithful friend was waiting with my family there until we could all be together once again.

8

My Stubborn Father

After moving in with us, my granddad made friends with an old couple called Mr and Mrs Harding who lived in an immaculate white pebble-dashed bungalow opposite our home. Mrs Harding's legs were in a terrible state as they would swell up almost to capacity with extra fluids, stretching the skin like elastic and making her veins pop out. I often visited them too, as Granddad had become very close to them. On one of the days I visited, I had been asked by him to pass on a message saying he wasn't attending his club that afternoon as he was feeling a little poorly. He often went there with the Hardings. So I knocked on the back door. As Mr Harding opened it I saw that his wife was struggling to put on her shoes. He invited me in while I chatted about Granddad's message and exchanged the usual pleasantries.

Mr Harding helped to put on his wife's shoes, bending down to fix the buckle. A pang of pain must have tweaked his back as he said, 'I will have to wait a moment, dear, my back has gone. I'll be OK soon.'

'Don't worry, I can do them,' I volunteered, and kneeled down to buckle up her shoes.

Instinctively I could feel the tension and pain in her legs from all the extra fluid. 'Do you mind if I give some healing to your knees and legs?' I said matter-of-factly. I knew she welcomed healing because my granddad said that they'd had many a chat about my gifts and she always found the subject fascinating. There certainly didn't seem to be any animosity after I'd made my request so I placed my hands on her leg. Already my palms were burning with the healing energy. Mrs Harding told me that today her legs were worse than ever and giving her terrible trouble.

As I administered healing to her knees and legs, I also felt that her heart was ailing. 'Do you take tablets for blood pressure?' I asked. She nodded her head, and as I continued I felt the blood pumping sluggishly around her body, as if it was having difficulties.

'Do you think your doctor might take a look at you?' I suggested. 'Because maybe he needs to check your blood pressure?'

'Funny you should say that,' she said, smiling. 'I have just this morning made an appointment to see him. My blood pressure was sky-high last week. He has given me tablets for this fluid retention but they're not working so I am going back to him.'

We finished my little mini-healing session and I went home.

It wasn't until Mr Harding came across to speak to Granddad one afternoon a while later that I understood what I had achieved. My parents were at work and I was at school so Granddad and Mr Harding often had a game of cards together while Mrs Harding took an afternoon nap. This day he was very excited and Granddad relayed his story.

His wife had attended the appointment with her doctor as arranged only to find that the swelling in her legs had greatly subsided. The doctor checked her blood pressure and even that was normal. Of course he maintained the tablets he'd prescribed had done their work well, but as Mr Harding said to Granddad, before I put my hands on her they had not been doing anything. In fact, his wife's legs had seemed to grow worse. How could they have recovered so quickly when she had been taking the prescription for two weeks with no outward benefit?

Granddad gave me the thirty pence Mr Harding had left so I could buy myself some sweets. 'There you go,' said Granddad, 'you have had your first healing patient!'

My granddad moving in with us was the best thing that could have happened as far as I was concerned, although there did seem to be some tension between my parents concerning our new lodger . . . even if he was my mum's dad. Granddad was a quiet, unassuming man, very gentle and not at all outspoken, so I never really understood why his presence was a concern. However, when Granddad and I were alone together, we would sit and chat for hours. Although I had always been close to him, we were now becoming even closer.

By the time I reached my final year at school, the building works there were completed and I didn't have to travel here, there and everywhere just to be educated. Finally we had state-of-the-art fully equipped science labs, beautiful new classrooms and a fantastic new sports hall. A new sixth-form block had also been provided and I looked forward to being able to study peacefully for my A-levels there once I had completed my O-level examinations.

My teachers were all very pleased with my academic progress. I was in the top three of my year in all my subjects bar needlework. The teachers had their sights set on me achieving my aspiration of becoming a veterinary surgeon.

My O-levels approached and Denise and I started on the hard slog of revision. As per usual the token parents' evening was arranged by our year tutors, to discuss our studies and future prospects. My head of year had already had an informal chat with me about what career path I should take, and now it was time to talk to my parents and explain what qualifications I would need to help me achieve my aim.

I felt that because my mock exams had gone well and I was riding high with good results, I stood a good chance of continuing my education into the sixth form. There I could gain my A-levels and hopefully acquire a place at a decent university.

But when the subject of my studies was brought up at home, Dad always chirped up that I should be a secretary or a hairdresser. To me this was a pointless conversation as I had no plans to be either. My sights were set on a much higher aim. I wanted to be a vet or to work in veterinary research, helping fight disease and improve animal welfare.

I knew that for a girl like me this was a tall order because I would have to achieve the best academic results and stay in full-time education, something my father was dead set against.

Sam was no help, I thought. Every time I asked him what I should do for a career, he simply smiled and said I had already chosen my path and would be healing people in a way I was yet to discover. I thought he was referring to becoming someone like a doctor or vet as he often brought spiritual doctors into my bedroom at night to explain healing to me.

I had already written to Bibby's Agricultural Company to see if they would employ me on a 'sandwich course', which meant giving me a job placement while I studied at university. I wanted to be in their agricultural department, but this was during the days of unabashed male chauvinism and they replied saying that there were very few vacancies for women in their workforce, and that jobs for the fairer sex within the area I had chosen were rare.

I did feel spiritually that my future role would somehow involve white coats, and over tea one afternoon my Granddad Joe and I discussed how I could achieve my goal. Undeterred by my father's negativity, I called Mr Lambert our old vet and explained that I would love to be involved in veterinary work. He agreed to let me have a job placement within his surgery for a few weeks during school hours. I had always had an affinity with animals ever since I used to play outside with the vicious dogs as a very young child. Although working at the vet's certainly gave me a chance to see first-hand the more emotional and messy side of the business other than stroking cute puppies and kittens. Some animals were downright nasty and snarled at the vet through pain or maybe even dislike. Others were too weak to fight and were pitifully ill. But this was not the problem for me. Sam told me one night, after I had worked in the surgery, that all animals recognised my healing gift. My problem was that each time I entered the surgery, visions of Gyp's final hours would keep playing in my mind, and I wasn't sure if I had the ability to control my feelings.

My parents knew nothing of my career aspirations, only that I had a couple of weeks' job placement during school hours. They had no idea it was with Mr Lambert. I managed to keep this information to myself. Even so, I wished I could have told them how much I'd loved the challenge, and how I was now more determined than ever to fight for a place at university, to study something related to healing animals.

My teacher knew about my high aspirations and keenness to study. But that was about to change after the parents' evening.

During my night-time spiritual tutorials, I would often ask Sam why I had to experience so much negativity from my parents. Why it seemed to be always such a battle for me to achieve what I wanted to achieve. Usually he gave me a warm smile and looked at me knowingly. Silence was apparently the order of the day, as if this was a lesson yet to be learned. All well and good, I thought, but it wasn't helping me right now, was it?

Parents' evening arrived and it seemed my father had already pre-determined my role in society. The biology teacher tried in vain to convince him to let me study further, with no success. She tried to explain to my parents about my plans for what I would eventually like to do once I left school, but I could see the disapproval in my dad's eyes. He argued that it was a complete and utter waste of time for me to be educated further than O-levels due to the fact I would be in my twenties by the time I finished university. By then, he said, I would probably have met the man I wanted to marry and maybe even have had a child. All that education would then go to waste. For practical reasons it was far better I should set my sights at a more modest level.

I couldn't believe my ears and burst into tears in front of my mother, father and teacher, with fellow students and parents looking on in horror. I think they thought the teaching staff had said something awful to me, when in fact it was my father who lost my respect that night.

No matter how hard my teacher defended my rights to an education, he argued to the contrary. He was defiant in his insistence that I would not be educated any further and would be leaving school for good at the end of term.

I was beginning to understand that women were just finding their feet as far as equal rights were concerned; unfortunately even then a huge amount of chauvinism existed in the workplace, and even the home. Men in general believed it was their right to be looked after by the females of the household, whether the women worked outside the house or not. Making cakes and homemaking is something we women tend to be good at, and very nice too doing nothing else if you choose to and can afford it, but surely it is down to the individual woman to decide what exactly she wants to do with her life. Why do so many men feel they can dictate to women what they should or shouldn't do?

Even though we are talking about only thirty-five years ago, life was very different in the 1970s. If you are a young person reading this chapter you may not understand the restrictions forced upon women back then. Even nowadays it's fair to say they have to fight their way to the top of the ladder in most professions, when they are in fact perfectly suited to and effective in that particular career.

In those days a woman could achieve, but the truth was that to do it they had to work more than twice as hard as any man, enduring endless opposition in the workplace as they did so. That's why we did not have a woman Prime Minister until Margaret Thatcher came to power in 1979.

My father certainly never believed that I would be able to talk to you in a book like this. In fact, I don't think he imagined I would achieve anything in life other than maybe marrying a good man with a steady job. That to him would have been the definition of success for a daughter.

When I watch my own children, I realise how lucky they are to have the opportunities they do in this world, and get very upset when they cannot recognise how fortunate they are. So many children really do not see the sacrifices parents make, with finances and personal happiness, to give their offspring the chances in life they themselves never had. This applies to my parents too. They were trying to provide a new life for us all, pulling themselves up from the council estate they lived in by working all hours to save money and buy their own home. The problem was they restricted the chances I was given so as to keep me at the same level. They never considered that what I needed most was a good education or, even more importantly at that time, a sympathetic ear.

The trip home from school was in total silence. Once we were in the house, I again pleaded with my mother to speak to Dad about changing his mind.

Through sobs, I shouted to my father that he could not control me this way and that I would study whatever he said. His reply was chilling and I still remember it clearly, word for word. 'This is my home and I pay for it. While you live under my roof, you will do as I say. You need to leave school and get a job. I cannot support you through any further education, and one day you will thank me for it. If you choose to study, then you leave this house for good and I will not help you financially in any way.'

Although his natural chauvinism came into it, unknown to me my father's decision was largely based on the information a consultant at the local hospital had recently given him. I later found out that Dad had seen him that week about a troubling chest complaint. He had been coughing for months. As it turned out my father was diagnosed with emphysema, a chronic chest ailment that would eventually kill him unless he stopped smoking and changed his ways.

I knew he felt unwell as Sam had been telling me for years to offer him healing, but it was totally off limits to try and talk to him about such things. Dad was having none of my 'spiritual mumbo jumbo', as he called it, and each time I spiritually felt his illness worsen, I knew he was drawing closer to his passing.

I was fifteen years of age and despite my healing abilities had never really looked into my father's illness with any spiritual depth. To me, merely observing as his teenage daughter, it seemed like he suffered from a persistent cough due to his chain-smoking habit. To be honest I didn't like my dad much at this point in my life and I was also very angry with him. He denied the existence of my Guides from the spirit world and crushed any ambitions I might wish to pursue.

Maybe he worried he might not be able to support me financially through my studies due to his illness, or perhaps he really was a die-hard traditionalist in his attitudes towards women. I tried somehow to rationalise the way he felt towards me. Maybe he genuinely believed women served no proper place in the workforce and were best suited to be good wives and mothers. Those women who chose to work should, to his way of thinking, be employed as secretarial staff, if they were bright enough, or hairdressers if they were creative. Those were the two options he reiterated to me over and over again. Perhaps, in retrospect, this hard-line attitude was exaggerated and used as a façade to cover his fear that his own working days were limited due to illness. Maybe it was tough love, making the decision it was far better for me to leave school now than be forced into abandoning my dreams halfway through university.

Being a lively teenager and feeling that it was not only my spirituality that was being suppressed but now my entire life, I rebelled violently.

I hated my father so much then. Maybe it was the surge of new hormones that made me so aggressive; maybe I had taken enough of the constant negativity. I don't know how I mustered the courage to confront him verbally. All I did know for sure was that, despite loving my father, I was disgusted by him and from that moment onward refused to speak to him.

Granddad became very upset when he heard my parents dash my hopes, but he never said anything to them. After all, he was living in Dad's house.

By this time I had learned to control my night-time spiritual visitors as Sam had taught me how to cleanse my bedroom myself. Even so, a mixed bag of light helpers (that's a term I use collectively for all manner of Guides) over the following weeks suggested I offer forgiveness to my father. Maybe it was because I was getting older and more independent-minded, but I felt I should make my own decision about that and was in no mood to listen to them.

Not long after the parents' evening, apparently the head of my year called and pleaded with my parents to reconsider and allow me to continue with my studies. My teacher's pleas met with deaf ears and a stony heart.

My O-level exams were only a few weeks away and, furious with my father's obstinacy, I took all of my textbooks and notes outside into the garden and burned the lot! My parents were out at work at the time and, no matter how much my granddad protested, I kept loading the incinerator, sending sheets of flame into the air as the books went up in front of us. I had only ever seen my granddad cry once before, at my nana's funeral. Half hidden by the smoke, I could now see tears trickling down his face for a second time.

'I don't care any more,' I declared to Granddad as he looked on, helpless.

By the time my parents returned from work I had barricaded myself into my bedroom so that they could not get in to speak to me. I wanted to block them out despite Granddad's pleas for me to come downstairs and have something to eat.

The next day at school I asked my teacher if I could have a private word. I explained the circumstances and she seemed shocked when I told her I had burned all my notes and books and would not be revising further. Nor would I be sitting any of the exams.

After that I broke down in tears in her office and she was ill at ease, not knowing what to do next. I had a feeling she wanted to be a fairy godmother to me and wave a magic wand to make things better, but she and I both knew that was impossible.

The teacher sent a pupil to find Denise so she could take me to the canteen to have a drink and calm down. By the end of the day the teacher had accumulated a pile of new books and photo-copied notes and asked me to continue with my revision. I thanked her but said there was no point. My father would not let me pursue my dreams. Anyway, I didn't care any more and was hell-bent on showing him that, once and for all.

During the two-week run-up to exams, I never once looked at one of the books the teacher had kindly replaced, and although I did agree to sit the exams, I walked in on the relevant days with little hope of passing anything. I had basically given up.

Sam was not pleased with me and reiterated on many occasions that I had to overcome my darkness within and keep positive. He explained that my energy was so strong that darkness would envelop me unless I broke free and kept my true positive path.

But I maintained there was no point in trying; my future would be the same no matter what level I achieved in my examinations. Soon after they had finished, I was called in to see the careers officer as I had now been listed as a school leaver.

I clearly recall the careers officer asking me what job I intended to do now that I had made the choice not to study further.

In front of her on her desk lay a huge book with what seemed to be every job in the world listed inside. Next to each job title was a short description. As she asked her questions I defiantly picked up the book, flicked through the pages in a random fashion and stopped haphazardly. I opened the book, and looked at the page I'd selected by chance. It was entitled 'Dentistry'. The picture of a white-coated dental nurse seemed to jump off the page at me.

'OK! That's what I'll do. I will do that,' I said, tapping my finger against the photograph.

The careers officer looked at me in astonishment. 'You do know that you will need five O-levels even to consider taking on a dental career?' she said, then sucked in her breath, obviously about to lecture me. 'What's more, Helen, I think you are being rather foolish. You haven't even given this any proper thought. You just picked up that book and chose a page at random.'

Looking back at her in a rude and confrontational manner, I casually answered: 'So? Are you suggesting I won't get five O-levels?'

The careers officer was red with embarrassment. Clearly she had not expected anyone to react to her advice so rudely. After all, surely the clever students were all staying on at school to do A-levels. To annoy the careers officer further, I wrote to every dental practice in Chester asking for a job.

We had to wait until July to receive our exam results. During that time, despite the fact I was only fifteen going on sixteen, my father suggested that I find a summer job to tide me over until I decided on more permanent employment.

In spite of my mother trying to lighten the atmosphere at home, conversations between my father and me were now cooler than ever. They consisted of very brief sentences, and meal-times were painfully quiet. Poor Granddad was feeling uncomfortable and openly stated that he felt like piggy-in-the-middle.

One Saturday while I was shopping in town I walked past Argos and saw how busy it was inside. Sam's voice came into my mind: 'Be positive. Think positive. You are what you send out into the world.'

To hear such strong direction from him was a wake-up call.

Be positive . . . OK, I thought, and bold as brass entered the store and asked to speak to the manager. A young man came to the front desk, asking if there was a problem, and I coolly replied that he needed me in his premises to help at weekends.

He was so taken aback by my statement, he offered me a job on the spot, asking me to start in the warehouse above the shop floor the following Saturday.

My dad was ecstatic when he heard the news and said how good it would be for me to take a job and what it could lead to. I didn't crack on that I was actually pleased to be offered it.

After a couple of weeks I found that I loved the independence of going out to work, and for the first time in my life I had my own money. I did my job with such ease that I was offered a full-time job working on the cash-desk and dealing with customer complaints. They seemed to like talking to me. In fact, the manager even commented that some of them had made very positive comments about my way of dealing with them.

When the end of term was imminent, a letter arrived for me from a dental practice called Bank House, asking me to attend an interview with a dental surgeon called Mr Sowerby. Secretly I was rather excited, though naturally I kept my interview a secret from my parents, as I did most things in my life by now. I took a day off school without their knowledge to attend it. (My lack of attendance hardly mattered anyway as we were in the final countdown to leaving and to be honest most teachers had little care whether the pupils were there or not.) Those who turned up for school were only there because they had nowhere else to go, so it was more a case of seeing friends than a good work ethos.

My interview went rather well, I thought, despite the fact that I was shaking like a leaf.

'How do you know you will pass your O-level exams?' the dental surgeon enquired.

With an air of self-confidence I was far from feeling, I coolly replied: 'Well, why wouldn't I pass them?'

He gave me a condescending look and said I was very young to feel so confident, and maybe he needed someone with more experience.

Little did he know that inside I was not confident at all, but quick as a flash I replied, 'How does anyone ever get that experience unless a person is prepared to give them a chance and employ them?'

Mr Sowerby smiled. He had obviously never met such a feisty fifteen year old. I was battling my corner in order to be given the chance of becoming his dental nurse. I didn't want my father to have the satisfaction of seeing me become a secretary or hairdresser.

Two weeks passed and I was beginning to think I would not hear from the dentist. Then there it was, a letter in the post saying that someone with more experience had filled the vacancy. This time the secret was out; my parents had caught sight of me picking up the letter. I had to read it out loud to them and they were shocked that I had been for an interview without their knowledge.

My dad said smugly, 'I told you, it's best you look towards other jobs. Something a bit more down-to-earth.'

Rather than have another confrontation with him, I went upstairs to be alone in my bedroom – yet again. Once I'd calmed down, Sam made his entrance. 'You didn't finish reading the letter, did you?'

Reluctantly I went back downstairs and retrieved it from the kitchen worktop. Another few minutes and it would have been in the rubbish. As I read the letter again, I saw that it finished by saying they would keep me on file for a later vacancy as the dentist had been really impressed with me at interview. I wasn't convinced, though. Such remarks were probably standard politeness so as not to upset the rejected applicants.

Despite my disappointment, Sam comforted me by saying that he was proud of me. He said it was often hard to pull back from depression or disappointment, and that I should keep thinking positive and keep my goals in sight. It would all come right in the end. After all, he concluded, the letter didn't give a direct no, did it?

I continued with my shop job, wondering whether this was

going to be all that was available to me now I was officially a school leaver.

While I was burdened with these thoughts, in his nightly tutorials Sam started to explain something he called a Step to the Sacred Truth.

'At times like these, when you feel lost or diminished, you need to stop and consider the truth. Helen, *truthfully*, what do you want your life to be?' he demanded in a paternal manner. 'Truthfully . . . what do you want to achieve?'

I thought long and hard about his question. I found that I could visualise myself and the work I wanted to do. In my mind's eye I could see myself sitting speaking to many people, using a microphone. I could see myself on TV. I could see myself writing then speaking on the radio. I could see myself in a white coat, holding my hands over people. How can this be possible? I thought. How am I to achieve this? The vision caused more confusion than clarity in my mind.

Sam smiled with such wisdom in his eyes, as though he knew something I didn't. Of course, now I know he did!

Then he sat down beside me and spoke in soft tones as he explained that above all I had to *believe*.

'There are times in a person's life when they have to believe in themselves and have faith that the path will be opened to them. This is nothing to do with choices,' he said, 'although you do have to make those when opportunities present themselves. This is to do with believing in yourself. Whatever energy you have within you, and whatever energy you send out, is transmitted like radio waves and bounces right back to you. If you think negatively, then negative thoughts and actions bounce back. Think positive, chile,' he pleaded. 'See your goal and *believe* it will come to you when it is meant to. Keep hold of that positive thought.'

Sam kept repeating that the dental career was not my ultimate path and soon I would know what I really wanted to do. In the meantime I must wait. He told me to imagine that the decisions in my life were like a four-sided lantern. As I journeyed through life I would be tempted to force the lantern's windows open to reveal the light. But he explained that the doors must never be forced, however tempted I might be to open them. They had to be allowed to open freely and easily on their own, when they were ready: then they would clearly light my way.

Imagine my surprise when two or three weeks later a letter arrived on the doorstep at 7 a.m. The morning sun shining through the front door spotlit the envelope, as though it contained a very special announcement. The letter was from Mr Sowerby in Chester. It seemed he genuinely had been impressed by me and was now offering to employ me as long as I went to night school to achieve my DSA (Dental Surgery Assistant) qualification.

The course was two years in duration and meanwhile he was happy for me to work in his private practice. I would be paid a low wage, and he would support me through a college night-school course. I was ecstatic and felt very proud of myself when I showed my parents the letter. They sat at the breakfast table absolutely stunned and silent. Apparently a stranger had seen more potential in me than my father was able to.

I shocked them further when I told them what I ultimately intended to achieve. My granddad smiled to hear it, and so did Sam standing right beside him. I heard him say in my mind: 'You have to have many experiences in your life first, Helen, so that you can become who you are meant to be.'

So it was that I started in Bank House dental practice after my sixteenth birthday in late August 1975.

Bank House was a beautiful detached Georgian residence situated in Whitefriars in the heart of historic Chester. The new law courts have since been built just around the corner, but at that time the city centre remained intact with ancient cobbled streets and many historic buildings, some with a ghostly past.

That night Sam sat on the edge of the bed for my evening tutorial and spoke definitively to me: 'Remember, positivity conquers everything. You must always keep that in mind when you think about your own problems and when you speak to others of theirs. Since energy bounces back to you, so it is important always to send out positive energy. When times are hard, think to yourself of three good things that happened in your life that day, no matter how small they may seem. If life seems difficult, keep focused on those simple thoughts.

'Those three good thoughts will then grow into three huge forces for good as the energy you send out becomes stronger. Instead of saying I *need* something to come into my life, or I *want* something, think, *I am achieving* this in my life, and visualise yourself doing that particular act. All creation begins with a thought – and a thought has the power to create!'

Sam's lessons to me were becoming gradually more profound and I could not help but benefit from them.

9

Path to the Sacred Truth

Working at Bank House surgery was good exercise, especially for a trainee dental nurse. I must have run up and down the stairs at least a hundred times a day. There was certainly no need to use a gym or suffer the pain of dieting in those days. Sam rarely bothered me during work hours as I was always so busy but there were odd times when he must have decided either that I needed him or he had something to say and he would arrive unexpectedly. As I walked across the garden one day he joined me, saying he would see me later. Strange, I thought, he never said why he had come to see me. I brushed the visit aside and carried on with my mission.

Bank House had a lovely walled garden at the back and Mr Sowerby's rooms overlooked the neat lawns. At the far end of the garden was a large converted outbuilding that housed the technical laboratory with its six-man team. To reach this building, you had to take a short walk over the cobbled path leading through the garden. Once you arrived, it was necessary to climb the steep steps leading to the first-floor laboratory.

Underneath the building was a large storage area secured by two heavy doors, where most of the dental supplies were kept under lock and key. Huge wooden gates blocked off the outside world, but were opened up when necessary to allow delivery vans to unload.

Inside, the laboratory building was divided into two large areas where the six-man team busied themselves like lab-rats. The smell of acrylic setting on dental moulds and the acrid acidic varnish hit my nostrils and made my eyes water every time I went into the place.

How the men could cope with these working conditions baffled me, it was a wonder they didn't all end up high as kites from the chemical vapours. Not surprisingly, they seemed happy in their jobs, humming and busily working away listening to the sports results in the background while they used their laboratory skills to perfect all sorts of artificial teeth.

It was amazing to see all the high-pitched grinding and polishing machines at work. I was beginning to appreciate the complexity of dentistry.

The buildings were very old and dated back hundreds of years. There I could feel the echoes of many people who had previously passed this same way, long before the days of laboratories and dental practices.

I entered the lab and shouted out for Harry. One of them looked at me and pointed to a large well-built man sitting on a stool in the far corner of the room, scrutinising his work intently.

As I approached Harry, I noticed that he was wearing goggles and ear protectors. The man sitting alongside him was working feverishly as though in a race against time to finish his project, and I noticed he only wore goggles. Harry looked up and I saw he had a friendly round face with a welcoming smile on it.

'Hi, Harry,' I said, a little shyly. 'I am Helen. Well, my name is Helen, but I have to be called Sarah.' He laughed out loud as he remarked so the whole group could hear: 'Make up your mind, little girl, are you Helen or are you Sarah? Hey, lads, we have a good one here. She doesn't even know her own name!'

Embarrassed and red-faced, I explained: 'I have to be called Sarah here because Mr Sowerby says there's already a nurse working in the surgery called Helen. He thinks the partners will become confused if we both have the same name. So I chose the name Sarah, after my Uncle Kevin's wife.'

My Auntie Sarah was new to the family and seemed intelligent and pretty, so I thought naming myself after her might reflect well on me.

Harry laughed again and quipped: 'Typical of Charles! Always has to make life easier for himself.' Strangely, the other men never said a word, just looked intently at Harry's lips as he spoke.

Despite my young years, I wanted to behave professionally with the men. I explained in a businesslike way that I had been sent over to retrieve a crown for a patient who was about to come in for an appointment. Harry glanced over and gestured towards a man he called Ken.

He was the youngest of them all. In fact, all the other men looked pretty old to me, considering I was only sixteen. Ken was in his early twenties and extremely handsome. I blushed as I made my way across to his workstation.

All the men then roared with laughter as they listened and watched while I pleaded with him for the crown. No matter how hard I tried, Ken totally ignored me. I had no idea that he was deaf! Apparently two of the lab men were completely deaf, and Ken was partially deaf. That was why they didn't have ear protectors on.

To the men looking on it seemed like a hilarious joke, catching me out, and they all had a good laugh at my expense.

'Come back over here,' Harry beckoned me. 'I have the crown right here. We've not finished it yet, so you'll have to go and tell Charles it will be at least another hour.'

This was not at all what I'd expected.

Standing there dumbfounded by his answer, I didn't know what to do. Mrs Williams' appointment was at 3 p.m. and it was now 2.50 – what could I do? Mr Sowerby was adamant I must not go back into the surgery until I had the new crown in my hand.

'Sorry,' I spluttered, 'I know I'm new, but Mr Sowerby specifically said that I can't go back until I have that crown in my hand.'

The technician laughed out loud. 'I know, I know . . . just teasing you, Sarah. Welcome to the team! I have Mrs Williams' crown here! Now be careful not to drop it.'

This episode certainly seemed to have broken the ice as every time I went over after that all the men made me very welcome and always had a little chat with me by writing notes because some of the technicians were dumb as well as deaf.

Everyone except Harry, of course, who always had plenty to say for himself!

I had never held a fabricated tooth in my hand before. It was strange to look at, completely perfect, and it was going to be fitted into a person's mouth in just a few minutes' time. Carefully I walked back across the garden, ready to place it in the surgery for the patient's arrival.

The garden was pretty and enclosed within an old red-brick wall that was currently covered in climbing roses, giving the whole scene a colourful yet homely feel. A wooden bench was placed at an angle in one corner, for patients and staff to sit on if the day was warm enough.

As I was walking I couldn't help but notice a stranger sitting on the bench reading a book. I thought nothing of it at first as people often popped out into the beautiful garden for a breath of fresh air, especially if they had to wait in between appointments. What really caught my eye was the way this visitor was dressed. As I looked harder, I noticed a familiar glow surrounding his body, which I recognised from Sam and the other Guides. Instinctively I knew this was no ordinary man but a spirit visitor.

He looked up from his book and smiled at me. I didn't quite know what to do at first because delivering the crown to the surgery was my priority. I really didn't have time to talk, not now, I was in a rush . . . and this spirit person was about to walk over and greet me! I quickly glanced at my watch. It was five minutes to three. We had a little time. Maybe I wouldn't find myself in trouble after all.

The stranger waved to me in a friendly manner and closed the book he was reading. That's it, I thought, as he walked over to meet me. I am definitely going to be late now.

'Don't worry, my dear,' he said, as he drew nearer. 'I won't keep you very long.' I looked at his attire and felt sorry for him; he looked more like a tramp in old clothes than the usual beautifully robed figures in spirit I was used to seeing.

Despite this shabby attire, though, brightness shone through the gaps in his ragged clothing, with thin strands of bright light radiating through the holes. To say his garments were basic and worn was an understatement, but he had a kind, sympathetic face and seemed intent on speaking to me, so really I had no choice.

'I know you don't have very long, so my visit will be brief. I am the bearer of a special message, dear child, one that you must store in your mind for when you have need of it.'

I was puzzled and agitated. I had to get back into the surgery with the crown or I might lose my job.

'I will only be a moment . . . You have a very good Guide in Sam. He is here to help you and keep you on the path you have already chosen. Life is not a journey but a choice. It is a pathway towards *the one sacred truth*. I am sending you healing and guidance, my dear, along with many others who wish you well. This is sent directly from the Angels to help you.

'You, and in fact all mankind, can create and change anything you wish – all you have to do is take the first step. The first step is that you need to *believe*, really believe, that you can make changes for the good of all. When it is aimed out into the universe in this powerful way, then the energy will ripple back just as strongly, if not more so, towards you and all the people, animals and places you come into contact with.

'Many think spirit is a separate world but it is not, it is a continuation of life. When small steps are taken and you believe, really believe, that you can accomplish this task, then you will succeed. It will be in a small way at first, but once you hit your stride it will escalate to greater success. Be positive, be strong, and *believe*. This is the first of the sacred steps: soon I will bring you more.

'Remember Sam telling you to be positive about this job you have now? Well, it is the same principle but on a much larger scale. You, my dear, can reach out with more positive energy on a far larger scale than you can ever imagine.'

I nodded silently to acknowledge his teaching as I didn't want any of my colleagues to notice me standing there seemingly talking to myself. The messenger continued: 'You carry a message of hope, my dear, a message that can change and help all those in need. A message that can change and help your environment, and all you come into contact with. Your Guide Sam has already explained to you that your energy sends out a frequency that transmits outwardly to the universe and bounces back. I have explained it to you again. I cannot stress enough to you the power of this action. The energy mankind is sending out needs changing, or what is bouncing back will in time have a devastating outcome. Changes have to be made in many ways. But don't worry . . . they will be shown to you in good time.

'There are other spiritual people who will open doors for your voice to be heard – and people will listen. You will reach into their hearts, Helen. Their breath will be your breath; their pain will be your pain; their joy will be your joy.'

My eyes welled up with emotion at what this messenger was instilling within me. The link between us remained strong and his message crystal clear.

'Fear has become an everyday part of your world. Fear of not having enough, fear of losing your job, fear of not having material possessions in life. Fear if you don't achieve . . . fear of failure if you do. But fears are created by choice. Think more simply and the fear itself will disappear. Instead of craving, look to create; instead of wanting, look to give. Love will always find those who open their heart in this way. Love is always around us, protecting each and every person. Explain to those you meet that love is only ever at a distance if they believe they do not deserve to be loved. Be happy with today and what is around you, and look to what you can do tomorrow to make it better. A simple smile at a stranger can produce the most profound effect. Study the ripples in a pond.

'Now be on your way, dear girl. We shall meet again, I am sure. Other Guides will come to speak about another of the Sacred Paths to Truth. We all love you here in the spirit world, dear girl. Remember, you are capable of anything. If you believe then you will succeed.'

These were profound statements yet surprisingly easy to understand. I couldn't afford to give my full attention to them now, though. I feared I was late. I had to be in surgery to give Mr Sowerby the crown I held firmly in my hand. I looked at my watch. It still read five minutes to three. I was confused. How could the messenger have said so much and the time remain the same? Despite our long exchange, no time at all seemed to have passed.

I left the smiling stranger in the garden, and as I looked back saw him walking down the path towards the laboratories. Once I was in the surgery, Mr Sowerby smiled at me and said: 'Well done, Sarah! I was wondering how you would manage the men over there.'

I liked Mr Sowerby. He was a caring man with a lovely family, a wife called Liz and two gorgeous little boys. They often called in after school just to speak to their dad while he was working.

It wasn't long before I was excelling in my new position. The surgery records were immaculate and even the more difficult patients felt relaxed with me. As the dentist himself said, I seemed to put people at ease. Little did he realise it was as a result of all the spiritual tutorials I was receiving. Gradually I acquired a unique way of empathising with people. I felt them in my heart. Whatever troubled them, I felt. Whatever ailed them, I felt. Whatever made them suffer, I felt.

Within the surgery I also worked alongside the chief nurse, Natalie, who had been with Mr Sowerby for four years before I arrived. During my first few weeks there I wondered whether she perceived me as a bit of a threat professionally because she would always give me the menial jobs she didn't want to do. I could tell by her body language that she was upset even though I was being particularly nice to her.

She often distracted my general routine by making me tackle the dirty jobs that everyone else avoided. I suppose she felt entitled to the easier ones because she had been working there longer; that was the general pecking order in most work places. Mr Sowerby seemed to notice this for himself one day when Natalie snapped at me to fetch her something from the stock rooms.

'Sarah is not your slave, Natalie!' he snapped back at her. 'If you need something for your work, please go and fetch it yourself and let Sarah assist me.' Mr Sowerby certainly put her in her place, and after that she changed her attitude and we became good friends, going for lunch together and often meeting up after work to socialise.

On one particular day, Natalie and I were off on our lunch break, walking into town, when we noticed a seagull on the ground in front of us. Some men were passing by, laughing as it stumbled to one side, dragging its wing along the ground. It was squawking loudly but still managed to look menacing.

Seeing its obvious pain, I said to Natalie that it was hurt and we needed to take it to a vet. She told me to ignore it. We only had an hour for lunch and wouldn't get to the sandwich shop and back unless we hurried. I felt I had to help the poor bird which was obviously injured, but Natalie insisted: 'I'm not stopping.' I just couldn't walk past the poor creature, despite its vicious nature. I bent down and grabbed the bird from behind, putting my hands to either side of its body. Somehow I managed to close the broken wing against its body. It squawked some more and tried to struggle, but my grip was steady. Meanwhile Natalie was screaming out I would get hurt or catch a disease.

My spiritual senses automatically took over and the healing energies started to tingle and warm the palms of my hands. The bird seemed to calm down as if it now recognised the safety I represented. I spoke to it in a soft tone, explaining that I would not hurt its wing. While I held it in both hands it seemed to become limp and trusting, almost as though it understood.

Natalie gasped as I announced: 'I'm running the bird down to Mr Lambert's veterinary surgery. Grab me a sandwich and I'll eat it later.' I turned in the opposite direction and dashed as fast I could with the bird in my arms to the vet's. It took me fifteen minutes to reach the surgery, with many strange looks from passers-by. I have to be quick, I thought, I have to get back to work. Fortunately the vet's receptionist was in the office. She was shocked to see me holding the bird, but I explained what had happened.

'I have never seen a seagull act like this,' she said. 'They usually try to peck you to death! They can be quite vicious.' She went and found one of the special ventilated boxes that vets use. 'Pop it in there until Mr Lambert arrives back from lunch,' she said. 'And who shall I say has brought it?'

'Oh, Mr Lambert knows me. I'm called Helen. He treated my dog Gyp some time ago, and I did a short work placement with him.'

'OK, I'll tell him. He has your telephone number?'

'Yes,' I said, 'but I have to dash back to work now.'

Later that evening when I arrived home from work, Mr Lambert rang me explaining that the bird had indeed broken its wing and he'd had to place a splint on it to aid recovery. He had handed it over to the RSPCA after that, and thought in time it might be released back into the wild. It had been very dehydrated and disorientated, he said, and not at all the sort of bird people normally rescued as it was capable of giving a vicious peck. He thanked me for being so caring.

I awoke early the next morning as it was my turn to do the Saturday half-day at the surgery. To my amazement, I found a single white feather on the pillow next to my face. How it arrived there I had no idea. As I picked it off my pillow, I heard a voice very clear in my head: 'The gift of humility and compassion is always there within you, my dear.'

Perhaps that was the spirit world's way of saying thank you!

Every Saturday morning the practice was open for an emergency surgery. Nurses took turns in a rota to work this extra half-day, which we did for no extra pay. We were assigned to whichever dentist happened to be on call.

Head of the practice was Mr Jones, a sweet man who seemed old enough to be ready for retirement. His surgery was next-door to ours and commanded a beautiful view over the garden, just like Mr Sowerby's. The only problem was that it was antiquated. Mr Jones was the last of his generation still to be practising. Bless him, he lived in the past, with his aged dental chair and antique furniture. Naturally, it was all kept immaculate and sterile, and looked very good despite its age. To me, his surgery resembled a scene from a period drama on TV and I was very nervous to be working with the senior partner today.

'Hello, Sarah, it's the first time we have met, I believe,' Mr Jones greeted me. 'Well, I don't think we'll be too busy, but I do have a rather special gentleman arriving this morning to have a crown fitted. It is the Duke of Westminster.'

I was speechless at the thought that I was to assist in the treatment of such an aristocratic patient. Almost royalty!

Mr Jones continued: 'Now, when you go into the waiting room to collect him, you must address Lord Grosvenor as "Your Grace", but please don't think you have to curtsey!'

I must have looked rather stunned because old Mr Jones smiled at me and said: 'Don't worry, dear, he won't bite you.'

He was right. When I did meet the duke, Lord Grosvenor, he was very courteous and even had a short chat with me as Mr Jones filed away at his teeth. What I found most interesting was the spiritual entourage that followed him. They were all dressed in fine clothes with fur collars and tasteful jewels; aristocrats related to the duke. It was 1976, and although I didn't feel he was leaving us just yet, I knew it wouldn't be too many years before he would be joining those he loved in spirit.

One man who smiled and showed himself particularly

forthrightly from spirit was Lord Ebury, the first Baron Ebury, but he also said that some called him Robert Grosvenor, or that's what it sounded like to me. As I walked with His Grace into the surgery, spirit relatives joined us. The spirit of Robert Grosvenor explained that he too had a leaning towards natural medicine. He said that he found my healing abilities fascinating and told me that when he was 'alive' with us, he was a fervent supporter of homeopathy. So much so that he had been patron for both Dr Curie's Homeopathic Hospital, and Dr Quin's London Homeopathic Hospital, and he had even spoken up for the practice in parliament.

It was very difficult to keep up with his excited chatter but when he then went on to say he'd died in the winter of 1893 in his nineties, I realised that he must have been a very honourable and principled man to have taken such a stand over what was then considered a dubious practice – homeopathy. Like myself, he had worked on the threshold of people's awareness and helped to bring about changes in public opinion, to allow the science to be practised today. Without him, who knows? Maybe we would have waited another hundred years for it to be introduced.

My life at sixteen proved to be very interesting, and it was made even better for me when I met my first boyfriend, Stephen.

When I first saw him he was asleep in the waiting room. I called out his name and jolted him back to consciousness. Well, I suppose it *was* only 8.30 a.m. To me this was normal enough. Many of our patients were bleary-eyed in the morning, especially as we opened the surgery ready for the first of them at 8 a.m. When Stephen opened his eyes and smiled at me he looked so handsome it made me tingle to my core.

Natalie was arriving late that morning so it was my turn to

assist Mr Sowerby. As I stood gazing down into Stephen's gorgeous brown eyes, my boss must have sensed the chemistry between us and came straight out and told Stephen that I didn't have a boyfriend.

I went cherry red and lightly kicked Mr Sowerby under the chair. He laughed, obviously revelling in his teasing of love's young dream.

His appointment over, Stephen left without saying a word to me. I thought that my boss's statement had sent him off in embarrassment.

Later that afternoon the surgery phone rang . . . it was Stephen! My heart fluttered as he asked to speak to me personally. After a short conversation he had officially become my first date. Mr Sowerby thought it was hilarious.

Natalie was furious as apparently she'd had her eye on Stephen for some time. It seemed like a whole group of the younger surgery nurses shared the same feelings. They'd all been hoping he would invite them out. Why me? I wondered.

Stephen was twenty – over three and a half years older than me – and was doing a sandwich course to train as an architectural technician for a large corporate practice.

Every time we went out, girls would stare at him. He was so handsome. Unfortunately he suffered badly from asthma and often had to stop walking and use his inhaler. Without thinking, I put my hand on his chest one day as he wheezed for breath during an attack. I think he thought I was being fresh with him but didn't stop me from touching his chest. Within a few moments his breathing had returned to normal and he didn't use his inhaler. He smiled and said, 'That's a first! I've never known my chest calm down so quickly before, and the tickle has completely gone too.'

I smiled but was too scared to tell him about my healing

ability. I didn't want him to think I was strange and be frightened away.

After we had had a few successful dates together and I felt secure enough, I asked Stephen why he had chosen me to take out when he must have known the other girls in the surgery were lining up for him. He smiled and said that he'd thought I was different. I had a sort of glow within me that shone out. He couldn't describe this feeling properly or put his finger on it, but when he met me he'd felt that he should be with me.

Oh! How could any girl resist that?

Stephen was such a romantic and always charming, always the perfect gentleman. My parents loved him and he quickly became a permanent fixture within our family group. He seemed to be able to talk to my father in a way that made him happy. Maybe it was because I'd explained that I found my dad hard to get on with, Stephen tried that little bit harder, for my sake. No matter. All I knew was that there was nothing he wouldn't do for me, and my parents loved him.

We talked of what we wanted to do in the future, where we would like to travel. We always found happiness in each other's company. I started to think that maybe my father was right about me not studying to go to university . . . perhaps it was my destiny to settle down in a steady relationship and get married young. It seemed a very appealing prospect.

On his nightly visits Sam kept telling me that as lovely as we were together, I still had a lot to learn when it came to relationships. He said a lot can happen in people's lives to change the way they feel about each other. Although he was trying to protect me, I certainly didn't want to hear what he was saying. All I wanted to hear was that Stephen would love me forever. That's what Stephen said, so what could go wrong?

I finally plucked up the courage to mention my spirituality to

Stephen, and was surprised when he accepted my healing abilities as a natural phenomenon. He was interested to learn more and introduced me to his grandmother, who happened to be a great believer in spiritual matters. She explained that she'd had healing for her knee some years ago when the doctors had told her there was nothing they could do apart from medication or surgery. She actively encouraged Stephen to have healing from me whenever I felt the urge, saying he was a lucky boy to have me in his life.

We had now been together a whole year and my college studies were going well. I was contented at work and ecstatically happy with Stephen.

There was just one problem: I kept having stabbing pains in my stomach and left side.

As usual, before a doctor could give his diagnosis, my Guides and Angels were on hand to advise me. Despite their warnings to me to have medical treatment, I ignored their advice, mainly due to the fact that my father was just returning home from another spell in hospital. This time he was recovering from a nasty bout of pneumonia and I didn't want my mother to have to worry about another member of her family.

Although my dad was only in his late thirties, his newly diagnosed emphysema was fast becoming a real problem, as Sam had warned that it would. Naturally I was worried for him, especially after my prediction of his early death. I think my mother was secretly worried too as we both witnessed a general decline in my father's health. He often suffered from pneumonic episodes when he caught a chill. He still smoked like a trooper and we would catch him chain-smoking! I have to admit my patience ran thin with him over that. It seemed that he was bringing much of his suffering upon himself . . .

He had been in hospital for a week's convalescence, the third time this year he'd had to be admitted, and my mother was beginning to suffer from the strain. The last thing she needed on top of his illness was a sick daughter too. So I reassured her everything would be fine, there was nothing to worry about.

As Dr Charles, the specialist, chatted to my mother about the condition of my dad's chest, he advised taking a family holiday – as if it would act like a magic cure-all.

If the doctor said this was what he needed, then my dad was ready to listen. Just the ticket to put him back on his feet, he thought. He would not accept that my Guide Sam and a mêlée of Healing Angels were standing right beside me ready to attempt that job. No matter how hard I pleaded to give my father healing, he still refused to agree and pinned his faith on science and the medical profession.

One day as my father lay in bed, my mother and I sat beside him flicking through the Thomas Cook brochures. Sam was with us, once again begging me to speak to my dad about his smoking habits, reiterating that no holiday in the world could prevent cigarettes from affecting his lungs. I could feel panic rising in my chest as the desperate tone of Sam's voice convinced me this was a serious warning. Dad *had* to stop smoking now before further damage was done and it was too late. I couldn't ignore this any more so I decided to tackle him then and there.

Just talking to a parent might sound simple enough, but my father was definitely not the easiest person in the world. Well, not with me, it seemed. Sitting by his bedside, I mustered up the courage to broach the subject of his cigarettes and what Sam had said about them.

My father flew into a furious rage, telling me to watch what I said as it was not the cigarettes that were causing his illness. His problem was stress – and I was giving him more of it. In fact, he told me to stop talking about my hocus-pocus healing too!

Fighting back tears of anger and frustration, I picked up a magazine and pretended to read it rather than bother to argue with him. I flicked through the pages and stopped at an advertisement for winter sun in the Canary Isles.

'That's it,' Dad commented, breaking the awkward silence between us. 'We are going there!' So the Canaries it was. 'Whether we can afford it or not, we are all going,' he continued, almost defiantly, as though this visit would definitely bring about his cure. So it was that a trip to Gran Canaria was booked, and two weeks later we were on our way. My dad was sure his optimistic cure-all holiday would work, but from the corner of my eye I could see Sam shaking his head in disapproval, confirming to me that it wouldn't.

Although I was sad to leave Stephen, he seemed to understand that our separation was necessary. My dad needed some time in the sun. Stephen knew I was feeling pretty ill myself so sent me on my way with warm kisses, telling me to have a good time, to rest and get well.

What is it about sunshine that instantly makes you feel well and makes you smile? Such warmth on a March day was unheard of in dreary, cold, wet England. Perhaps Dad was right. It felt like this was going to be the best tonic in the world for him as we walked off the plane on to the scalding tarmac runway.

Going abroad thirty-five years ago was a big event. Hardly anyone ordinary did, especially in winter. The working classes typically went to places like North Wales, Devon or Cornwall for their main holiday – if they were lucky – and always at the height of summer.

As soon as we all stepped off the plane we were greeted by the scent of lemon balm. The heat of the sun on the asphalt created a shimmering mirage as it radiated off the dense black surface.

Wow, I thought, this was great! However, the nagging pains

in my stomach constantly reminded me that everything was not OK. Strangely, Sam was also accompanying me every step of the way and trotted alongside me no matter where we went.

With sightseeing in mind, we looked at the possible places to visit. Apart from the usual trips to the market and the occasional barbecue, we also chose to visit the site of an extinct volcano high up in the black mountains.

This trip was quite an expedition and took all day. I don't think it was any great distance away, but in order for the travel company to justify what they were charging they were adding in several stopping points. This included a compulsory sangria tasting and winery tour, plus visits to traders in flamenco dolls, wirework matadors and flock-covered bulls. Actually at seventeen years old it was all very exciting to me.

Before setting off that morning I had been feeling unwell but had kept quiet, knowing that Dad was really looking forward to this trip. The tour members were to meet in the hotel lobby first thing, where we were given a packed lunch to take with us for the day. My stomach groaned and churned relentlessly. Once again, Sam was giving me one of his 'something is going to happen' looks. He then directly told me it might not be in my best interest to travel that day. Despite the pain, I chose to ignore him.

About thirty people boarded the coach with shows of enthusiasm and excitement. We then had to make our way to another hotel to pick up further passengers. With each minute that passed the pain inside me seemed to grow more intense.

What do I do now? I thought. Fortunately the seat next to me remained empty and this allowed me to spread out. That didn't stop Sam from pacing up and down the aisle as he became more and more concerned for my welfare.

Despite having a microphone, the tour guide raised her voice as she battled to be heard over the passengers' chatter. My eyes became heavy and I fell asleep, hypnotised by her dulcet tones. I vividly remember speaking to Sam during my sleep.

I don't know if you have ever had a moment when a dream seems so real that you think you are awake? That was what I experienced there. During this sleep Sam explained to me that I had to have medical help. He implored me to tell my parents I was very ill.

The coach pulled to a halt and I was jolted awake. Did I just dream I was speaking to Sam and going to be ill? And why was he speaking to me in a dream, when he could easily do so when I was awake? It was all very strange, I thought, wondering why he hadn't just spoken direct to me if he was so worried. But, of course, he had. Was I really *that* ill?

The thought of serious illness at my young age was hard to take in. Yes, I had a bad stomach ache, but surely nothing worse was going to happen to me?

As the passengers disembarked, I was one of the last to leave the coach, waiting to let everyone else off first, mainly because I didn't want to move. As I got up I felt a stabbing pain sear into my left side. My legs felt shaky and I was a little light-headed. My parents had already disembarked so I couldn't say anything to anyone. I stumbled down off the bus in the vague hope it would pass.

I could hear the guide talking to the group of people by the coach. 'OK, everyone, this is our first stop . . . let's all gather by that pagoda on the right just next to the restaurant and we'll start our tour from there.'

I took the last step off the bus . . . and plummeted straight on to my face in a dead faint. I groggily came to with the awful stench of strong-smelling salts being wafted under my nose by the coach driver. A few people had gathered around as my mother mopped my grazed brow. I was mortified!

'It's OK,' I said. 'I'm OK.' But, of course, I wasn't. My face had turned an ashen shade of grey under the reddening bruise from where I had fallen. I felt awful. 'I'll wait in a bar while you all walk around,' I said. 'I'll be fine in a moment. It's probably because I haven't eaten much today.'

This seemed like a reasonable suggestion and my mother and the tour guide seemed relieved to hear it. I was given somewhere to rest in a nearby restaurant, a lovely little place in the square where the bus had just parked. It was clean and friendly, and the tour guide settled me down in a comfortable lounger chair that allowed me to rest with my feet up. She told the owner to look after me until she returned.

Fortunately I had Sam with me and he decided to cheer me up. It amazes me how he can always bring the right ingredient to the table, whatever is required. As he always says: when there is a need, that need is always answered.

He told me to close my eyes, saying he would show me a wonderful sight to lighten my day and help me feel better.

Following his instructions, I closed my eyes and rested. I still heard the various noises in the background as people ate and drank and chatted around me. Behind the general cacophony I could also hear the tweeting of the birds and some Spanish pop music, melting into the background. I focused on Sam in my inner vision. Despite my eyes being closed, he was the same in my mind's eye as he was when I saw him right there beside me, only in my vision he seemed to glow even brighter. He spoke and I started to wonder if it actually was him speaking. Doubting my own Guide, I half opened my eyes and he told me, 'Relax and trust in me, Helen. I told you I was taking you to a special place. For this journey I need you to reach a different level of consciousness. So close your eyes – and relax!'

The noises around me started to fade into insignificance as I saw Sam again in my mind. This time he was holding my hand.

He started to walk me towards a huge building. We crossed a beautiful meadow to where the building stood, tall and proud. Around it was a magnificent garden with a small ornamental lake of crystal-clear water reflecting colours so diverse and vivid they were almost unrecognisable to me. The walls of the building were smooth like marble but were made of no material I recognised.

Once we were inside, the building seemed to have many corridors leading off in all directions, with rooms off them to each side. I knew by the height of the building that there must be many more floors to it. I continued to let Sam guide me through our shared experience.

'Where are we?' I asked in my altered state.

He smiled. 'This is one of the Great Halls of Learning, it is specifically for healing,' he whispered. 'Did you say *one*?' I answered.

'Yes, there are many. Here in the Great Halls, much important work is achieved. Healing is sent to ease suffering on earth, and doctors and surgeons, chemists and advanced spiritual minds, continue with their medical studies and research, and instruct students who wish to learn from them. I am bringing you to see the doctor who came into your bedroom once. His name is Dr Clarke and he once practised at Guy's Hospital in London.'

I saw many spirit people were going about their business and then suddenly there he was, the very man who had stood in my room when I was a child and watched with Sam as the outline of a skeleton appeared on the page before me. I knew I had my eyes closed and I was still in the restaurant but this seemed so real – I was also here in this magnificent place. I touched the walls and they felt solid to my touch. Was I asleep and imagining all this or had I been somehow transported to a spiritual realm? Logic said this was a dream or else imaginary. My senses interpreted every-thing around me as real.

Sam broke into my thoughts. 'Concentrate, Helen. I need you to listen to what the doctor has to say.' Dr Clarke took me into one of the many side rooms, where there was an examination couch. I was asked to climb up on to it and he examined me, putting his hands high up on my stomach. After a few moments of moving them in a hovering motion to left and right, he eventually called Sam over to speak to him in the corner of the room, out of earshot from me. I could hear a little of their muffled conversation, but not all, and was becoming agitated. 'I am going to open my eyes now, Sam,' I threatened.

'Wait just one moment!' the doctor spoke out – this was the first time I had heard him say anything. He walked back to me with Sam.

'My dear,' the doctor announced, 'you need an operation. You have a large cyst directly over your left ovary and it is twisting, periodically cutting off the blood supply. I will help you today and throughout your holiday, but you must seek medical advice immediately you are home. Unfortunately healing alone cannot remove the cyst on this occasion. You need surgery as soon as possible . . . by which I mean physical surgery.'

I nodded, acknowledging that I would do just that as soon as I got home.

Sam sat beside me as the doctor told me he was going to perform a spiritual healing session on my painful body. It was so soothing, whether it was in my mind or not, and I was grateful to be out of pain for the first time that day. I could feel energy flowing through my body and see the soft hues of the aura as its colours wafted before my vision. Violet, blue, green, yellowy-white, orange, red . . . they made a rainbow floating across my mind's eye. Even though my eyes were closed, I could feel the heat from the doctor's hands as he held them just above my body.

Once he had finished the healing and we had said our

goodbyes, Sam told me we were going to walk back to where we'd started. In the next instant I knew I was resting back on my lounger in the restaurant and could hear the sounds of the people eating and drinking around me. I opened my eyes. I could still hear Sam although I could not see him.

'The journey is complete, Helen,' he said. 'The doctor has given you enough strength to help you through your holiday.'

Had I just imagined the whole scenario or had Sam taken me into a spiritual hospital where Dr Clarke had performed a healing?

Once I was alert again, one of the local Spanish ladies offered me a drink of orange and in broken English explained I had been asleep for half an hour. Perhaps I was dreaming, I thought.

Sam appeared by my side as I would normally see him and without any questioning from me explained why we had taken our journey to see Dr Clarke: 'Without his healing help you wouldn't be able to stay here on holiday,' he explained. 'You will still have to take it easy. The healing will help but you are chronically ill – fortunately not critically ill.' What's the difference? I thought naively.

The rest of the holiday was affected by my illness. With each day that passed my condition became worse. Dark shadows appeared under my eyes. Strangely, although I felt ill, the pain had dulled and I seemed to be able to cope with it. Sam kept repeating that I needed medical treatment immediately I returned home.

The power of healing certainly helped me through the pain, but it didn't solve the underlying problem. Sam explained that when something mechanical goes wrong with the body and it needs removal for fear it may cause other organs to deteriorate, it requires a surgeon's hands to cut out the problem quickly and healing hands to expedite recovery.

There are times when I myself have known an organ respond to healing all on its own, but usually only when a condition is in the early stages. When the illness is more advanced then urgent action is required and you must take whatever route necessary to achieve recovery.

I have never, even in my younger years, thought of spiritual healing as an alternative to conventional medicine – I have always regarded any form of spiritual healing as complementary or adjunct to the conventional path.

When it comes to our health, I feel we need to tackle any serious problem immediately, especially if it could become life-threatening. I could tell that the pain I was suffering on holiday was out of the ordinary, and it was getting worse. Having my premonition and then an examination by a spirit doctor, whether in sleep or not, convinced me that Sam was right and I should listen. The funny thing is, you never think you might be at risk of dying. Even when you feel desperately ill, there is always the stubborn belief that you will get better. I was still only seventeen so I suppose the thought of actually dying from an illness had never crossed my mind, no matter how many times Sam pleaded that I should take it seriously. Maybe it was because I was so young and fit previously that I decided I could bear the pain and wait for it to go.

We returned to the UK from our two weeks of supposed rest. The day after we arrived, I was taken to the GP's surgery by my anxious mother. The doctor's examination confirmed my spirit friend's suspicion. I had a rather large cyst on my ovary, and I needed to see a consultant – fast. Apparently, however, the waiting time to see this particular specialist was over six weeks . . . not very comforting when you are in pain.

'Surely Helen can see him sooner?' I remember my mother saying. 'After all, she is only seventeen and she shouldn't be in this type of pain.'

The GP assured her that a six-week wait on the NHS was normal, but if we could afford it maybe it would be better for me to see a consultant privately as I would probably end up in A & E before then. I suppose that's the NHS answer to jumping the queue, its new slogan: *Dying for quick service*!

I knew this would cause a problem for my parents as things were tight financially. Burma Oil in Bromborough had closed and my father had been made redundant. Plus he had been ill again during the holiday, so now my poor mum had both of us to worry about.

I tried to reason with her, saying she couldn't afford to pay privately for a consultant's appointment, but it was no use. She was determined. I think she had made the decision to have me seen privately by the consultant gynaecologist, Mr Bender, because I was the one person she could help. My father was generally so stubborn that he was impossible to deal with. At least with me something could be sorted out quickly. A private appointment with the gynaecologist was made for me at his home in Curzon Park, Chester, and I was going the next day! Amazing what money can do, I thought.

Although I had been working at the dental practice for more than a year now, I was worried about taking any time off despite my illness. Fortunately my boss knew Mr Bender and was very sympathetic when he heard that I had to see him. At least he believed me and knew I was not making up stories.

Mr Bender had the most beautiful house I had ever seen. It was Victorian and set in lovely gracious gardens. His wife answered the door, and my mother and I were ushered to a quiet seating area and told he would be a few minutes as he was finishing with another patient.

This was just like the dentist's, I thought, as I waited patiently. Eventually Mr Bender arrived in the doorway and introduced himself. He looked like a little penguin with his rotund stomach and funny bow-tie. What a strange man, I thought, not at all the god-like person that everyone seemed to revere whenever they heard his name mentioned. He did have a warm, sincere smile and I could tell by his aura that he was a genuine healer at heart.

This was the first time I'd ever had a gynaecological examination, and I was petrified. I had never had sex and now I was going to have to expose my intimate self to a strange man, even if he was a doctor. My mother stayed in the room to give me moral support. After examining me, he wasn't as cheery. The news was not good.

'Sorry, Mrs Sparrow, but your daughter not only has a large cyst on her left ovary, I think she has polycystic ovaries as well. This would explain the pain she is experiencing, and there is a good chance the ovary may have twisted, causing complications.'

I had heard my spirit doctor say the same, but now it felt different. It had been confirmed by a living doctor. He continued: 'Her chances of having a natural conception in the future could be considerably reduced, if she can conceive at all. She hasn't had a period for six months and sometimes there can be more than one cyst on the ovary. We need to operate as soon as possible to see what damage has been suffered. Do you have private medical insurance?'

Sam sat on the floor cross-legged, watching the doctor. Then he stood up and walked over to him. He leaned towards the consultant's ear and smiled at me meantime, putting his finger to his lips, then he whispered to Mr Bender. I never said a word as I watched Sam, wondering what he was doing. Could the consultant actually hear him?

My mother turned a paler shade of grey and looked to be in worse condition than me as she shook her head and said, 'No, we have no medical insurance.' Then in an outburst of emotion she exclaimed, 'I don't care if we sell our house, I just want Helen to be out of pain and well again.'

I was shocked. I had never heard her make such a statement without consulting Dad first. I started to cry, telling Mr Bender that my mother couldn't afford even this appointment because my father had been made redundant and was constantly in and out of hospital with emphysema.

Mr Bender seemed genuinely moved and spoke in softer tones. 'No need to go to those lengths, I think, Mrs Sparrow.' He lightly touched her shoulder. 'I will speak to my secretary tomorrow and put Helen at the top of my NHS list. After all, this is an emergency. I will ask my secretary to phone you later with a date for her to come in once we have sorted out where I can do the operation. I am sure it won't be much of a wait.'

I was still in shock from this statement when he ushered us out, gesticulating towards his door, shaking hands with us both and finishing with a matter-of-fact statement.

'Don't worry, Helen, you are in good hands, my dear. But you will need six whole weeks off work so tell your employer, please. I may need to do a hysterectomy.'

This is serious, I thought. Six weeks off work? The operation can't be that bad, can it? Looking at the expressions on Sam's and my mother's faces, it obviously was!

True to his word, later the next morning Mr Bender's lovely secretary rang and confirmed I was to go into Chester City Hospital just two days later. My mum came back from the phone after speaking to her, looking quite white.

The following day dragged by due to the prospect of the impending operation, and I had to face Mr Sowerby and tell him the bad news that he was going to be without a nurse for at least six weeks.

I didn't even qualify for six weeks' holiday, let alone an extended recovery period, and I trembled as I requested the meeting with my boss. I thought he would sack me there and then, and find a replacement. Thankfully he didn't.

Fortunately Mr Bender had phoned him that morning and explained my poor state of health. So when I finally had my chance to explain to Mr Sowerby, he was kindness itself and told me the important thing was to get myself well. Talk about relieved! All the staff at work were so kind to me. They all wished me a speedy recovery and even asked to pop in when I was strong enough for visitors during my convalescence.

I think the impending hospital stay was making me question my own mortality and life's purpose, and I wanted some answers. I couldn't help but wonder why Sam was with me. Why was he always around, telling me about the spirit world? Why had I been singled out to see – and hear – and apparently heal? Why was I not healing myself? Come to think of it, why was I ill at all? If I had been given a choice, I might have chosen not to see spirit . . . so why did I have no choice about having this gift, and why was he here to educate me in it further? So many questions – so few answers.

When I went to bed that night, Sam was waiting for me in my room.

'Hello, my dear,' he announced. 'I know you are a little scared about your operation and I want you to know I will be by your side the whole time. I also know you have been asking many questions and that you feel a need to know more about yourself. I think it is time we had a talk about your life choices. There are things you need to know about me, too.'

Heck, I thought. What now?

'There are things I need to tell you and I feel you are ready to hear them. Now is the time to listen to me, chile.' I knew as soon as I heard the word 'chile' that this would be a kind, loving talk . . . hopefully!

'Well, the truth is, when you befriended me in the spirit world, you asked me to look after you on your journey here, to guide you through life when you had no recollection of who you really are.'

I couldn't stop laughing at his statement, but he was deadly serious. The pains in my side were aggravated by my amusement. However, Sam continued to talk, sounding a little upset and wounded by my response.

I needed to clarify this. 'So are you saying I have employed you to work for me – am I your boss?'

Patiently he replied: 'No, what I am saying is that you are from a higher place . . . one that I cannot visit. You have decided that caring for and being a Guide to you in this earthly way will form part of my learning and spiritual progression.'

I was speechless.

He was deadly serious, though, and by the look on his face I knew this was no laughing matter to him. He sat beside me and softly relayed our story. I was still wondering why, if I was such a good healer, I was so ill. Sam just smiled and said I needed to hear what he had to say. By the seriousness of his tone I knew it must have some bearing on my life.

10

My Guide Sam — His Story

Despite the seriousness of Sam's tone, I found the notion of my ever having employed him ridiculous. I might only have been seventeen at the time, but I was certainly old enough to understand that what he was really talking about was some form of reincarnation. Now that's a topic that can start to play real tricks with your mind and open up a can of worms. I was just settling into my life as Helen the teenager, I had recently fallen in love for the first time in my life, and Sam, whom I implicitly trusted, had come along and suggested that I was in fact a whole lot older – maybe by a couple of millennia! My parents would certainly sign the section papers to have me admitted to hospital if I discussed any of this with them.

This will take some digesting, I thought then. Thirty-five years later I am still digesting this piece of information without, as yet, reaching a final conclusion. Despite many tutorials, I still struggle to accept that I am anything more than the Helen I am today. I don't dismiss the notion of reincarnation; many religions talk openly about it, so the concept is well established. It's just that my Western upbringing makes me wary of the idea – though it would certainly help to explain my clarity of spiritual sight, the empathy I share with many different people, and the intensity of the healing energies that, where appropriate, flood through my body. It was tough to take it on board then, and it's tough for me now as a mature adult. I don't discount the possibility of reincarnation, but I am content to be the Helen that I am in the here and now.

However, my seventeen-year-old mind was teeming with questions, not just about my alleged previous life, but all manner of other curiosities. 'Does the spirit world have a hierarchy?' I asked.

Sam replied: 'It is fair to say that there is an order and structure ranging from the very top to the very bottom of the chain of energy. At the very top is the source or supreme energy. Beneath this entity are many authorities of higher and then lower energies, or vibrations as we call them. So it is the case that some in spirit are more progressed and attuned than others. To ascend to the top naturally requires a great deal of work. We all have different gifts and abilities here in the spirit world. The difference is we don't think of our work as being hierarchical. We know that we all come from a source of pure love and light. We always work together for the same beneficial ends and never try to compete with one another. Why would we want to, when we have all freely made our choice? We want to continue in this world full of love, bonded together, developing and growing in our aspiration to reach the higher realms.'

I asked: 'Do you as my Guide help many other people in the same way as you are helping me?'

'Each person has a Guide but they also have a Guardian Angel. Unlike a Guide who teaches, the Guardian Angel acts as a sort of doorkeeper: protecting, overlooking, generally keeping a person's life in order. The Angel can be called upon and asked to help, but they never act in the same way as a Guide. One is to protect; the other to teach. I am your Guide for as long as you need me, although I do also help other people find where they need to be if their crossing into this world is difficult and as new spirits they can't find their way. That is my part-time position.'

I laughed openly at the thought of him moonlighting while looking after me.

'So you are a full-time Helen Guide, part-time finder Guide: similar to when a group of tourists becomes lost and they need to be gathered together to be shown around!'

'Yes, something like that,' he said, smiling. 'When someone is lost because they have entered the spirit world quickly, and their Guide or family who are trying to reach them can't find them fast enough, I or someone like me will be the first person that they see. Although their Guardian Angel may protect them and steer them into spirit, helping them to overcome fear and giving them a blanket of love, they will need someone like me to guide and teach them their first steps.'

'Wow,' I said, 'you must be kept very busy?'

'No, apart from me there are many thousands of us doing the same work. It is quite an honour really and a big responsibility, because quite often the person who passes into spirit is so traumatised when they arrive they don't even realise they are dead. You have to be technically very adept to be allowed to treat and direct a soul who is entering into spirit in this way. Once their own family and Guides have caught up with them, they then take over the role. This transient period is often the most traumatic for a soul to adjust to, so I suppose I am good at my job.'

'How many years have you been in spirit?' I enquired.

'Over two hundred in your years. However, I was only

awarded the privilege of being your Guardian Guide when you, Helen, decided it would be good for me.'

I was still confused, and laughed to hear this. 'Oh, yes,' I said, rolling my eyes, 'I forgot . . . I am your boss! Tell me about your past, Sam. Your life here on this earth. I want to know more about you.'

He frowned. 'You said there would be a day when you would make me remember this! You said I would only have to speak of this once, Helen, because I have moved forward from those painful days. But you made me promise to tell you, saying it would affect your own personal life choices in some way.'

I hadn't a clue what he meant, but I listened anyway. This sounded surreal.

Sam spoke in hushed tones, as though it was a long-held secret we were sharing and warranted some reverence. 'I too had a family once in this earthly world,' he began solemnly. 'Life in it was bitter for me, filled with heartache and suffering. Thankfully I have been reunited with my family in spirit, and now that I am learning my role as your Guide, I can come to terms with and understand evil ways.

'My name is Samuel Bartholemy as it is said in English. In my own language I am known as Se-se Samba. (Bartholemy was the surname my brother used, and which I later adopted.) My name is pronounced "Seh-seh" but my mother would often call me by my second name, Samba. Se-se means "God has heard", or "God hears", and maybe my name was chosen with this journey in mind. Who knows?

'I was nineteen years of age when I died on the cobbles of Liverpool Docks. My body was emaciated and racked by illness. I believe your doctors now call the illness tuberculosis, but back then it was considered a terrible plague, sweeping through many lands.'

I was eager to know what he once did, and in what circumstance he'd ended up in Liverpool. And most of all why he had died.

Sam described the village where he grew up as a child in Africa, and how a large boat filled with men from a different land arrived there and herded his kin together like animals.

'They beat us and bound us together with wooden yokes around our necks, and chained our hands and legs with iron, like wild animals. Our parents were killed and our homes burned so that we would have no one and nothing to try and escape back to. All the young men, women and children were gathered and separated into different groups, similar to some of the ethnic cleansings I have seen mankind practising since my day. Women were separated from their husbands even if they were pregnant. Blood flooded our land as the elders were brutally murdered, and the screams of those we loved are still etched into my mind as we were torn from our families.

'It was barbaric, inhuman, leaving many in ignorance of who among their kin was still alive and who was dead. We were human beings and yet we were treated worse than beasts. I was a man with a different-coloured skin, but a man nonetheless. What crime had my kinfolk committed? Why were we being punished for living? It took me several generations of understanding and forgiveness within spirit to come to terms with man's inhumanity and the crimes he is capable of committing.'

Sam continued his story in a low voice. 'My siblings and I were kidnapped and our parents murdered by the slavers. I was bound in chains and sent to be sold to the highest bidder. My three sisters and two brothers were also taken. All but one of them was lost to me when we were divided amongst the various ships carrying live cargoes. I had no way of knowing what had happened to them. It was my duty as the eldest son to protect my family – a duty I could not fulfil. One brother was chained alongside me, a mere seventeen years old at the time. He was put with me into the hold of a huge ship along with hundreds of other black souls. My three sisters were aged fifteen, thirteen and eleven, my youngest brother only six years old, but they were all chained and dragged away, screaming and whimpering like dogs awaiting a new master.

'I had no idea at the time that we were to travel by sea for several months. Before we had even boarded the ship many of us were already suffering physical and mental abuse at the hands of our captors. Once we arrived at the docks in America, we were stripped naked and examined by the Captain, or the "man with knives" they said was called a surgeon. This was where they decided whether slaves would be sold to plantation owners or moved on to another boat for a further journey. We were placed into groups and classified by age, looks and possible fertility. The pretty young women were singled out by the masters into yet another section, to be sold on as concubines. Sturdy men and young boys fetched the highest price for their muscle power.

'I thought my awful journey to America was the last I would see of a boat and at least I was on dry land. Then I and many others were sold on to travel on another ship bound for Liverpool. Once more we were packed together below deck to be treated worse than animals. We all knew this was going to be a long journey.

'Conditions aboard the ship were horrific. We were secured by leg irons in a cruelly confined space. We were rarely fed and kept in total darkness in the hull of the ship. We were lined up side by side, the air so thick around us we almost suffocated. We had very little range of movement. Our muscles wasted, causing spasms of cramping pain so acute that it seared into our bones, and every part of our bodies ached as we lay flat on the bare, stinking wood. We hardly saw daylight and the pit of the ship's belly was hot as an oven – or what I then envisioned as the depths of hell. It was a floating prison filled with the innocent. Urine and faeces trickled down through the planks from the bodies lying above us. The stench around us was an unbearable mix of excrement and vomit, that would turn the hardest stomachs. Epidemics of dysentery, smallpox and other illnesses spread quickly through the boat.

'When the weather was good and the putrid smell became too insufferable for the Captain and crew to bear, we were taken above deck. We stumbled up there as the crew beat us with iron rods, and our eyes smarted as we were blinded by the sunlight. They would untie a whole string of us at once to be washed down with buckets of salt water. Sometimes we were hauled into the air by a noose around our feet and tossed upside down, to be dunked over the side of the ship for the crew's amusement. Some of the men were dying and were hauled overboard for the sharks. Others who were refusing to eat would be force-fed by crew members, who would hold them while they rammed a steel funnel into their mouths and poured gruel down it.

'Maybe twenty or thirty men were bound together by the ankles and wrists, with chains threading them into what looked like a "snake style dance" of men. Only they were not dancing, they were all contorting with pain. The crew loved to see the agonised men jumping about in pain. It was entertainment for them.

'Salt water eats into the skin and sears open cuts and bruises as they absorb the saline solution. The water burned like acid on our skin as we saw daylight again for a few brief minutes. In the sun we thought of our homes and family. Then we were put below again and it shattered our memories of home and freedom. We knew we would never be free again. We were told to scrub below decks and to wash the excrement from where we lay. Then another batch of men endured the same fate while we listened to their agony and finally they were herded back below into the dark pit of the hull's belly.

'How could our fellow men do this to us? Were we not men ourselves? My thoughts would rage around the same questions for days. Why, why, why? Am I not a human being? Who would choose to torture and take away a person from their own kin? Steal their offspring to be sold on like animals or objects? Who made the choice that I should be in this living hell? Had I no voice to speak out and be heard?'

Sam continued speaking with tears rolling from his eyes. 'We were all petrified. Some tried to escape but ended up being beaten nearly to death. Some even committed suicide, they were so desperate. The Captain would often scream out to his crew not to damage the cargo as we were only worth money alive, not dead! I was nineteen years old and the young man next to me only fifteen. The voyage was killing us, not only our bodies, but our minds and hearts. We didn't know which was worse. To die during the long journey or once we'd arrived, as none of us knew what was going to happen to us next and the constant fear was agonising.

'The only thing that kept me alive was the prospect of seeing my beloved family alive at the end of the journey. To see my sisters and brothers once more. I did not even know if the brother who had boarded with me was alive. Although we were bound on the same ship, in the same hold, we were separated from each other as we embarked. This was because we were arranged below deck according to our heights. Every man, woman and child was measured so that every square inch was taken up with human flesh or cargo. The smaller areas were filled with women and children while the longer ones were filled with men. He must have been placed on a different level from me as he was not as tall.

'There were hundreds of black souls shackled around me. I tried calling out to my brother several times, but could never make myself heard above the moans and wails of terror. I even tried to pass a message from man to man, but it never worked properly as so many had the same name or were too distraught to co-operate, rendered speechless through shock.

'Men sobbed uncontrollably as they wept for the dead family of their homeland and for the family trapped on board the many ships. Our grief was incalculable. Little did we know it was just the start of what lay ahead for us! A combination of disease and inadequate food took a heavy toll on the captives and crew. One in every five Africans died on board ship.

'It was 1797 when I arrived in Liverpool Docks. I was very unwell by the time I eventually disembarked. Wealthy families in Britain would congregate at the docks to buy slaves as fashionable status symbols. The prosperous merchants of the area saw them as luxury purchases with which to impress their friends. The fact that I was ailing by the time I arrived meant that the Captain didn't know what to do with me. To hide my sickness from the visiting buyers, he chained me to a wall in a quiet area of dockland out of sight, along with a couple of other men and women who were similarly ailing.

'I was coughing uncontrollably and blood oozed from my mouth each time I did. "We have to kill him," the ship's surgeon told the Captain. "He is too dangerous, he will contaminate the others." The language was foreign to me at the time – the tone was crystal-clear.

'I could hear the crowds thronging around as they were selling off each slave by name and age. "Who will give me a good price for this young boy?" The auctioneer called out a strange name and

I knew instinctively it was my youngest brother who was being sold. No, I prayed it was my youngest brother. He had survived! He was being sold to someone, hopefully a family. Maybe he will sleep on straw tonight, I thought. Then a gun exploded, putting a bullet in my head. I don't remember any more about my life on earth.

'I awoke to find the sea lapping against my skin. This time it did not sting. The sun was shining on to my chest yet I felt no burning from it, only warmth. As I stood on the seashore, the soft sand under my feet, I heard people's voices behind me. I turned around to see my mother, father and youngest sister running towards me from the distance. They were shouting my name loudly. I was home! Home in the spirit world. That is where I began my spiritual journey.'

There were tears streaming down my cheeks as I heard what Sam had endured. I was also relieved that he was united in spirit with his family.

'When did you decide to be a Guide, Sam?' I asked with respect.

After he had composed himself he continued with his account. 'After I settled in spirit, I decided to spiritually progress and become a Guide because I felt that no man should ever have to undergo the inhumanity and horrors I'd had to endure. At the time of my death, two men called Thomas Clarkson and William Wilberforce in your world felt the same way. They led a campaign against slavery, collecting evidence against the atrocious trade. Despite winning the cause and achieving the abolition of slavery in Britain and other countries, illegal trading in slaves continued until eventually, sixty years later, it was totally obliterated. Liverpudlian ships were responsible for transporting over half of the three million Africans brought across the Atlantic.'

'Were you spiritually part of the influence upon these men,

Clarkson and Wilberforce, influencing them to campaign against slavery?' I asked, riveted.

'Sort of.' He smiled. 'Those men already had a desire within their hearts to change the white man's way of thinking. Helping them was easy as they wanted to make things better. Today, in your era, things are different. The powerful sometimes choose to overlook evil acts in other countries. Even today people with my African roots are still filled with hatred. No peace can ever last until love binds people together again and they believe they can be united. Throughout time, man's greed has fed his belly with hatred and the lust for power consumes him. When will the destruction end?'

He broke down and sobbed for a few moments then resumed talking.

'I met you in the Great Halls of Learning. Although I know you do not believe you have lived before, you are a Guardian of light on the right of the divine spirit, and your energy is that of pure light. You were reading inside one of the Great Halls. There are many hundreds of such places where the perfection of the different senses may be experienced. In some you read; some you stand and listen to penetrating music that you feel throughout your being. Some are filled with sadness to teach an under-standing of grief; some are filled with laughter. The list is endless. I met you in the Halls of Understanding and Compassion. Helen, you are indeed a very old soul.

'My first tasks were to help those who were lost when they entered spirit. Like I said earlier, I meet and greet when families or Guides are slow to catch up with them. I did this for quite some time. Then one day you asked if I was ready to take on more responsibility. You said you would be my child and I would act like a parent to you. When you felt the time was right, you would be born to a family and I would be your Guide. I would only tell you what you needed to know, and you insisted you must always be allowed to make your own decisions, no matter what the consequences. Those were your rules, Helen. You would not tell me when this was going to happen, it just would, and when that day came you said you would not know me straight away. It would be only with time that you would start to trust and speak to me. That was to be my task until you rejoined the spirit domain. I was to guide you.

'It felt like quite an honour for me, but you instinctively heard my thoughts and said the honour was all yours. So now I am here with you. I stand by you and try to guide you, even though I know you can guide me! You explained to me that love is the bond. Love is the invisible energy that cannot be seen or measured, but is felt by the heart and soul. Love drives nations with its passion and pride, and makes us feel wanted and cared for. Love develops a belief system that is unstoppable, although at times it can become misguided, when it is mixed with other constants such as politics or religion, for instance. Pure love is the powerful energy, not the manipulation of it.

'This invisible, unbreakable bond is far stronger and more precious than any rare diamond. At times we don't even realise how real and true love's value really is. We frequently take it for granted. Even I am guilty of that!

After that we both sat quietly as I sobbed for a whole hour. My poor Sam.

11

Healing Love

Chester City Hospital was a huge red-brick Victorian building resembling a workhouse more than a twentieth-century place of healing. In fact, years ago, that's what it was, a Poor Law Union Workhouse, built to house the city's poor and orphaned.

After the 1930s it was renamed St James' Hospital, and then in 1948 it was transferred to a hospital management committee following the inauguration of the National Health Service and finally named Chester City Hospital. It specialised in treating seriously ill people – and I was about to be admitted.

As we approached shivers ran down my spine as the energies of hundreds of people in spirit passed through my soul. Sam was waiting by the entrance as I made my way to the ward. 'It's OK,' he soothed me. 'The spirit world will look after you'. I love Sam and his encouragement, but at this moment in time I was too nervous to be easily comforted.

After about an hour of nurses telling me to put this on, take that off, have my blood pressure read, blood tests, questions and more questions, I finished up looking a right sight in my blue open-back hospital frock complete with bed socks and white hat. Not quite the fashion statement a seventeen year old was looking for! I arrived outside the operating theatre. The thick, sickening smell of anaesthetic hung in the air. The anaesthetist introduced himself, voicing a little shock that I was so young and yet having such a major operation. He read my medical notes with interest. That was encouraging, I thought, in a negative way!

A drip was hooked up and a needle was inserted into my hand by the anaesthetist. 'Now count down from ten!' he commanded. I managed to reach eight.

Within the blink of an eye, it seemed, the operation was over . . .

As I opened my heavy eyes, still drowsily drunk from heavy anaesthetic, the searing pain from my newly acquired stitches burned like a jellyfish sting. A tight sensation pulled across my midriff. Having an operation is such a strange experience. It makes you immobile and stiff, unable to function in a normal way as your brain battles to reassert its autonomy and reason.

Drifting in and out of sleep, I blearily noticed the nursing staff busy around me before I slid back into oblivion. Although I was seriously ill, I didn't think of it as a life-threatening situation, but rather a matter of being weary. I chose not to fight my illness – I just went with the flow.

I had no idea how long I had been asleep when I opened my eyes and looked at the nurse sitting on a chair by my bedside. She seemed such a kind lady, soothing me as she held my hand when the spasms of pain came.

I heard her explain that I was very ill and had lost a lot of blood. She said she was going to sit with me until I felt out of pain and more restful. 'Try and sleep, my dear,' she said. 'You need to rest as much as you can.' I noticed how softly spoken she was and how calm she made me feel when she held my hand.

Some time later, I woke again and spoke to her, asking for my mum. I felt so ill, I cried and begged to see her. 'I know, dear,' she said, 'but your mum isn't here yet. The other nurses have called your parents to come in and be with you because as you have lost so much blood, you are quite weak. I am going to sit with you until they arrive. My name is Nurse Mary.'

Just then another nurse came into the room and checked my drip and pulse. She leaned over me, smiled in that dissociative manner that nurses often have, and said she would be back in a moment. I couldn't understand why I had to have two nurses. I distinctly remember Nurse Mary standing up in the other nurse's presence and looking at her. Neither of them spoke to one another, so I naturally thought Nurse Mary must be the senior nurse and that she was keeping an eye on her junior. I did notice, however, that they wore different uniforms. Nurse Mary must be the senior as she wore a much larger hat, I thought.

Eventually, I felt a little stronger and mustered up enough energy to speak to Nurse Mary again, as for some reason her hat intrigued me.

'You have a pretty hat. It's more like a bonnet,' I said. 'Are you the senior nurse?'

Again she smiled sweetly, and answered my question. 'Yes, dear,' she said. 'I am much more senior.'

Sleep overcame me again.

When I awoke, I noticed Sam by my bedside, talking to Nurse Mary. Wow! I thought. She can see and talk to him. They continued deep in conversation, walking into the corridor just out of my sight. Within seconds of their leaving the other nurse came back in to take my blood pressure and pulse again. Seeing that her hat was different, the first thing I said to her was, 'Where's Nurse Mary gone?'

'Who?' she said in a puzzled way, frowning.

'The nurse who was with me earlier. You saw her. She was here with you a little while ago. She was sitting beside me and stood up when you came in. She said she was called Nurse Mary and she was holding my hand.'

Just at that moment, like some sort of scripted drama, my mum and dad rushed into the room all gowned up and in sterile facemasks. Despite the masks I could see how worried they looked. I felt a glimmer of satisfaction to have them there with me. This was one of those occasions I wanted my mother to put her arms around me and make it all go away – though I knew this wouldn't happen.

Trying to make conversation, I explained to them about the nurse and her hat, saying how kind she had been, holding my hand. Then in the ward entrance I caught a glimpse of Nurse Mary standing with Sam: they were both smiling at me.

I finally realised the reason why she was with Sam. Nurse Mary was from the spirit world! From then on, least said about her the better, I thought.

My parents just sat there. I felt like crying, not talking. As I was too weak to offer much in the way of conversation it made it easy for them to sit and say nothing. Eventually they said how pleased they were that I didn't have to have a hysterectomy. Nonetheless, they were aware I had undergone serious surgery, taking out cysts and my appendix together with a jar full of massive gallstones from my gall bladder.

The nurse made another check on me and while doing so seemed to access something in her memory. 'What was that nurse's name again?'

'Nurse Mary,' I said, still feeling weary, and went on to

describe her uniform to help jog the other nurse's recollection.

'Actually, there is a hospital story that there was once a nurse called Mary on these wards. She died some years ago. The uniform you have just described is the old nursing uniform we once wore. In fact, from memory, Mary was in charge of the Heart Ward right above us.

'There have been stories over the years that she roams the wards, searching out the very sickest patients and nursing them back to health. You'd be surprised how many of the staff have said they have seen her over the years, walking up and down the corridors. Even some of the doctors have commented on seeing her when they have been here on nights. But to be honest, I have always passed it off as a trick of the imagination. Well, well! You have been nursed by the famous Nurse Mary.'

My parents looked at me in disbelief. I was very pleased they'd heard all that from the nurse and not from me. If others had seen her, like the nurse said, my parents couldn't blame the anaesthetic for giving me hallucinations. In my mind I thanked the spirit world for taking such care of me.

After a while my parents left, satisfied for the moment that I was recovering. They promised to return the next day. They came and went for a while. I slowly recovered enough to go home and convalesce.

When someone is ill it must bring out the best in other people because everyone was very kind to me after my operation. I found that my work colleagues and friends were supportive, and my family unexpectedly so.

Many of the staff at work invited me home for tea. Some offered to take me out shopping once I was on the mend. It was lovely to feel so wanted and cared for by so many people. It was something I'd never expected, but I was touched that they took the trouble.

I had noticed however, that since my operation, Stephen was being evasive. I thought he was giving me space and time to recover. It never occurred to me that he was withdrawing from the relationship. Why would I think that? I was in love.

Apparently while I was in hospital his parents had a long chat with him about his future and said they felt he should reconsider having me in his life. As a parent of three growing boys, I can now understand what they must have been thinking. After all, he was a handsome lad with a good future ahead of him. He could have his pick of girlfriends. I can only assume they were concerned I couldn't have children or had long-term health issues.

Or maybe Stephen was tired of waiting for me to mature as he wanted a sexual relationship without any lasting commitment between us. Although I loved him, I was not ready to agree to his demands and had said I was happy to remain a virgin until I was ready for marriage. Whatever the reason he left, I was so sad he'd finished with me that I cried for weeks. As a young girl in love my heart was broken by him. He did eventually pluck up the courage to visit me at home and bring a bunch of flowers. So, being naive, I suggested we remain friends even though I was crying inside.

Once I felt well enough to resume work, I started back as a dental nurse. I was grateful that Mr Sowerby was very considerate and gave me only light duties until I felt completely strong enough to run up and down the stairs again.

My operation had been a great success, but it had left me with the threat of a major trauma. I had to face the fact that I might never be able to have a family of my own. Mr Bender was quite adamant in stating that it would be difficult, if not near-impossible, for me ever to conceive. At the age I was, the enormity of that took a while to sink in. Thoughts of feeling less of a woman as I matured slid through my mind when I contemplated my future. What were the chances of anyone else wanting a relationship with me if I couldn't have children? Who would want a barren wife?

Sam would always be on hand then, dismissing my negative thoughts and saying that the Angels and many higher spiritual helpers were sending me intense healing for my potential fertility problem. Still only seventeen, I struggled to cope with all the implications, and unfortunately they overcame me one day while I was eating lunch in the Bank House staffroom with Jane. She and I were happily chatting away when I unexpectedly burst into tears. It was the first time I had actually voiced my fears of infertility to any of my work colleagues. Up until now I had not told anybody at work of Mr Bender's prognosis. Jane, a married woman, seemed to understand.

She was beautiful with a petite figure and well-groomed hair. She had a natural grace to her and a beauty that shone out every time she smiled. All the men turned to look at her when she entered a room, and she and her husband seemed blissfully happy. However, my spiritual radar detected all was not as it should be and detected a glimmer of sadness within her.

We had seen each other many times, crossing paths in the surgery, and naturally always said hello out of politeness, but we'd never really had a good chat to each other. This was mainly because I was the new girl and still in my teens whereas Jane was a married woman in her early thirties. She most probably thought I was too young to socialise with, but now, for some reason, everything seemed different. Maybe it was because I'd had such a major operation at such a young age. Maybe she had heard a rumour about my ability to communicate with the spirit world. Who knows? But suddenly we were having an in-depth conversation about her belief in my spiritual abilities. That was out of the blue, I thought. I hadn't really mentioned my abilities to anyone while working at Bank House, so I was a little curious to learn how she had found out.

Her saying she was interested was all the catalyst the spirit world needed to light up the room with Jane's family from the other side. Straight away I could see a man standing beside her chair in the staff room. He did not have the brightness of a Guide so was most probably a family member.

I had to tell her that there was a spirit visitor wanting to talk to her. As far as I could tell she was too young to have lost anyone close to her, but maybe I was wrong? Each time I went into further detail about the spirit world, the young man smiled at me and politely asked if I would tell her more about him.

Eventually, after about five minutes of talking, I finally mustered up the courage to tell Jane that the young man looked like he was in his early thirties. She seemed startled and asked who I thought it might be.

The man was eager to communicate and called himself David: he spoke about his brother Neal. He seemed relieved that Jane was going to listen to what he had to say and said that he was her *new* brother and that he had died in a tragic accident involving a huge kite!

Who flies a huge kite? I wondered.

I didn't know how she would react to the message but the room suddenly became silent and Jane started to dab tears from her eyes.

'I know who this person is, Sarah,' she said in a whisper. 'It is my husband's brother. He died nearly two years ago in a terrible accident.'

On hearing her acknowledgement, the man in spirit became excited as he went on to talk about himself and his brother Neal. He told me that he was a natural sportsman, always on the go, and often took up dangerous hobbies like jumping out of planes. One of the sports he became interested in was paragliding. It gave such an adrenalin boost, he told me. Although he considered himself to be an experienced flyer, nothing had prepared him for what happened the day he died.

Naturally all the equipment had been checked and double-checked, in the standard safety procedure. The weather seemed perfect and the group of paragliding enthusiasts was set for a day of high-adrenalin adventure. The moment came for him to jump off a mountainous plateau when unexpectedly a thermal current snatched him up then plunged him to his death on the ground below.

Jane was now crying buckets as she continued to listen to her brother-in-law communicating. 'My family will be so pleased to hear from me,' he said. 'And I am so sorry to have wrecked your big day. You looked as radiant as a bride could ever do. Please tell my brother that I love him and he is a lucky man having you as a wife. I am sorry I was not the best man at your wedding, but I heard my brother's speech and what he said about me.'

Jane's weeping turned to sobs. She must have used a whole roll of toilet tissue during our chat, leaving her eyes bloodshot and very red.

'I can't believe it, Sarah. You are amazing. My brother-in-law died over a year ago, one month before our wedding. He was going to be our best man. In fact, it is coming up to the anniversary of his death. At first we didn't know whether to cancel the wedding or not, but we went ahead in honour of him and made a toast on our wedding day to remember him by.'

In reply I commented: 'Well, what he has said today certainly sounds like he heard everything you said about him on the wedding day!'

'Oh, Sarah, I am so happy he has spoken to me. Neal will be so pleased, but to be honest I don't quite know how to tell him.

It's not that he won't believe, it's just that it is so hard for him to talk about his brother. He loved him so much.'

Sam entered the room then and put his arm around David, as he had started to have a little weep, watching over his sister-in-law.

'Oh, you will,' I said, 'you will find a way, I am sure.' Sam gave me a little wink. He walked over and sat on one of the staff room's worn leather chairs to listen to what was being said. David in spirit smiled and mouthed the words, 'Thank you, Helen.' I watched as the young man disappeared in front of my eyes.

Jane heaved herself out of her chair and flung her arms around me, planting a big kiss on my cheek. 'You are an angel,' she said to me. 'You have no idea what this will mean to Neal. You know nothing about me . . . you haven't even been here long enough to know anything about my wedding day. You can't have made this up. Just look at the state of me, Sarah! I'll have to go and put on some make-up before we start back to work.'

Sam and I sat alone in the deserted staff room, feeling that we had done a good job.

Jane and I never talked about the incident to anyone else. She made me promise to keep what had happened between ourselves. I was quite relieved because if the others had found out, I felt I would never have a quiet lunch break again.

A week passed, and I had put the impromptu sitting to the back of my mind when Jane caught my arm one night as I was leaving and invited me to her house to meet her husband. 'Please come for tea one night, Sarah. Neal wants to cook for you, to say thank you. I will take you home with me from work and run you back to your house later.'

What could I say? I was flattered that she wanted to

introduce me to her husband. Jane was always the posh one of the nurses and I doubted she invited any of the other staff over for dinner as she kept herself very private. I excitedly but nervously accepted.

The evening arrived and Jane, as good as her word, drove me to her house after work where her husband greeted me like an old friend. Neal was so pleased by his messages that he had made me my favourite meal, spaghetti Bolognese, and by my table setting was a bunch of flowers and box of chocolates as a surprise.

It was a wonderful evening. Neal told me that the messages had given his family so much comfort and hope. He explained that his mother especially could now sleep at night, knowing that her son was safe. It was during the table talk that I noticed a little child sitting on a chair beside us. Unlike a normal child, this one glowed with such brightness you would swear she was Tinkerbell's sister.

The child smiled at me. She was angelic. To say she was beautiful would be an understatement. The beauty radiated from within her tiny body with an intensity I had never seen before. She had long blonde curls that tumbled down to her waist, sparkling as if each strand were adorned with a thousand crystals. Her clothes were not traditional in any way, but it was as if strands of pink and white coloured energy had been woven into a perfectly fitting one-piece tunic. Her eyes were the palest of blues and yet they were not the eyes of a child, they were the essence of pure wisdom looking straight back at me. As I held her stare, a blast of emotion ran through my body: I wanted to cry.

I heard a voice say in my mind that she was a Healing Angel and she had been watching me work with Sam. I couldn't tell if the voice was of the child or of a spiritual Guide. No matter, the message was perfectly clear. 'You are a healer. Your healing voice will be administered not only through your hands into the mind and bodies of those in need, but through your smile, your actions and your intentions.'

Still smiling at me, she vanished almost as quickly as she'd appeared. It was from that moment onwards that I realised: whether I was giving healing spiritual messages or physical healing through my hands, this healing energy was derived from the one true source.

Now my friend Jane and her husband could start to move forward and heal from their dreadful loss. It was a powerful moment for me, made even more profound by the Angel's words. Now I truly knew I was here to change lives.

Back in the 1970s there was no procedure similar to the keyhole surgery we have today. I'd been left with a scar right across my abdomen. Nowadays surgery is much less dangerous. While medical science is moving on in leaps and bounds, so equally is our thirst for spiritual knowledge. We are now entering an era of great changes in our spiritual awareness.

Quantum physics has already established that the dimension of spirit can exist. General science may not yet have proven the existence of the spirit world, but believe me when I say it won't be long before they do. Just as in the mid-seventies we could never imagine doctors having the expertise routinely to conduct lifesaving transplants as they do now, so it will be that one day we will see science and spirituality as part of the same spectrum, rather than opposing disciplines.

For the time being we have to feel the world of spirit with our hearts and offer unconditional love. For that is the greatest of gifts . . . love is what fuels everything.

When the rest of the staff found out I had visited Jane's for dinner they were all very curious as to why I'd been there. I passed it off, saying it was a kindness due to my operation and recent parting from Stephen. But Jane and I knew the truth. It was because a special gift had been given to both of us . . . the ability to carry on with life and to live it to the full, thanks to the consolation offered by the spirit world.

12

Crash, Bang, Wallop!

I hadn't long been back at work full-time from my major operation when the strangest event happened, turning life in the whole surgery literally upside down.

Everyone had gathered in the kitchen for the usual tea break at 11 a.m. As usual we were all spitting feathers for a cup of tea by then.

Mrs Copeland the caretaker, fondly known as Mrs C, always placed a huge plate of McVitie's digestive biscuits on the table as she distributed mugs full of strong tea. This break was important to all the girls as we nurses had usually been on the go with patients for about three hours by then.

In the large kitchen there was a small separate area where a couple of open shelves held the crockery, next to a sink set against the wall. I think it had formerly been a pantry and had been added on to the main kitchen as there were at least eighteen of us using it for tea breaks, so we needed as much space as we could get.

The whole house was something of a throwback to a grander Victorian era. It contained many antiques, and even the kitchen had a huge old pine dining table which we all gathered around, huddled together on small spindly wooden stools.

To the sides, along the longer walls, were rows of narrow filing cabinets. There must have been at least forty of them, all crammed to capacity with patient record cards. Computers were not commonplace back then, so all record-keeping and filing were done by hand.

These particular filing cabinets belonged to Mr Johnson, our resident orthodontist, and two other dentists practising in the downstairs surgeries. I always felt I worked in one of the better surgeries because only Mr Sowerby and Mr Jones, the most senior partners, occupied the upper floor of the house.

Breaktime was coming to a close. Mrs C had finished her chores and gone back up to the top floor, into the flat where she lived, when Lesley and Jean, latecomers for tea, hurried in for a quick break.

Jane, who was Mr Johnson's nurse, was now back at work and busy with filing patient record cards while I continued to finish my tea at the table. Lesley and Jean were washing some leftover dishes and putting them away on the shelves while waiting for the kettle to boil.

Something strange started to happen. Each time Lesley put a piece of china on the shelf, it seemed slowly and precisely to edge its way to the end and drop off on to the floor. At first we all laughed and said that the shelf must be a bit warped, but Lesley, looking puzzled, said that it was perfectly straight and she didn't know why it was happening.

'Look!' she said, as she put another plate on the shelf. Lo and behold, it slowly edged its way to the end, teetered for a second, then dropped to the floor with a crash.

'I'm not doing anything,' she exclaimed, 'it just seems to be moving on its own.'

I looked up from my mug of tea to catch sight of a male spirit, chuckling to himself, standing directly beside Lesley. In a moment of telepathic recognition, his awareness focused directly on mine, he looked into my eyes, and I knew that he knew I could see him. Before I could say out loud to Jane that I thought there was a spirit man among us, he picked up a plate Lesley had just placed on the shelf and threw it across the room, hitting the wall inches away from Jane's head. She stood riveted to the spot in fear.

All hell broke loose. I can't remember who screamed first, but I know we all did and ran out of the kitchen as if our lives depended on it. Even I was trembling, and I see spirits all the time. As it happened this was the first occasion I had witnessed a spirit able to affect our earthly dimension, and it was just as much of a shock to me as it was to the other girls.

We all stood outside the room, looking in fearfully from the doorway. I bravely said I would go back inside while the others hid behind the door, too scared to look. As I stood in the doorway, not crossing the threshold, I saw the spirit yet again, howling with laughter, not in an evil way but more out of impish delight that he had shocked us and that we knew he was there. I quietly and calmly spoke to him in spirit: 'Who are you?'

Bold as brass, the spirit man smiled back at me cockily – then slammed the heavy kitchen door shut in our faces.

We all screamed again and Lesley continued to sob uncontrollably. This was certainly an out of the ordinary occurrence; it was utter mayhem. With all this commotion going on in a place where loud whispers were the preferred means of communication, it was no wonder that patients and partners came rushing out to see what could possibly be going on.

Astonishment and disbelief were expressed, but four witnesses to any event, however bizarre it may seem, are not easily discounted.

Despite seeing all manner of spirit from a child, I had never experienced anything of this nature before. Although I now understand that many have experienced these unruly sightings, they are not always the work of disturbed spirits. Yes, there are cases when the underlying intention is evil, but I didn't feel this from our particular spirit at all. All I could feel was a sense of pent-up frustration and anger, as though he was trying to reveal something to us. What and why, I don't know.

Maybe by showing us he was there, he could find a solution to his problem. Maybe our acknowledgement that he still existed was all he wanted.

Jean, the wages secretary and office manager, announced to the partners that they had to do something, and pretty sharpish, or they would not only have an unfriendly ghost to worry about, but no staff to run the surgeries!

No one quite knew what to do, but all eyes seemed to be on me. Why? I thought I had kept my spiritual gift undercover quite successfully. Apparently not. I can only assume Jane had been talking to the others about me. It must have seemed to them that I would have had some experience in dealing with the problem.

Taking Jane to one side, I assured her that this sort of encounter was as alien to me as it was to her. I had no idea what to do for the best and did not want to call attention to my spiritual abilities before my bosses.

The senior partner made a decision on our behalf. He calmly announced that he was ringing the Cathedral Chaplain to see if an exorcism could be arranged – all very matter-of-fact, as if he were telephoning Rentokil to tackle a rodent infestation.

I don't know if any of you have ever visited the City of

Chester? If you haven't, then put it on your to-do list, as Chester Cathedral is one of the most beautiful you will ever see. It is situated near the Town Hall in the middle of the city, surrounded by the medieval old town. The whole area oozes history, so it's not surprising that it would have many hauntings and instances of spiritual activity.

Our boss seemed to be well connected. Cathedral clerics came to the surgery within the hour, most probably because the partners realised we wouldn't go on working unless the exorcism was arranged quickly. A meeting was called (not in the kitchen I might add!) and the partners and clergy decided that all staff members had to be present during the ceremony. An exorcism was arranged for the following morning before we started work.

No one, including myself, had ever come across anything like this before and I have to say we were all pretty nervous of what lay ahead. The consensus amongst the staff, who I might add became specialists on the subject within an afternoon, was that we had had an encounter with an unruly spirit or poltergeist. The name originates from the old German for 'noisy spirit'. Traditionally they are neither ghost nor spirit, but they do exist and are a type of loose spiritual energy, causing chaos and destruction at different levels depending on their psyche.

When I arrived home and shared the day's unusual experience over tea, I can't say I met with any sympathy from my parents. My father just laughed at our foolishness, though my mother stayed silent. My father insisted we all had too much imagination and the partners were just playing up to us by inviting the Church to participate in the whole charade. In retaliation, I argued that the partners, who were very educated men, thought the visitation was real or why would they have the building exorcised? Dad was at a loss for words, but his scepticism remained unaltered.

Sam, however, despite not making an appearance throughout

all this activity at work, said the spirit was trying to catch my attention because it knew I was aware of spirit people.

Arriving at work the next day, we all gathered outside in the car park until the priest who was to perform the exorcism arrived. My father gave me a lift to work; maybe curiosity about our conversation the night before had taken hold or maybe he didn't believe this exorcism was really going to happen. His mouth dropped open when he saw the partners and staff assembling for it. The priest was already there and I thought I was late, but my friends cheerfully announced as I climbed out of the car that they were all bright and early for this extraordinary event. I could see by my dad's expression that he was a little startled by this. As I closed the car door, he asked me, 'Helen – will you be OK?'

I smiled back and said: 'I'll have to tell you tonight!'

I could feel by the tension among them that everyone just wanted to have this experience over with. The priest gave each of us a blessing with holy water before we entered the building. As he looked at me before sprinkling on the water, he peered deep into my eyes as though he could see into my soul.

'There's something lovingly different about you,' he said openly, in front of all the others. I felt embarrassed. He had said nothing to anyone else. Perhaps as a priest he could sense that I possessed the gift of healing.

Now it was official, the exorcism was about to begin and no one knew what to expect. We had all had our blessing and it was time to enter the building. The priest said he wanted to start at the top and work down. The top floor contained the attic room, the flat where Mrs C and her husband lived, and several stock rooms.

Every room received a prayer, and the priest blessed each of them with holy water.

Surprisingly I couldn't spiritually sense a thing, nor could I see any spirits. Of all the times I had been in the stock rooms before, this was a first – not to feel anything strange.

The upstairs stock rooms had a reputation for feeling eerie and cold, even when the heating was on full. From my own experience, it always felt as though something wasn't quite right up here. On occasion the ceiling light had a habit of switching itself off for no reason, despite the partners having had an electrician in several times to attend to the problem. Sometimes there was a cold draught coming from nowhere, and once the door slammed shut of its own accord behind me, despite there being no draught. One might blame this all on our over-active imaginations, but the staff felt it was much more than that as they had all felt the same misgivings. If any of us had to go up alone to fetch supplies, we would rush in and out as fast as we could.

So the upstairs was spirit-free and duly blessed. Even Mrs C's big fat tabby cat, which hardly ever moved from the landing, had had a sprinkling of holy water. Everything was going fine as we proceeded a floor lower, to where Mr Sowerby and Mr Jones had their surgeries. That too went without incident. When we started to descend the stairs to the hallway and reception area, that was when I started to feel the hairs on the back of my neck stand up.

I couldn't see anything, I just felt cold. Very cold. We were now outside the room where it had all started. Slowly the heavy door was opened to reveal the kitchen exactly as we had left it yesterday. We all braced ourselves, expecting crockery to come flying out. But as the priest said his prayers, nothing happened and we breathed a sigh of relief.

However, when we started to walk out of the kitchen and back into the reception area, the hairs on my neck started to bristle again. Whatever we were looking for was here.

The priest stopped in his tracks as though he too sensed a change in the atmosphere. Melodramatically, a sudden beam of sunlight came shooting through the large sash window and brightly illuminated our faces. The priest held out his Bible and started to pray again, a little more earnestly and an octave lower, as if a spirit had silently confronted him. I am sure the other girls were having the same adrenalin rush that I was experiencing: however, some wanted to giggle, some to cry. The girl next to me was trembling with fear. We all huddled close together as if our lives depended on it.

What the priest failed to realise was that the soul he was praying for was not in front of him but directly in front of me! I stood riveted to the spot as the priest directed us all to move forward once he had ended the verse. The priest knew I was sensing something so he held up his hand to stop the movement of the crowd and asked if I was all right. Not moving a muscle and staring straight ahead of me, I remained motionless. The others saw that I was not responding and the priest asked me if I could feel anything. I stared blankly, unable to speak . . . the spirit was that of our plate-thrower. He was a young man dressed in a leather waistcoat, with a dirty white shirt and dark brown-black breeches beneath. I could tell by his clothing that he was from a different era; to me it looked like the Elizabethan period, or possibly the late Middle Ages.

The spirit of the young man started to yell at me in what at first sounded like a foreign language, though on reflection it was most probably an Old English dialect. Nonetheless, I couldn't understand. He kept turning around, looking over his shoulder as if he were scared. I had the feeling others were chasing him. Spiritually, I sensed his predicament and images appeared in my mind. He had been accused of stealing something from this household – a clergyman's house.

My eyes flickered momentarily towards the window and the car park beyond, but what I saw was not parked cars but a tall wooden gallows erected outside with a man – this man – dangling from a noose, surrounded by a mob of onlookers cheering with approval.

It felt as if I had been standing watching this sight for ages, but it could only have been a couple of seconds in real time.

The patch of ground where Bank House stood was originally known as Whitefriars after the monastic order that had built its residence there around 1277. Over the years the monks acquired the land to build seven more houses so that they could expand their order and then build themselves a church. The White Friars' priory became a popular burial place for the richer members of Chester society in the Middle Ages, but later fell into decline. It seemed as if our spiritual visitor dated back to this era when he had suffered a violent death – though whether this was justly or unjustly, I had no knowledge.

The link was broken and my access to the spiritual realm had gone. I didn't know what to do. Talking openly to the crowd about what I had just witnessed was going to throw me into the spot-light, and right now, I didn't want to appear any different from my peers. My days at Bank House were spent seeking to be noticed for who I was, not for what I was.

Looking directly at the priest, I forced a smile and said, 'Oh. It's nothing.'

Looking sceptical, the priest turned around, the volume of his prayers became noticeably louder and the holy water was sprinkled with more fervour as the Bank House staff were led like sheep onto the next room.

Finally, after about forty minutes of rambling around the building, we seemed to reach the end of the exorcism. The mood had become lighter because everyone but me thought we had successfully concluded it.

My senses were telling me that the spirit person felt scared, cornered, and angry. I thought he believed some sort of injustice had been committed, though I still couldn't quite understand if he was guilty or not of a crime. In the Middle Ages people were often put to death for stealing. Maybe this poor soul had taken something he believed to be trivial, but ended up on the gallows for it.

The priest said a final prayer and we were all told to go to our surgeries and resume work. I never saw the apparition again after that day.

We had no more plate-smashing in that room; nor did we feel cold upstairs in the stock rooms. Now, the radiators' warmth could be felt everywhere at long last. Bank House was at peace.

Had the young man's soul finally been laid to rest?

I suppose we will never know for sure.

13

The Second Step

Apart from all my college activities I also started to attend the local Spiritualist Church because I was desperate to meet other people who could see what I could and mix with people who were similar to myself. How wrong I was! Please don't misunderstand me, the church was a meeting place for many lovely people, but they weren't at all what I expected. For starters, I was just a teenager and the average age of everybody else was about sixty. From my teenage point of view, they were all old people – very old people. Secondly, I wanted to meet people who could see the spirit world and speak to their Guides in the same way as I could. I wanted to discover how they were treated at home by their parents and family, and any other people who might not under-stand about spiritual sight.

It's not easy going around feeling that you are odd or different, especially for a teenager. I had experienced prejudice for as long as I could remember from the very people who were meant to love me the most: my mum and dad. The trouble was, there wasn't anybody else at the church who could actually see and talk to the spirit world in the way I could. What made it worse was that the members themselves had an unofficial hierarchy of those who could 'see a little' to those who could 'see a little more'! Nobody liked the way a teenager came in with her stories of healing the sick and in-depth tutorials direct from a spirit guide!

In one of my early visits to the Spiritualist Church I was offering healing to a young woman called Jenny. She was about eight years older than me and had hurt her neck in a car accident. The seniors at the church asked if I could help her as she was in terrible pain. On reflection I believe they were testing me that day, to determine whether I could offer healing in the manner I had told them.

As soon as I put my hands on her ailing neck and shoulder a room full of spirit doctors appeared by my side. One of the doctors said that I should look at her shoulder and, despite her being fully clothed, I would *see* within my mind's eye the muscles and inner workings of it. Jenny closed her eyes and I started to heal her. With the laying on of my hands, I could feel the intensity of heat travelling through my body and into my palms as I worked. Then, with no warning, my eyes refocused and I could *see* for the first time the actual muscles and nerves, like a detailed 3D anatomical picture. I was shocked as one of the spirit doctors proceeded to walk over to me, pointing to her shoulder and saying that a nerve was trapped, causing her pain.

'Look,' I heard him say to me as he pointed to a particular area of her shoulder, 'can you see that?' I nodded. 'Can you see the nerve and can you see where it is trapped?' Again, I nodded silently. Then I administered the healing instinctively as I normally do, healing the damaged tissue within, gently moving and releasing the nerve.

The doctors in spirit congratulated me. 'You have done well

Helen, but this is just an introduction to your potential abilities.' I was shocked, because to see into the body as I had just done seemed amazing to me and yet my teachers were implying it was a more basic skill. One of the doctors further explained, 'You are able to look through the body and focus to any depth required, as if the bones, muscles and organs can be sliced for you to observe.'

With renewed enthusiasm, I tried to focus my spiritual sight at different levels of Jenny's upper arm muscle. At first it appeared thick and large, and I didn't know if I was actually doing the observing correctly. Then it happened, everything came into focus and no matter at what depth I was viewing, the area became clear with exact detail. It was as if the muscle itself was made up of thousands of layers of thin-sliced tissue. Within the body I could also see the blood vessels and the blood flowing through them, one pump at a time. Even more remarkably, the blood itself became visible, as if I could see each and every particle of its make-up.

It wasn't too long before no matter where in the body I focused, I could see every detail of its organic constitution.

The spiritual doctors were pleased at my progress and added, 'Soon, you will be able to see into the mind and determine the level of hormones and chemicals that are released into the body and then in time alter the amounts to balance the body.'

Despite my excitement, I couldn't help questioning the feasibility of such skills. Although still young, I noticed that as I matured, an inner part of me had started to question my spiritual growth. It wasn't that I didn't trust my spiritual teachers; it was that as a young adult I was not as accepting of everything as I had been as a child.

The doctors must have sensed my doubts, because they reassured me by saying, 'It is right that you question everything.

By questioning you will intuitively affirm your abilities and then they will expand and become easier to use.'

My spiritual senses scanned Jenny's body and for the most part, apart from her trapped nerve, she seemed fit and healthy.

Jenny's session ended and I thought no more about it. A week or so later my senior at the church notified me that Jenny was feeling much better. Apparently she was so tired afterwards she went straight home to bed. When she woke all the pain, and the feeling of pins and needles she had suffered, had gone. If that was a test by my seniors, I believe I must have passed with flying colours, although they never said so. However, Jenny contacted me personally and told me that her healing was a miracle as she had been suffering for a whole year before that.

Another miracle that happened around that time was the way I didn't strangle the laboratory staff at Bank House when one of their famous practical jokes went wrong one day, leaving me locked and afraid in an underground cellar.

The staff in the laboratory had a habit of playing pranks on me. Some were harmless, like when they planted rubber biscuits on the plate during breaktime or gave me a bottle of mustard to open and a furry object flew out as I unscrewed the lid.

Some were not so nice, but the laboratory men thought they were such fun!

To be honest, I took the pranks in my stride. After all, there are only so many rubber spiders you can be scared of before it becomes boring, even for middle-aged men. The one prank that definitely did backfire was when they locked me in the cellar.

Underneath the surgery a cellar housed all the hydraulics for the dental chairs. Part of my job involved draining off the excess pressure that built up from using the high-pressure drills. Once a month, it was a nurse's job to release the air – and, as I was the junior, that job was my pleasure alone.

I hated going into the cellar as the stairs going down were very steep and releasing the air was a messy job. Being down there was certainly a bit scary, especially as a couple of months before we'd had an exorcism ceremony in our workplace.

What was most disconcerting about the job was the noise. It was similar to that of a pressure cooker when it was hissing, only this pressure cooker was much larger and much louder. Imagine having to bleed air from a machine as big as a double cooker, while crouched down on your knees, fiddling with a tiny valve. On reflection, I'm surprised I was allowed to do this kind of work. Health and Safety must have been non-existent in those days – and maybe we were better off for that!

On this one occasion, I left the cellar keys in the lock with the door ajar, as I always did, and went down to complete the task. As you can imagine, in such an old building the cellar reflected a lot of history. You could plainly see remnants of structures from different eras dating back hundreds of years. Most prominent were some bricked-up arches that may once have led to an underground walkway, which many believed the monks and priests of a bygone era had used to navigate their monastic buildings without anyone seeing them.

As a joke someone had left an anatomical skeleton we used for training sitting in a discarded dental chair, as though a patient had been there for years waiting for treatment and had wasted away. I chuckled to myself. Poor Larry the skeleton!

Focusing on the fact that there is nothing to fear but fear itself, I kept my mind solely on the job. Suddenly, halfway through the task, the lights went out and everything went pitch black. I heard the upstairs door slam shut and someone locked it behind them with the set of keys I had left in it. I was trapped!

My fingers were still holding the valve so, even though I couldn't see, I immediately turned it back to its original position.

It was too black for me to make out anything, so for safety's sake I stood up and started to shout out that I was down below working and would someone please open the door and put the lights back on? I waited. I shouted again, a little louder. Again! And again! Nothing happened.

The steep stairs up to the ground floor were impossible to see even after my eyes had started to adjust to the blackness. There were no light sources so in effect I was blind. The only way out was to find the stairs and climb up to the door. I tried to visualise the layout as I had been down there several times before. Despite my best efforts at recollecting it, I groped around the walls like a blindwoman, becoming more disorientated with each movement I made.

In the silence of the cellar I heard a noise. All my senses were affected so I couldn't make out if the noise was of the physical or spiritual kind. From the dark the smallest of glows appeared, revealing what I can only describe as a monk standing by me reciting a prayer. Rigid with fear, I screamed at the top of my voice, yelling and demanding to be let out! Eventually I realised no one was going to help me.

Fortunately, the monk disappeared as quickly as he'd appeared. Once again I was alone in the darkness. How long would I have to be here before someone noticed I was absent? I felt the objects around me, trying to work my way towards the staircase. This was hopeless.

I was terrified, locked all alone in the darkness of the cellar. I daren't move far as to do so might cause me injury, but I had to find a way out. I started to cry. As I couldn't find a tissue on me and no one was looking, I wiped my nose on the back of my hand.

In my mind I begged for Sam to come. As a general rule I

never call him. In fact, he usually arrives of his own accord at such times. Maybe he was here and I just couldn't see him in the darkness. That would be a first, I thought, as Sam can usually light up anywhere!

The next instant I knew he had arrived. Not that I could see him, but in my mind's eye I could spiritually sense his presence. Not only could I sense Sam, but also a second person with him. Maybe by the spiritual intensity the visitor radiated, I discerned this visitor was an Angel. Knowing I had company, albeit in spirit, I was not as fearful despite the darkness.

Sam began to explain the purpose of their visit: he told me his visitor was similar to the spirit Guide who had visited me in the Bank House garden, offering teaching about the Sacred Steps to Truth.

He continued with fatherly pride in his voice: 'You are right to discern that the visitor is an Angel. This demonstrates how progressed you are becoming.'

Very flattering, I thought. But if this really was an Angel, why didn't he light up the room? As if in answer to my question, Sam said it was best if I only sensed him. 'While in the darkness, we have your complete attention.'

As if to acknowledge my inner fear, he tried to settle me. 'Don't be afraid, chile, no harm will come to you.' That was all well and good, I thought, but was this really the time or place to meet an Angel, especially in the dark?

As Sam talked I could feel myself starting to calm down. I intuitively realised he wasn't here to help me escape, he had actually come to give me one of my spiritual tutorials. Why that time in particular I don't know! That is one of the spiritual abilities I find most difficult to explain – that you just know something is true without being told.

As it happened I didn't need physical light to see Sam or his companion. By focusing on their spiritual presence I could see them both quite clearly in 'my mind's eye'. Both Sam and the Angel looked at me, smiling, radiating a compassion I was not able to put into words.

Sam spoke softly in his teaching tones, explaining that not all Angels or higher Guides look as I imagined them to; neither do they all have names given to them by the living world. He told me that Angels in their truest form in fact don't have names, but meanings or reasons to visit.

'Angels bring different forms of energy according to the gifts they possess. Some may give healing, some may give loving thoughts.' Poor Sam, I thought, he may as well be talking to the wall as I was barely taking in what he was saying. All I needed to know was how I could find a way out of the cellar. I wasn't in the mood to be entertained or educated, even if his visitor was an Angel! Despite my thoughts, (which I knew he would hear), he continued talking, ignoring my intolerance. 'You have met this Angel's messenger before, in the garden when you first started here, do you remember?'

My thoughts returned to my first days here, to collecting the crown and having a strange conversation with a shabbily dressed man who said he was a higher Guide. 'So *that* Guide was the messenger for *this* Angel?' I confirmed, hoping this might be the end to the conversation.

'Yes, that is correct,' Sam continued. 'The content is so important that the Angel is delivering the message directly to you because you need to feel its urgency. It is a message of hope for the world to adopt compassion and humility, then they will understand the Second Step to the Sacred Truth.'

My patience was running thin by this stage. All I wanted was to escape from this cellar; it was not the best time to talk to me – Angel or no Angel! I was confused . . . I could now hear people above me, walking about in the surgery. I could barely make out their muffled voices. Work must have started, which meant I had been stuck down in the cellar for about ten minutes.

The Angel never spoke. However his presence was in my mind; somehow we were linked as one. I could see thoughts and pictures flicker fast past my eyes like a slide-show. Images of the earth and of children starving. Images of people suffering illness, seemingly with no basic health care, being left alone to suffer and die. Other images included visions of the poor, depressed and lonely – people unable to cope with life. Images of children being beaten, abused or abandoned, crying out through lack of love and attention. Areas of woodland, wasted, grey and lifeless, with large machines ploughing through more green land, creating only devastation. Animals and habitats destroyed, disorientating and starving thousands of species. The visions just went on and on – unrelenting. My heart raced with adrenalin.

It upset me and I couldn't help but start to grow panicky. 'Why are you here? Why am I seeing these images? Why now?' I cried to this Angel and Sam, as I watched the phantasmagoria float past my eyes. 'Why are you showing me all of this?'

Sam smiled kindly. 'This Angel is here to bestow compassion and humility, Helen. By feeling this energy, you will radiate it out towards others. You see, these visions are not only for you to understand and feel, but more importantly for you to pass on to others. Your home, your life, your love for humanity, is being destroyed by your fellow man. It is up to you along with certain others to try and educate through your healing messages.'

Educate . . . me? How can I educate anyone, I thought, I am only a young girl?

As if in answer to my thought, Sam smiled again. 'You will know one day . . . you have to grow spiritually first.'

This was the mid-seventies, so what was Sam talking about? The world looked fine as far as I could see.

He continued, 'I speak for this Angel as there is much to look forward to and you will help bring this message of hope. It has to be heard for the earth to survive.'

Survive what? I thought.

Insistently he continued talking: 'The message of hope is the message to love and respect yourself, plants and animals, everything . . . you will help teach how to work spiritually towards this in the future. This is the Second Stage of the Path to the Sacred Truth.

'Your nations of people must work harder and take a greater responsibility for their actions. To believe that things will improve is a positive thought, and to implement it by working to achieve that outcome is accepting your problem. Many understand this already by seeing the planet as it really is. For every problem there is an answer, but sometimes we do not like to hear that answer, nor do we like to initiate sweeping change. Good and positivity will come to you if you think positively, but you also have to recognise where the problems are. No matter how hard they are to solve, you have to rectify them. The ripple of small changes then expands into positive waves. In the next fifty years you will be mopping up the mess that man's thoughtless profiteering has created.'

I heard what Sam was saying, but didn't fully understand all its implications – how could I? And I was feeling a bit scared. It all sounded very far-fetched to me. We had only just acquired a new colour TV. Astronauts had landed on the moon a few years before. Great progress was being made, so why should earth start to suffer so quickly? No one I had ever spoken to had mentioned any adverse changes going on around us. There was nothing in the news that said times were bad in our world – apart from when it came to paying taxes. All my father moaned about was the price of petrol, which was robbery at 76 pence per gallon. He maintained the world as we knew it would change if petrol reached £1 a gallon – but no government would ever let that happen!

Sam went on, regardless of what I thought, obviously intent on getting this Angel's message across to me: 'Let me try to explain further. For instance, let's say someone was overweight and they knew they needed to lose weight in order to look better and feel healthier. It is not an easy task for someone to lose weight. Going on a diet, changing the foods you eat, means altering your thought patterns and routine. If you think positively and really believe you can achieve this goal, then of course that will give you the strength actually to make the necessary changes. However, you are the only person who can do this. It cannot be done for you. *You* have to understand that it is you who has to change your diet. No one else can do it.

'Likewise, the spirit world cannot make technological changes for mankind to alter its environment; it is something that has to come from you, the people! Energy and positive attitude starts the process off by nudging you, helping you to visualise and achieve your goal. Ultimately it is your efforts that will bring about changes for the better.

'Helen, think of the world as though it has to go on a diet. On a larger scale, this may mean political regimes and politicians negotiating extreme policies to change society and the way it acts and thinks. This doesn't mean indoctrination, it means people collectively recognising that the world needs their help. It may even be an unpopular and difficult medicine to administer as these changes can only take place if the collective will understands and respects the fact that change is needed in order for the world to survive in the way they want it to. By this I mean still having plentiful food, oceans that are unpolluted, water supplies, animals and medicines. They have to understand there must be a greater knowledge and respect of life itself to achieve such an outcome.

'Everything we do should have the intent of love connected to it. Your generation and future generations will be cleaning up the mess in the world for some time to come. What is important is that you know the Angels in spirit need this message to be heard, and fast. They want to help. There is urgency.'

My mind was now in overdrive. 'What about killing animals to eat?' I asked. 'That doesn't have intent of love – only hunger.'

Sam smiled as if I were asking a puerile question. 'Yes, you are right, but your intent of love is to feed your family. Harm and greed only occur when you take too much. There is a cycle to everything, you know this. It is when that cycle of life is put at risk through man's own greed that the laws of balance start to implode, and it is then man faces his own worst peril . . . himself. The earth will continue to function whether you are here or not. It will reshape itself in some form or another, but you will not survive as human beings in that case. The earth is precious and needs help – now!'

I was seventeen and hearing that my world was about to face such chaotic changes was terrifying. What could I do to help? I have to tell someone, I thought – but who would listen? I was overwhelmed with emotion. I wanted to cry. I felt humble, guilty, sad, almost ashamed. I didn't understand why I felt like this.

Sam brought our tutorial to a close.

I wasn't sure if I was relieved or not. Suddenly I felt uneasy. No one had ever talked to me about any sort of planet-wide problems. At Christmas charitable organisations collected for Africa and Pakistan as there were wars raging and children were starving. I remembered seeing heart-rending pictures on charity envelopes, encouraging me to give money, but that was about all I knew regarding the world's problems.

I was overwhelmed. All I wanted at that moment was to reach the stairs and get out of the cellar. As if they heard my plea, Sam and the Angel materialised in front of my eyes. Their auras became bright and the Angel stretched out an arm. I could now see the Angel's soft, gentle face. She looked graceful and beautiful. Her robe was shimmering as if made of the thinnest luminescent golden thread. From her shoulders, bursts of energy shot out, as if her back was engulfed in spikes of rod-like flame. As the spikes emanated they dripped thick golden energy in a waterfall down to the floor. I could see the steps leading to the cellar door now. My escape route was clearly lit. The Angel smiled lovingly at me, but not one word was spoken.

'Go now,' Sam said, 'get yourself cleaned up.'

At that moment I could hear Jean on the other side of the door, turning the key in the lock. I called out to her, she opened the door and turned the light on. She howled with laughter when she caught sight of me running up the stairs.

I looked back but there was nothing there except the usual dreary contents of the cellar. My visitors had disappeared.

I had inadvertently touched the walls before I could see any light and then put my hands on my white overalls. My hands were now black and grimey, and my nice white uniform had handprints all over it. Even my face was smudged with black where I had wiped my nose or touched my hair. I was a real mess.

'Who locked you in?' Jean asked. 'Oh, Sarah, look at the state of you! How long have you been down here? One of the patients screamed when she was sitting in the dental chair waiting for the team, and came running out to reception, saying she could hear voices from the cellar! I think she thought she'd heard a ghost.'

Little did Jean know I just had.

I looked at my watch. I couldn't believe it. I had hardly been down there ten minutes, but it had seemed like hours.

As it turned out, it was Ken from the dental lab across the garden who had locked me in. He had seen that I was cleaning out the compressor, thought it would be a hilarious prank and locked me in. Like all jokers, he didn't think his actions through and realise that I would be terrified.

Mr Sowerby was furious that I had to clean myself up and change my uniform as it held up my work for the morning. The partners did not appreciate the prank and Ken was reprimanded. He, however, still thought the whole incident a hoot and laughed about it for weeks.

The next time I had to make a collection from the laboratory all the men were a bit sheepish. Ken silently handed me a note. On it he'd written: '*Sorry . . . it seemed funny at the time.*'

As Ken was deaf I wrote a note back and placed it on the table next to him, '*Still friends . . . But don't do it again!*'

Now I think I do understand a little of the Angel's message given to me that day in the cellar. We do need to send out a message of hope and love towards ourselves. It needs to reflect first within us, then towards others, and most of all towards helping our planet – for it is *now* it needs to heal.

In the thirty-five years since this message was relayed to me, the earth has undergone great changes by the introduction of technology. I never thought so many changes would happen in so short a time, but obviously the spirit world knew better. The love the Angel spoke about is, I think, a form of moral respect for everything we come into contact with. Without such respect and loyalty nothing has any value. A relationship, a job, our life, the earth . . . they all need to be treated with loyalty and respect.

The images the Angel showed me that day in the cellar have remained vivid in my mind to this day. The message to show compassion and humility has achieved its purpose. I now understand that unless we show these qualities towards the earth, its environments and all its inhabitants will certainly endure some sort of natural destruction. During the seventies the television and radio weren't filled with media messages of doom and gloom prophesying environmental tragedy; apparently at that time we all felt we had nothing to worry about. And yet, thanks to the Angel's teaching, I was made aware at that date of much that has become of pressing concern in later decades.

Predictions are funny things, it seems to me. We all want to hear them, but we rarely really want to listen.

I have.

Have you?

14

Blind Date With a Stranger

My escapade in the cellar caused hilarity within the staff room. It was talked about for weeks. Of course, I didn't tell any of them about my encounter with Sam and the Angel. Having said that, I did feel a greater sense of spiritual urgency thanks to what I had learned. Maybe this is one of the reasons why I felt as though I had to start telling more people what I could see.

It was a dilemma, because on the one hand I tried to keep a low profile at work, as there I could just be me, and on the other I had the spirit world urging me to speak out to a wider audience. Also, on the more practical side, I had enrolled to take my DSA (Dental Surgery Assistant) qualification and was studying hard for my first-year exams. This meant having to travel to Liverpool for a night-school course every Thursday evening. Life was pretty busy for me already without taking on more commitments of the spiritual kind.

Having enrolled late in the course I had either to study for an extra year or study harder and take my chances that I could catch up the six months I had already missed.

My Colleague Natalie had passed her exam and, being about three or four years older than me, had received a salary rise from the surgery. I was determined not to be outdone by her, so decided to cram my two years of studying into just eighteen months.

My mother made my father drive me to Liverpool for my course, and although he never complained about making the journey I felt quite guilty, as sometimes he really wasn't well enough to take me. This prompted me to start taking some driving lessons, financed by my meagre wages.

Although I was only seventeen at the time, driving was something I took to straight away. My mother decided it was time she should learn too, and in an attempt to encourage her, my father bought an old Vauxhall Viva. Jokingly, he said that the first person to pass their test could have the car. That was music to my ears, and all I needed to encourage me.

Eventually the day of my driving test arrived. I had arranged with Mr Sowerby to take two hours off from work. Neither of my parents gave much thought to my test over breakfast that morning, but in my mind I had already decided the car was mine.

As my test started, in the rear-view mirror I could see Sam in the back of the car. I had a little chuckle to myself, wondering what the examiner would have made of the tall black stranger in the passenger seat behind, if he could have seen him.

Everything went well and I was ecstatic when my examiner announced I had passed my test – first time!

On my returning to work, Mr Sowerby asked, 'Well, Sarah, how did it go?' and seemed to beam with pride when I told him the good news.

When I arrived home that night, I was so excited my stomach was fluttering with butterflies. Granddad was the first to hear and proudly wrapped his arms around me, telling me how wonderful it was and how being able to drive would change my life.

Mum and Dad arrived home an hour later, but neither of them bothered to ask the result of my test. Eventually I had to prompt them: 'Well, aren't you going to ask me how I got on today with my driving test?'

My dad looked at me and patronisingly replied, 'Well, never mind, love. I'm sure you will pass next time.'

I couldn't believe my ears. Yet again he seemed to have a complete lack of faith in me. I burst into tears and shouted at the top of my voice: 'No, Dad. I passed actually!'

I dashed out of the room and into my bedroom so I could be alone. Some time later he did come to see me and apologise.

Natalie was a little jealous when I started to come to work in what I called my new car, as she hadn't passed her test. However, she was much happier these days due to dating a guy called Selwyn, with whom she seemed totally smitten. It was the first time I had ever seen her like this, all demure and giggly, acting like a little girl whenever she mentioned his name.

At each break or lunch hour we talked about Selwyn . . . or rather Natalie did! He was a good old Welsh lad, with a thick North Wales accent. Every time he called the surgery on the phone at breaktime she would glow with pride. Flowery thoughts filled her head and our ears. She never stopped talking about her new beau.

When Selwyn was in Chester working with the town planners, he took her out for lunch, much to Natalie's pride. We would peep out of the window, watching them walk hand in hand up the road, like love's young dream. Natalie was truly in love and would float back into work on a cloud of joy.

It wasn't until about seven months later that I had my first encounter with the beloved Selwyn was when I met him and

Natalie in the local coffee shop we all frequented. As I was introduced, I caught the tail end of their conversation. It appeared that Selwyn wanted to take Natalie out to a dance that weekend, but he had also promised to meet his best friend. As they sat, locked arm in arm, he proposed a blind date between his friend and me.

Within an instant Sam was there, demanding my full attention. I had never felt him jump into my senses so quickly. 'Are you sure you want to go along with this idea?' he questioned me. I wondered why he would even want to discuss it.

Selwyn pleaded, saying that if I went along to accompany his friend then Natalie and he could still meet up and they would be grateful to me for ever.

What do you do in a situation like this? Do you let your friend down and decline the proposal as she sits looking adoringly into her boyfriend's eyes? Do you ignore his pleading? Or do you throw caution to the wind and go out for the night? It was only one date after all. What could go wrong? In silence I stood frozen as the sounds of the hissing coffee machine blended into the background. I felt numb for some reason, I had no idea why, but eventually I agreed to their demands just to keep my friend happy.

I don't know if you have ever been on a blind date? If you haven't, then I have to tell you it is a very strange experience. The prospect of spending an evening with someone I had never even spoken to before made me really nervous. This feeling was compounded as something inside me hinted that this was going to be a life-changing experience, and I wasn't sure if it was one I should really have.

Setting my fears aside, I decided to ignore my inner doubts, for Natalie's sake, and just go with the flow. She assured me that I only had to stay a couple of hours, then I could make an excuse and leave if I didn't like him. According to her I didn't ever need to meet him again, and Selwyn was buying the meal and tickets for the dance so at worst it would be a free meal out. I have since learned there is no such thing as a free anything in life!

That's how I met my first husband, John.

I can't say it was love at first sight, but he was a nice, good-looking polite man and something must have clicked between us and we were soon a courting couple. I was quite flattered that somebody from what seemed to be a more traditional and privileged background was so interested in me, and we did seem to enjoy each other's company. Also, I suppose I was dazzled by his aspirations and confidence. Although not in awe of it, he didn't have a problem with my spiritual sight. After all it was part of who I was and if we were going to be a couple he had to know something about this special part of me. It was still early in our relationship so I restricted the conversations we had, never really going much deeper than talking in general terms. I liked him and having experienced my parents' lack of understanding, I didn't want to risk yet more rejection. By his request, though, we did not discuss my abilities in front of his parents.

When I was taken home to meet his mum and dad, it was a novelty to meet a mum who could stay at home, prepare dinner and bake cakes all day. I am not saying that his parents were rich or that they hadn't had their own tough times. After all, they were farmers and worked long hard hours during parts of the day when we were fast asleep. His mum often had to feed droves of men who came trudging through her kitchen during harvest time or lambing. But her children never had to let themselves into an empty home or wait for their parents to return home from work. John's tea was waiting on the kitchen table, with the house all spick and span, when he entered the door.

In my mind, I had always held the notion that when you met

your soul-mate, Angels would bring out their harps, bells would ring in your head, and pangs of love would pierce your soul like a thousand arrows. No such thing happened, but I did feel that we loved each other in a practical way. A way where we knew we could work together in harmony. I waited to see if our love would develop into the all-consuming passion described in romantic novels.

Part of the attraction was that he seemed to be a good man at heart. A man of integrity, a man whose family had solid roots. In my father's eyes he even appeared to be a man of means, as he held down a good job in the architectural department of a growing supermarket chain.

He seemed to offer what I craved: security. And he did seem to love me very much, so it became easy to strengthen our bonds in many ways, including supporting John's hobby of rally car driving. On one occasion, I went out into the depths of a bitterly cold night armed with hot soup and snacks, to watch a rally championship. For several years John had driven rally cars around the North Wales hills, but he also loved to watch the professionals at work.

We positioned ourselves in a designated marshalled safe area to take photographs, but before long Sam appeared and urged me to move from our spot, as I would be in danger. I know from experience that Sam only makes such statements with good reason, but I hesitated, unsure how to tell John. In retrospect, I should have told him everything, that way he would have known at a much earlier stage in our relationship how important Sam was in my life. Sam continued to be insistent that I move well away from the viewing place we had chosen and, as a compromise, I moved back three metres to a field's gate just behind us. I told John that something was telling me that the edge of the road was dangerous and we should stand behind the gate for safety, but he laughed at me saying that we were perfectly safe, as there were no corners for the cars to navigate and they were just going in a straight line.

We could hear the roar of the engines in the darkness as the cars sped towards us. Ahead of us, there was a dip in the road and as the cars drove over it they lifted slightly off the road. One car lost control and swerved in a bid to rectify the deviation. However, it veered right to where John was standing. Fortunately he made a dive behind a tree for protection and the car slammed into it. The occupants were unharmed apart from the car having a nasty bump down the side and without hesitation the driver quickly negotiated their way back onto the road without a second thought for John standing in shock behind the tree. The marshals came running over to see if he was all right.

'Phew!' he said. 'That was a close call.' Then the reality hit, I would most certainly have been injured or possibly killed if I had remained in the spot next to John. I made a remark about how he should trust my spiritual instincts, but he insisted it was just a chance occurrence. We had only known each other for a couple of months and we were becoming close, so I didn't want to push the matter in case it spoilt what was happening between us. Nevertheless, Sam, as usual, knew best.

Although we were growing strong as a couple, the beginning of my relationship with his parents was a little rough, mainly, I feel, because they wanted him to marry a local farmer's daughter. They were good parents and cared deeply for John and his two elder sisters, and they clearly had his best intentions at heart. However, it didn't really affect us and as the weeks passed, our relationship deepened, though, to be honest, I still wasn't sure if it was true love.

I had just had my nineteenth birthday, but my father felt it was a great move for me to settle down and be married. And to be honest I was tired of being at home where I felt continually downtrodden by my parents' lack of enthusiasm for anything to do with my life. Also, it pains me to say, my father was now becoming very ill, often needing my mother and me to nurse him when he had one of his many pneumonia attacks. Inside I was still very angry that he wouldn't stop smoking or have any healing from me to help alleviate his condition. At times I watched helplessly as he had a panic attack, gasping for breath. His deteriorating condition frightened me. My father was dying before my very eyes and there was nothing he would allow me to do to stop it. It was difficult to watch a person I loved so much, crumble to nothing.

Settling down into a relationship seemed a good solution; then I could be independent and less of a burden to them. After all we loved each other and my dad liked my new fiancé. I think he saw in him the same qualities as I did. In Dad's eyes it was a very happy outcome for his daughter to become engaged to such a solid man. Sitting here now, fingers on the keyboard, no matter how hard I try, I can't even remember the occasion of the proposal – that's how remarkable it was. How sad, when such a moment should be a monumental event, affecting the whole of your adult life. Maybe we just drifted into a decision about marriage – I can't remember. What I do know for sure is that it was only about seven months from our first meeting that we walked down the aisle together.

The October wedding happened two months after my nineteenth birthday. In the same week my father was admitted to hospital once again with his debilitating emphysema. Naturally I was devastated that my dad was going to be unable to walk me down the aisle and would miss my big day. However, on the morning of the wedding, unbeknown to me, he signed himself out of hospital and arrived home by taxi. 'I don't know how I have done it but I am here,' he told us. Sam winked at me as he stood by Dad's side, almost supporting him with one arm around his shoulders, and I knew that it was with my Guide's help that this miracle had happened.

It made me cry tears of pride that, ill as my dad was, he had dragged himself out of hospital, barely able to breathe, just to see me down the aisle. At that moment all the family problems we had endured faded away and I loved him more than I could ever put into words. He had shown how much I truly meant to him.

Everything was in place. Dressed in my white wedding gown, with my schoolfriend Denise and workmate Natalie as my bridesmaids, we laughed openly as we waited for Denise's mum to arrive in the Silver Cloud Rolls-Royce. She had taken it out of its resting place in the garage, polished it up, and was now acting as chauffeur for the day. She even wore a chauffeur's cap! Goodness knows where that had come from. I couldn't believe my eyes when she eventually rolled up to the door as Denise had secretly arranged it with my mother when they went to hire the cars without me.

Denise's mum was in the front seat, but unknown to my entourage Denise's dad in spirit was co-driver, sitting next to his wife. He had come to send his love to me and to his daughter, whom he said looked radiant as bridesmaid.

Dad and I had our last few moments together before we set off for the church, just the two of us for the final time with me as a single girl. We sat and chatted in the lounge before the car arrived back for us, my father still weak and barely able to move from his illness. Confiding in him, I said that during my engagement I had frequently asked myself if I was making the right choice and wondered should I call off the wedding? I wasn't sure. Not the sort of doubts I really wanted, especially as this was my big day.

His face paled, not only from illness but concern for my welfare.

'I want you to be happy, Helen. I love you and am proud of you, but you have made all these arrangements now and people are waiting at the church. It would be heartbreaking for the poor man if you didn't turn up. I am sure this is just nerves. The feeling will pass and then you will be very happy together. He is a good man.'

I listened to his advice, my eyes welling up with tears. Maybe he was right. It was just nerves, wasn't it?

The doorbell rang and Denise's mum Lillian stood waiting for us to parade in front of the neighbours who had all gathered to see me leave the house. A Rolls-Royce of this quality was rarely seen in these parts, so as much interest was shown in the car as it was in my dress.

My dad smiled and gave me a huge hug, telling me I looked radiant. I knew he really did say this from the heart. For the first time in years, he had managed to show me his feelings. Together we walked to the waiting car.

My father had given me the best big white wedding he could possibly afford, complete with a reception at the Chester Grosvenor Hotel in the middle of the city. The traffic stopped and crowds cheered as my new husband and I walked in on a red carpet like royalty. I think onlookers thought it was a society wedding as we stepped out of the Silver Cloud.

The day went by almost without a hitch. However, halfway through the meal I had my first run-in with my newly acquired in-laws . . . in the ladies' cloakroom of all places. On reflection, maybe I too would be inclined to want to voice my opinion if I felt my child was making a bad decision. So perhaps I shouldn't have been so upset when my new mother-in-law voiced hers. Even so, without that hindsight, her words reduced me to tears on my wedding day as she told me without hesitation that she felt her son could have chosen to marry someone 'better'.

Deep inside me, I felt there was an element of truth to this. Was that why Sam had shaken his head when Selwyn mentioned that blind date months before?

Our honeymoon in Cornwall lasted a week and then we returned to married life in a dormer bungalow we had bought in Prestatyn, North Wales.

My new husband seemed to have accepted the fact that I might not be able to have children. However, I am sure his farming family, knowing of my father's illness and my own infertility problems, considered I wasn't particularly good breeding stock. After a few months of marriage, imagine how astonished I was when, after my doctor's initial diagnosis of wind, I tested positive for pregnancy with my first child. Both Dr Howe and I were dumbfounded and struggled to understand how I'd become pregnant so easily. How could so many doctors have been so wrong?

I knew the answer was most likely because I had received so much healing from my Guides and Angels. They had told me so often enough, but still it was a total surprise to me.

This development was not something we had anticipated during our first year together, but one I embraced as a miracle. Fiona, my first child, was born thirteen months after her father and I walked down the aisle.

My new husband was attentive and caring, but it wasn't long before financial burdens came crashing down upon us. Having a baby so early on was not something we had budgeted for. We were now down to one wage. Luckily it was the boom days of the housing market, and our first home doubled in price within the first year. John decided he wanted to cash in and sell.

In spite of my reluctance to sell our home, he made the decision to do so. The prospect of moving with a new baby was an upheaval I could do without. But we needed to improve our financial position quickly, and my husband decided to buy two terraced houses out of the proceeds of the sale, renovate and sell them on. We would live in the first house while the second was undergoing its makeover. It all sounded like a good plan in theory but, as we all know, even the most meticulous of plans can go wrong. And while the first house was being modernised we had nowhere to live.

My parents had just bought an old bungalow to renovate. My architect husband had convinced them that he should design the renovations and carry out some work in exchange for lodgings for us . . . even though he had also to renovate our own houses.

We were due to move in with my parents. Days prior to the move, a group of gypsy people called at our house. The leader, a rather plump middle-aged lady, stared into my eyes at the door, offering to read my palm for a few pounds. In her hand she held a large bunch of purple heather, for good luck, she said, waving it front of my nose.

Without warning she suddenly lunged forward and grabbed my hand. 'Oooh,' she said, wide-eyed. I was a bit startled as she proceeded to tell me I'd just had a little girl and that I was not happy in my marriage. 'Your man is about to leave and travel a long way from you, possibly abroad,' she said confidently. 'All will change when he does and the life you know here will be no more. He will not be your husband for ever. You are destined for someone else. I will take this bad luck with me, and with it I will take him from your life.'

'No, no!' I spluttered, I was just married and had a baby. Why should she say such a thing?

Seeing that I was upset, she persisted in telling me that we were not destined for each other and that the heavens would decide whether or not we would stay together. 'You have seeing eyes,' she told me earnestly, 'you should listen more, my dear, to the people who know best. And it is not the living I talk of.' With that parting statement she went on her way, leaving me with a piece of lace and some heather which I still have to this day.

Could a whole life be changed and changed again by saying yes to one simple date?

My tutorials with Sam were less frequent now that I was overstretched as a mother and wife. I began to appreciate the sacrifices my own mother had had to make in order to provide for me as a working woman, but I was determined to stay at home and look after my only daughter.

When Sam and I spoke next, I questioned him about what the gypsy had said. He thought for a moment. 'Well, my dear, everything in life is for a reason. Each time you think something or do something, it is for a reason. There are no coincidences; everything is for a reason. Those reasons will direct you to whatever path you are meant to tread. If you are off course, then something will happen to direct you back on track. Maybe the path you have chosen is the longer route to where you need to be, but in time you will still tread the right route. That's the way it is.'

I was made a little angry by his statement. After all, he was the one who said we always had choices. Why was he now implying that we didn't? When I confronted him with this statement, I was surprised by the answer I received. 'It is not that you don't have a choice, it's just that those choices lead on to one road. Which path you take to arrive there *is* your choice, but you will get to the one road, no matter what!'

Oh, my goodness, that opened up my mind to more questions. I asked him if our road in life was predetermined, and if it was, where exactly were these choices he'd talked about?

Again the answer was not what I'd expected Sam to say. 'You need to see and listen to whatever signs the world of spirit sends you. There are no accidents or coincidences – only awareness.'

I was beginning to think that Sam despaired of me as once again he started to shake his head. 'You will see soon enough, my dear. Good can come from every experience, no matter how hard the process can sometimes be.'

My saving grace, I thought, was that at least my mother would be around after our move and she would see her grandchild more often. It was lovely that, through Fiona, my parents found a new way to demonstrate their love for me. As a family we had never been as close. Maybe I am biased, but I have to admit I was very proud of my new daughter. She was gorgeous, spiritual and smart even from an early age. It isn't easy sharing a house with your parents when you are a married couple. You lose your privacy and independence, and you have to adapt to circumstances around you. It's not that people don't mean well, it's just that two pairs of adults making decisions in the same place inevitably causes problems. I was grateful that my parents gave us a home when we had nowhere else to live, and I know they tried very hard to help us, but it was still an extremely stressful time.

The first terraced house in Shotton, Deeside, was finally completed and we moved out of my parents' home – only to find that we had run out of money to complete the second.

By the winter of 1981, I was twenty-one and we were well into our second year of marriage, but the gypsy's words nagged at me and I knew deep down that she was right. Now I had a husband and child, my nightly chats with Sam had largely stopped. However, loyal as ever, he would sit outside the bedroom each night, making sure I was taken care of. The only chance we had to chat now was when I was on my own, which happened rarely but most usually at bath-time. It makes me laugh to remember sitting naked in the bath, talking to my spirit Guide, but it was often the only part of the day I had all to myself. Although John and I often discussed spirituality in general, I didn't open up to all I could see and understand about the Spirit World. I think I was still scared of rejection. However, I don't think John doubted my ability to see and generally he was quite supportive of me. It was around this time, too, that I received the most glorious surprise. I fell pregnant again. I know my Angels and Guides had worked hard to heal me, but to have a second child in such a short time was mind-blowing. I felt honoured to be doubly blessed in this way.

However, as always in life, along with the good news there were also bad tidings. With the closure of the Deeside Steel works, my dear Uncle Bob lost his job, along with many men in the area. So many men's lives changed overnight that year; some committed suicide, and still more were lost to the depths of depression. My Uncle Bob came into that category.

It was the Christmas of 1981. The weather was bitterly cold. In the ice and snow, most people's houses had frozen up. My father, forever the plumber, worried about the very young and the infirm managing in such harsh conditions, when pipes burst and boilers broke down. He would go out on emergencies, no matter what time of day or night it was. Despite his ill health he still worked when he could, and this month seemed to be busy non-stop. The phone kept ringing and ringing as more and more people complained of leaking pipes or broken heating systems: the whole country seemed to be on overload!

During that time, Sam came to me, explaining that the bad weather was not good for my Uncle Bob's health and he must look after his toes. My poor Auntie Joan was suffering badly, because not only did she have my uncle's depression to handle, but their housing association had moved them out of the family home while it was remodernised, and put them up in temporary accommodation just down the road. There were several houses kept here by the housing association for short-term use by their tenants. I remember my cousin Debbie telling me that she hated the make-do house, but there was no other option. They had to live there while theirs was being completed. She said the house felt empty and unwelcoming; in her words – spiritually dead.

Despite my attempting to warn Auntie Joan, we were informed Uncle Bob had to have an operation on his foot; he had frostbite in his toes. In the week between Christmas and New Year his health seemed to be deteriorating fast. When I visited that Christmas, I shared my cousin's feeling that the temporary house was possessed by negative energy. We discovered many people had died there, even my uncle's sister Louise had died on the back step while bringing coal inside when she lived there. Then there was Uncle Harry who had died during his stay, just after his daughter had a bad car crash. The history of this house was filled with sadness, which seemed to cling to the bricks and mortars. I know it is a strange thing to say but I truly believe that houses have feelings. I know they are not living entities, but it seems that whatever life has been there leaves behind its own print or energy. This house stored negativity, and the sooner my aunt and uncle left it the better.

Uncle Bob and Auntie Joan found Christmas hard as they missed their son Peter so much at these family times. He had emigrated to Canada a couple of years before. Peter and his dad Bob had been great pals. Children sometimes don't realise what an effect emigration will have on their family. Those left behind often feel cheated of family moments that could have been shared like Christmas and birthdays. Such a loss can make parents grieve, even when there are other children at home. The other siblings also suffer, watching their parents' anguish, feeling that they too have a loss to bear as their family unit is destroyed, often for ever.

Now the New Year had started, my uncle's health had substantially deteriorated. One January morning he took a turn for the worse. Debbie ran as fast as she could to the phone box down the road, but before the doctor arrived Robert Hughes passed into spirit having suffered a heart attack. No one could do anything. As Debbie said, it was as if a light switch had been turned off. The house had claimed yet another life.

Their loss as a family was huge; my loss ran deep too. I had loved my Uncle Bob. He was always kind to me, always praised me, always loved me like a daughter . . . and now he was gone. So many happy memories. Thank you, Uncle Bob.

Sam was wonderful throughout this time, explaining that Bob had not suffered in any way but passed into spirit instantly with his Guardian Angel, Guides and family waiting to greet him as he arrived. He was definitely safe, but how could I tell my family that? My own father made me promise that no messages were to be passed to my aunt or any of her family. I held my tongue as I watched them suffer at the funeral, while I knew family in spirit and loving Angels wanted to comfort them.

After the funeral, Sam grew concerned about my Auntie Joan's health. I thought it was pretty obvious she'd be affected; after all, she had just lost her husband. He reiterated the same words over and over: 'Feel her chest pain.' I thought it was because she was upset and full of grief so I passed the message by. Well, I had to, I had been forbidden by my father to mention anything to any of the Hughes family about healing and the spirit world.

It wasn't until the eve of Peter's leaving to return to Canada after the funeral that I realised the full extent of Sam's warning. Peter had been out with his in-laws, drowning his sorrows, when previously he had arranged to stay at home with his mother and family for that final night. Selfishly, he had not considered his mother's feelings or that it might be years before he would see her again. Precious moments wasted in drunkenness. The next morning he rolled in with an entourage of in-laws, still under the influence, completely self-centred in his actions. He was laughing and seemed oblivious to the extent of his mother's grief. A huge row erupted between mother and son. My cousins told me they stood silently outside the closed door as they heard her verbally attack her beloved eldest son.

That morning Sam woke me, telling me that my aunt was now very ill.

What should I do?

Peter's brother then brought him to our house as my father had volunteered to drive Peter to Heathrow Airport. How could I approach my parents and tell them Sam was worried about Joan? As my father left in the car, Sam became most concerned and kept telling me to stop them as my Auntie Joan was critically ill. I tried in vain to tell my mother that this was serious, but she dismissed the spirit warning and kept on saying Joan would be fine once Peter had left.

About fifteen minutes later we had an urgent phone call from Vera, my aunt's neighbour. Joan had suffered a huge heart attack and was on the way to hospital by ambulance. The lights were flashing, and they didn't think she would make it. My husband urgently rushed us to the City Hospital. As we arrived Sam was waiting outside to greet me. 'Her heart stopped as they travelled here,' he informed me. 'They've revived her.'

Soon, we were at Joan's bedside. My mother asked Debbie whether we should call Heathrow Airport and stop Peter from flying off to Canada. 'What's the point?' was the answer. 'He has already left us, he isn't really part of the family any more.'

Her words moved me. Emigration can destroy the whole foundation of a family. It's not that there isn't love between its members because there is always love, but setting up a new life and not being part of the fabric of the old one can tear apart family bonds. It's not just the miles that separate the family, it is the lack of interaction. Those living far away have to make huge efforts to keep in contact and show their love by sharing the daily detail of their lives. For those left behind, the loved one's life being led thousands of miles away is like a carrot to a donkey. It dangles in front of your nose, but you can never reach it to taste! I promised myself that my own beautiful family would never have to go through that.

Sam sat and smiled sympathetically, as though he knew something I didn't. I looked into my little daughter's eyes – for once, I didn't want to know.

Fortunately, Auntie Joan proved tougher than we'd all thought and after hospital convalescence came home to be cared for by her family – except Peter.

After the sale of the two Shotton houses, we moved into a house with only one previous owner on a modern estate near St Asaph, North Wales. It was a great move as far as I was concerned as it now meant we had a much larger detached house with a beautiful garden. Despite its relative newness, however, the house needed substantial renovation, as the previous owners had not maintained it properly.

My second pregnancy was proving difficult as I had severe sickness from the start and my sugar levels showed that I had quickly developed a diabetic condition.

During my pregnancy I always seemed to have not only Sam watching over me, but other higher-realm Guides and Angels too. Maybe they knew what was to come because at only twenty-eight weeks the toxaemia I had contracted a few weeks earlier brought on early labour. The hospital tried to stop it and injected me with steroids to help my baby's lungs to strengthen. This time not only was my life in danger, but also that of my unborn child. I was put on complete bed rest, but even so managed only a few more days before I went into full-blown labour and had a little boy.

Fortunately my husband arrived from work just in time to see the birth of his new son. After his untimely entrance into the world, this little bundle only reached the length of his father's hand; he weighed 2lb 3oz and fought for life in a pint-sized incubator. For the first few days I was not even strong enough to visit him as the toxaemia and drugs given to combat my condition had made my face and body swell with fluid retention. For a while my condition was so bad, I was blind in one eye. I looked in a mirror for the first time in days and found myself altered beyond recognition.

Once I was stabilised, I was allowed to see my son. Arriving in a wheelchair because I was too weak to walk, I couldn't believe my eyes. In the intensive care unit, I saw a solitary Angel leaning against the Perspex incubator, peering inside to study my son.

On looks alone, I most certainly would not have thought this spiritual being an Angel at all. His powerful energies, however, identified him as Angelic and acting for the greater good. I felt he exuded an overwhelming compassion and love for my son as he studied him so closely. The essence of this love was a sense of stoicism, courage, calm and clarity, with unconditional strength to act no matter what the outcome, even if that ultimately meant the death of my child.

The Angel was incredibly tall, clothed in a red iridescent robe that was majestic in its proportions. I remembered seeing material similar to this before. It was not woven of conventional cloth but of what looked like strands of energy combined with light. The folds in it radiated not one but a multitude of shades of red, changing with each breath I took as if the slightest movement of air was enough to affect it. Wisps of red-coloured light energy (not plain red, but every conceivable variation and shade of that colour) flowed from his hair, body and clothes with spikes of energy bursting like sparks from his hair.

He stood over my baby's aquarium-like cot, reverent in silence but solid in defiance, strong in appearance. As he turned to look at me, I could feel in my heart even he was not sure whether this child's destiny was to live or to die. Once I saw the Angel's face close up, I was shocked to realise that he looked almost lion-like, with a red beard and hair surrounding his face like a lion's mane. It seemed to have a life of its own as each strand crackled with energy, pulsating with an electric current. He was not a pretty sight, more fearsome in looks as his skin appeared leathery and his forehead deeply lined, as though he had been weather-beaten withstanding years of storms. His face suggested to me that he (I say he, but even that I was unsure of) had seen much despair, and yet there was something about him that spoke of compassion beneath the strength. He would decide a person's ultimate fate: he was an Angel of Death.

His eyes made me shudder. They were dark with no colour to them at all. As I looked into his blank gaze, I felt as though I were looking through glass, and behind his eyes were another pair, then another, as though they were endless and bottomless.

The doctors gathered around, oblivious to the Angel, though he looked as if he was listening to their every word, even though I was unable to hear them. There was no smile from him, no words, as though he alone were making the decision. As the medical team gathered me up and ushered me into the office, they explained it was touch and go whether my baby would make it. At that time my baby was the smallest to have survived in that hospital. When I went to visit him in the special care unit I tried to express milk in the hope he might feed, but he would still not suckle when the nursing staff tried to feed him. After much counselling the doctors decided even this milk was unsuitable for fear the drugs I was taking to combat my illness were being passed on. It was now five days since his birth and the only sustenance he had was the drip keeping him alive with nutrients. The doctors explained that he had to take a bottle in order to survive as he could not live a normal life otherwise. They also said that because I had been desperately ill at the time of delivery there was a possibility his kidneys had been affected and that his body could not break down the protein. When they said this I noticed that the Angel looked straight at me, almost through me. He looked serious and there were no smiles as he casually leaned on the incubator roof. I knew, even though there were no words spoken, that the Angel was deciding whether my baby should live or die.

Although I heard the doctors' words, I found it hard to concentrate as I was still staring at my tiny helpless baby, lying in his warm incubator, fighting for survival. The Angel glanced at me, then at my new arrival. Had this being come to take him from me? Why was I seeing such an apparition? I wanted to hold my baby and give him my loving comfort. He had his mother's arms, here ready to protect him, and I desperately wanted my baby to live and to feel my love. A mother's love is precious. Was this Angel about to rob me of that joy?

I could only watch and pray to the Angel standing over my son that he would spare my baby and not take him. That he would give him the strength he needed to keep safe and live.

After a while I was taken back to my own bed where Sam was waiting to greet me. I was so emotional and upset that I bombarded him with questions. Why was it I had to suffer all this illness and pain? Why was it my son lay in limbo between life and death? 'You say I have the power to heal and yet here I am, sick and powerless even to hold my own flesh and blood? Your teachings seem to contradict my reality. Why do I feel this way? And who is that red creature watching my son?' I asked.

Sam began to reply: 'The Angel you have just seen is a deadly and very old soul. His name here on earth is Arch-Angel Sammael: focused on victory, stamina and leadership. I am most concerned when I see this Angel because his energies can go either way. He can take your son or he can fight alongside him for survival. There is no one more powerful.'

Sam continued: 'You are not suffering illness because of any action the higher source has taken. It is because your body was not strong enough to carry this child. His fate now lies within the Arch-Angel Sammael's hands. Your son is not in limbo, he is most certainly alive, and this Angel alone will decide his fate. If he spares him, then at some time during your child's life he will become aware of how special he truly is and will discover that he needs to find his life's purpose. Arch-Angel Sammael is a fighter who awards victory – in this case a win means life itself. You are powerless in this particular instance to help your son. At any other time in his life your healing will be invaluable, but for now we have to wait. It is up to him to decide if he will take up the challenge of the fight Sammael has put to him.'

Strangely, once the Arch-Angel had left the baby unit, Anthony took his first ounce of milk from the nursing staff and gradually he started to put weight on his tiny frame even though it was measured in grams.

The nurses soon named my little bundle 'Mighty Mo', their nickname for a fighting spirit. They said they called him this because he was the tiniest baby they had ever had in their unit, but with the strongest will to survive. I thanked Arch-Angel Sammael and the other Guides and Angels for helping bring Anthony, my new son, firmly into the land of the living.

It was a struggle to think of a name for my precious new baby at first, as I'd wanted to call him Sam after my Guide, and now, it seemed, a somewhat scary angel of a similar name. But my husband wasn't keen. Sam said why didn't I consider naming him Anthony after St Anthony? He'd performed many miracles, and after all this little man was just that . . . a little miracle! David Aitkin, the consultant obstetrician, was wonderful, so I decided to call my boy Anthony David, in testament to Mr Aitkin's care. So my little Anthony David fought his way bravely into this world.

Each time I visited my new son in the special care unit, the heat from the incubators left me gasping for breath. My blood pressure spiked, and my skin became engorged with fluid due to my condition, so I could barely stay for more than half an hour at a time with Anthony. It was many weeks after the birth before I stabilised.

Nowadays babies are born weighing much less than him, but at the time I had no way of knowing if Anthony would be able to lead a normal life or whether he would live with a multitude of ailments due to his difficult start. After tests, the doctors even confirmed that the placenta had been dysfunctional for at least three weeks prior to his early birth, so he was quite literally starved of nutrients to make his tiny body grow and was dismature as well as premature.

Fears that he would prove to have some sort of disability were uppermost in my mind, but his wasted body was at least starting to fill out the way a normal baby's should. I was just so happy that he was alive and appeared well, and each time I visited I would try to transfer healing into his tiny body. It was many weeks before I could hold Anthony in my arms, so for the first couple of months of his life I would administer the healing through a single finger, which I held inside the incubator.

The precarious life of my baby continued. After four months

of continual care by many nursing staff and doctors he was allowed to come home, weighing a mere 4lb 7oz, still only a fraction of what his real birth weight should have been.

Anthony was a miracle child of his time and I was so proud of him.

With such a will to survive and the fact that an Angel such as Sammael had stood over him, he *had* to be here for a reason.

My son chose life over death.

15

A Tutorial With Sam: The Balance Between Good and Evil

Being a new young mother with an innocent little bundle to take care of, I never wanted to give much thought to evil people or dark thoughts. The purest gift of all was lying in a crib in front of me. How could anything dark ever be allowed to enter his world? Despite my near escape from abduction when I was young, and having to experience my friend's murder by her father, I still retained the belief that people were basically kind. That was naive, I know. I didn't even consider back then that there were undoubtedly very evil people living in our earthly world and quite probably the spirit world too. All that was about to change. I would eventually understand that evil actually lurks everywhere. Fortunately for most of us, we remain oblivious to it and carry on with our daily lives, often brushing past great darkness, unaware that it could affect us.

As I looked across at my son, lying in his warm incubator, I could understand neither why my baby had to suffer in this way, trying to cling on to a thread of life, nor why such a fearsome Angel was standing guard over him. I now understand fully. But at the time it perplexed me, especially as Sam had explained that this particular Angel's energy could turn either way, towards fighting for either cause – good or bad.

Plus, despite my recent constant harassment, Sam still hadn't answered my questions about whether that 'all-consuming pit of fire and brimstone' actually existed in the spirit world. You know, the one we had all heard about from the pulpit of the church and from religious artwork.

Was Sam avoiding my request for more knowledge because this place actually existed, or was it pure myth and legend?

Either way, nothing was going to stop me from trying to wheedle out the answers. Every opportunity I had to speak to Sam resulted in me badgering him to tell me more about this evil secret society.

Why were there Angels who could act in either way? Had these particular souls been consumed with solely negative ideas? Did they not know the difference between good and evil, or did they like to dabble with both energies? Did they once have a choice or had they been fixed for eternity in the role they now occupied?

Though it scared me to contemplate the answers to my questions, I felt I did need to know more in order that I might be able to protect not only myself from such energies, but others too in the presence of evil.

Sam sat pondering for a moment before finally answering that I was right to want to know more about the depths of despair.

Ever since Janet was murdered, I had wondered why such innocents were taken from this world. It really tested my faith to the limit to try and understand. I dreaded to think what her close family must have experienced after her death.

To a parent, especially a mother, the loss of a child must be the greatest loss of all, especially if they are snatched away by an evil act such as murder. Then there's guilt at failing to protect those who were taken, being plagued continually by thoughts that things should have been different.

Looking at my tiny child, I wondered was I now to face the prospect of losing my own son? I demanded answers from Sam as to why this particular angel was standing over him. Despite my demands, Sam spoke calmly and quietly. 'Your gifts are developing to such a degree you are like a flame to a moth. Your brightness attracts and lures watchers from the shadowy depths, presenting you as a challenge for the underworld to conquer. I feel I can only tell you a small amount of what lies inside those depths. As you continue to develop your spirituality, I will continue to prepare you in every area of knowledge you will need. However, knowledge is one thing – wisdom is another.

'What I am about to tell you now will at least be enough to protect you from immediate danger. You should be able to determine more clearly "evil" energy when it comes close to you or others around you. You see, evil deeds can come from various different avenues, invading both your living earthly world and indeed both your living and spiritual life.'

As Sam spoke, I wondered if I was going to be able to cope with what he was about to tell me. Was he going to say something about my child? Had this Arch-Angel Sammael been a form of evil energy, sent to take my son from me? I listened intently.

Answering me, Sam explained why I had seen Arch-Angel Sammael. 'He has chosen to represent you with good reason. He is an Arch-Angel who has descended by choice from the highest energy source. He has not fallen from grace but has chosen to act in the way he does, and can work for good or evil, depending which way he chooses.' I shuddered, feeling uncomfortable at the thought of such an angel watching over my son.

Undeterred by my reaction, Sam continued, 'It is quite simple. He has the capacity to punish those who don't deserve and reward those who do.' I gulped in air, trying to weigh up this information. It was a shock to think of any Angel inflicting punishment.

Sam saw my fear and replied, 'He is perfect and an Angel of the highest order. He works through the medium of good intentions, fighting many causes. In this instance, he has fought to save your son and therefore you are blessed, my dear.'

As I continued to ask questions, I felt a need to speak in hushed tones, albeit in my mind, scared in case something or someone evil might overhear. 'So do evil beings come from spirit into our living world?'

Sam paused for a moment then resumed speaking as he studied me. 'Yes, Helen, from time to time they do try to dominate your earthly world, and Arch-Angels such as Sammael defend against such actions. Evil beings can enter into another person's space, by which I mean their psyche, and steal what they feel they want to take by infecting the thoughts and swallowing up the persona. When doing so, they can freely take an innocent soul or a trophy from them. But these occasions are extremely rare. In your world you call it possession.'

'What do you mean, a trophy?' I asked naively.

Sam winced slightly as he answered: 'I mean a life . . . by causing a murder or a death. To an evil being, that is the equivalent of obtaining a trophy.'

'Why would they do this? Why don't they just stay in their own darkness? Surely they have enough evil there to satisfy them.'

'Helen, you misunderstand. They do have much evil where they reside, but they are always looking to cause more harm, more terror. It's about control and kudos. The more they can govern and manipulate men and spirits by their evil actions, the more power they have within their own domain. Even there they have a hierarchy of sorts. It is all about what they want, not what they can give. They never stop to think about anything else. Their objective is to acquire more trophies at any cost.'

'Do they even try to steal good spirits . . . Guides or even Angels from the spirit world?' I asked, nervous at such a prospect and of the reply I was about to receive.

'Yes, occasionally they try to manipulate and persuade some from here in spirit too. That is a trophy worth a great deal to them,' Sam replied. 'However, Angels are rarely tempted by evil as they are the purest of all energy, particularly Arch-Angels. But if the evil entity manages to live within the psyche of a person in your earthly world, as a real person, then it would want to cause as much damage there as it could, provoking evil thoughts within that person and thus gaining control of another living soul. It guides the mind towards obscene sexual desires, greed, torture and murder in order to inflict as much suffering and pain as possible on other living beings. The ultimate quest is to acquire a spiritual token, which is the soul of an earthly life.'

As hard as it was for me to listen to this, there was something inside me that needed to hear everything Sam was prepared to tell me. 'How can they do this? Don't we have any defence against such evil? You say that they can tempt, corrupt or cause evil disharmony to living and spiritual beings. Was this Arch-Angel I saw with my child evil then?'

Sam smiled, 'It is very complicated for you to understand fully, my chile.' That was a term he had not used to me in a long time, I thought. He was talking to me again as though I was a child.

'Your Arch-Angel Sammael was weighing up what is right.

However, true evil can invade the psyche by infecting a person or spirit with its own vile nature in spiritual possession. This drains away any good feelings that person once had and drives them with the power of hatred. It can only do this when the earthly soul has a desire and tendency to be innately evil. All the spirit has to do then is invade and develop it.

'There are, of course, some earthly souls who do not need any tutoring in the ways of evil. They seem to have a compulsion to harm from birth. These earthly souls develop their evil ways in your world by free will, and when grown into adults inflict pain and suffering on their own behalf. So when they eventually enter spirit, they are evil in its purest form.'

'Do people think I am a demon, for seeing and communicating in spirit? Is that why my father won't talk to me about my spirit visitors?' I asked.

Sam laughed out loud again. 'Oh, my dear, if they think that then they themselves have no spiritual sight! All your life you have devoted your skills to helping others. I have yet to find a devil, demon or evil entity who has done that. Cast out any such fears. You will find it is the demon negative within them speaking out, trying to put you off course from achieving your good work. Do not doubt your own abilities. You are a true "light worker" of the highest order. When you come back to us and live in spirit once again, you will see glory in full once more.'

Hold on a minute . . . had I heard Sam say I would see purest glory *once again*? Did that mean I had lived on this earth before? This was the second time he had made a reference to the possibility of reincarnation. I kept such thoughts to myself, fearing to interrupt as his teaching was in full flow.

'Other dark forces work in more subtle ways, infecting minds and thoughts on a sort of one-off basis. These areas are very difficult to monitor or detect, and in most cases the deeds are totally camouflaged. For example, many can be manipulated through political means. These divide nations, causing earthly civilisations to experience starvation and wars. They are a very subtle way of causing mass evil simply via a prompting to action.'

Startled, I replied: 'Oh, my goodness. Does that include me? Am I manipulated in some way, Sam?'

'You could be,' he bluntly answered, 'but you are not. Do you know how I know you are not?' I shook my head, with no idea what he was going to say next.

He continued: 'You are not infected because you know the difference between good and evil. You know when you are about to use your own strength to manipulate others, and you never try to do that to cause harm intentionally. Granted, in a small way you may try and use your mothering skills to stop a child from doing something you don't want them to do, but that intention is through love. It is only when manipulation is used in the interests of greed, hatred or control that it has evil roots. Do you understand, Helen?'

'I think so, Sam. Are you saying that because I try to be a good person and help others, I have good intent within my heart, therefore any negative I have is outweighed by my good motives?'

'Yes, that's more or less it. You, my dear, have an innate history you have yet to discover. The Arch-Angel Sammael would not have spared your child if he didn't think you capable of doing great work. If you were a normal person I would say that was exactly right, but because you are a "light worker" you are automatically aware of evil more profoundly than most people. Your knowledge and understanding of good and bad is more finely tuned, but even you can be caught out.

'Some people, when they are in a position of power, want even greater power and crave the mass control that comes with it, regardless of whatever destruction it causes within your world for them to reach their goal. You see, my dear, the source, or God as you like to call it, works in mysterious ways – but so does evil. Remember, life is about balance. Fortunately, good deeds have more power to conquer than evil. Evil only rules in the minority, but when it raises its ugly head we as normal people feel its effects profoundly. In a way it is just like a school bully in a classroom. There are very few of them, but their actions can affect other people's personalities and confidence for the rest of their lives, as well as affecting the whole class at the time. Evil is not as prominent as you think, but the important fact to remember is, it is there.'

He paused and then took a deep breath before continuing. 'Helen, I can see your point about wanting to recognise this evil force when it does try to edge near to you. Evil will do that from time to time. It will try to inflict pain upon you, just as it does upon others. You are a bright beckoning light so any chance the darkness has to infect you or your thoughts, it will try to use with its entire strength. It will try to steal that which is important to you. The prize to such beings is not only to take what they want, but to inflict as much damage as possible upon the sufferer. For instance, it may take a life, a marriage or a hope, if it can't quite reach the true crown of another's life and soul.

'Remember, evil works through thoughts as well as deeds, so your path may be blocked from time to time by an evil energy trying to stop you from speaking openly or healing freely. Fortunately, even though you cannot remember your past, you have inherited an inherent spirituality that far exceeds that of most evil beings. So only the most cunning would succeed in polluting your earthly life. Now that we are talking about this subject they will be watching you, Helen, and you must be on your guard at all times.'

My ashen face must have said it all but I managed to splutter out the words anyway. 'Will I now experience bad things? Will I be in danger?'

Sam responded: 'Remember, your brand of danger may not appear as a threat to your earthly existence, more as someone trying to put obstacles in the way of your spiritual path. Evil can be as subtle as that. You need to reason out each time you are presented with a spiritual hurdle if it is there for good or evil. Sometimes the dark objective may be so disguised you will only realise the danger or stumbling block once you are midway through surmounting it. You are emotionally equipped to the highest degree, you just can't remember all you have experienced previously. When you are in danger of harming yourself or if others are presenting darkness towards you . . . you will remember! Something will show through.'

'Are you sure about that, Sam?' I asked doubtfully.

'We in the spirit world depend on goodness, but of late we have been worried that darker actions have been succeeding against human mankind. So as an earthly student I know you are asking these questions for good reason. You are back in this earthly world to try to send a message . . . a message of hope and love. Plus I have been instructed by you in your previous life to tell you everything you ask, but only if you ask!'

He was again referring to my having had a previous life in spirit and even here on earth – something that I had no recollection of.

'How am I ever going to be prepared enough to fight this darkness if it lurks in so many different places? Surely if it is so cunning and I don't see it coming, it will overwhelm me?'

Sam solemnly nodded his head. 'This is true, but some evil deeds are very subtle, as I said. They don't always result in possession or death. Manipulation is more common. Sometimes that manipulation is very minor. Fighting evil will come naturally to you, Helen. Trust me, it will. Just as the spirit world has Arch-Angels, Angels and Guides, not to mention the millions of other good-natured helpers, so there are different entities in the dark world, possessing different capacities for evil. Some are only adept enough to cause disruption and chaos. As I have said, they find a weak soul and enter through that person's thoughts, to cause doubt or disharmony, while in others they may cause fatalities.'

'Does this mean there really are such beings as devils or demons presiding over the whole evil arena then? You still haven't told me if it's true there is a hell of fire and brimstone!'

Sam laughed again. 'It never ceases to amaze me when I hear some of the stories people tell about the spiritual world. Quite often I have read and listened to writings about what people assume to know of this world. They even talk of Angels as though they are all knowledgeable on the subject!'

I laughed because I knew what he meant. I too had heard of many a spiritual book written by psychic people professing to know everything there was to know about Angels, Guides and such like. As Sam had explained to me many years ago, only a fool thinks he knows everything!

What I am telling you, my reader, is my life's experiences and the things the spirit world explained to me, so that you may think about them for yourself. I never profess to be all-knowing. I realise that I am on a continuous learning cycle. I may be more knowledgeable than most on spiritual matters, but in the scale of the universe I know only a tiny part of what lies ahead.

Sam continued to instruct me, stating, 'All Angels are pure of heart and intent; most only know within their consciousness the goodness of truth and light. Arch-Angel Sammael is different, I know, but there is yet one more type of Angel who is very different from these. Technically it is not even an Angel at all.'

I believed what Sam was trying to tell me was that while it is correct to assume that 99.9 per cent of the time, Angels are true beings of light, very occasionally they are not. This was a revelation to me.

'Let me explain to you, Helen,' he said, seeing the horror in my eyes. 'Firstly, all Angels are here to help mankind. Their work is only for good. But here in the spirit world we do have a special sort of Angel that we call a Redeemed Spiritual Angel. This particular entity has a very special gift, and although technically one could say it is not an Angel in the truest sense of the word, we feel it is deserving of that name. They are extremely rare among us, and even more rarely seen in your earthly world by someone spiritual like you. In fact, compared to the multitude of millions of Angels, Arch-Angels, Guides and helpers who aid people on a day-to-day basis, there are only a handful of Redeemed Angels.

'They very rarely interact with an earthly person, their work is usually purely connected to spiritual beings, but there are unique moments when a living person requires their specific help. They are special because they have fought their way back from the depths of despair and darkness. Because of that they possess extraordinary abilities very different from our normal Angels of light. They were once so deeply woven into the very fabric of evil it is hard to imagine how they could ever have escaped from that obscurity. They were part of an underworld where they had been totally engulfed in all that you would term evil. Even I would have feared to tread where they once dwelled.'

He continued with a slight shudder as though someone had walked over his grave: 'Where they originated was a dark and dangerous place, ruled by pure evil. Beings living in that world are so damaged they are capable of the most heinous crimes towards others. They see everyone as a mark or target whom they want to control. The souls residing in this place are natural predators. For the entities who decided they wished to be freed from such depravity, it would have required a commitment and determination of the highest order to turn away from evil. They would have suffered greatly for wanting to move towards the salvation of light. It would have taken even greater resolve to achieve their goal. Their journey to redemption would have been such an incredible personal transformation, demanding such gruelling ordeals, that we have to admire their achievement. Though, granted, their purity of heart can never be the same as the Angels of light.

'The true Angels of light saw the plight of these beings and watched the sheer determination with which they continued along the painful path to cleanse themselves from evil. Once they completed that journey they were awarded redemption, so that they could again feel the warmth of love and commit to the service of humanity. Sadly very few complete this journey from the pits of despair. To those that do achieve their aim, the Arch-Angels have given the status of Redeemed Spiritual Angel and they are allowed to reside within the light realms, providing that they continue with their quest and help mankind.

'Unlike normal Angels they cannot interact freely with us as their role is purely to serve mankind in a specific way . . . by protecting it when man is confronted with evil on the largest scale. Who else is better equipped to fight this cause?

'They will never be able to forget the depths from whence they came. These redeemed souls can still remember the atrocious acts perpetrated within that gloom. As they become "lighter", so their history will become blacker in their own eyes. They live with the scars of such knowledge. Only when they are truly purified will they be granted peace. Do not underestimate their ability. They are proud to bear their scars but they are fearsome creatures to look upon.

'If I was to try and explain what they look like then I would have to say they resemble more a twisted animal form, similar to those of your stone gargoyles adorning churches, rather than any human form. They are physically grotesque creatures, not a bit like the golden-haired, fluffy-winged angelic beauties you see depicted in religious art.'

This all sounded far-fetched to me – but why would Sam tell me any untruths?

'Surely I won't know if they are good or bad if they look like this?' I said naively.

Sam looked me sternly in the eyes. 'Don't mock, Helen, you never know when you may need such an Angel for assistance. They alone really know the depths of evil, and they alone can help fight against that true darkness. When you meet this Angel it will give you the guile to triumph over evil.'

'But won't I think they're some sort of demon, if they look so hideous?'

'It is difficult, I know,' he said, frowning, 'but they will offer you a prayer of light from one of the Great Halls of Learning. When you accept this prayer, the light around their body will glow a little brighter. Every service performed makes their light shine brighter. It is their new life's work to help. Each task they undertake aids their own development. They are redeemed to serve mankind.'

'How long would it take to repay such a debt?' I questioned.

Sam shrugged and looked serious. 'It depends to what depths they had sunk in their previous life. To have fought their way out and retrieved their light warrants our greatest admiration and compassion. However, you must always remember they would have caused great harm in their darker life, so never take them for granted.'

'What is a prayer of light?' I asked then.

'The light prayer which has been given to them from the Great Halls of Learning is a bond of love. We don't have prayers relating to any particular religion here in the spirit world, we only connect with love. Love protects, it binds and nurtures all of us. It enhances our deepest inner security. By receiving their prayer of love, you are bound together with that being. Therefore the Redeemed Spiritual Angel is bound to you with true love. By accepting this prayer offer, you in fact return that love. This is an empowering action, which will radiate and allow that being more strength to continue its fight for mankind and with its ultimate goal of being accepted back into the divine light of what you call God.'

I gulped and hoped I would never need to meet such a spirit . . . or should I call it an Angel?

'Are all Angels both male and female, and are Redeemed Angels male and female?' I asked.

'Angels may appear to be male or female when they show themselves, but really we are all part of the oneness. Therefore our gender does not matter.'

'Will the hideous looks of a Redeemed Angel ever disappear?'

'No, Helen. That will be their lot for ever, for all to see. These scars represent what they did to others, physically and mentally. We in the true light have not had any part in such a life. This was their choice before they lived amongst us. So it is their lot to wear that appearance for ever.'

'What about the fiery pit? Does that exist too? Don't you as Guides and Angels know about all of this evil, naturally, as part of your job?'

'I don't know about fire and brimstone,' Sam said openly. 'All I have ever felt is an austere cold that chills the very essence of your being when entering into the darker realms. I don't know whether fire and brimstone exist as I have yet to delve deep into the darkness. I think it is definitely safe to call it hell there! But you know, Helen, hell exists all around you in your earthly world too. You think of it as a single place in spirit, when in fact it is there amid your day-to-day life. Again, remember that life is about balance, Helen. It is when the balance tilts unevenly towards negativity that hell prevails.'

'So we can live in hell here in the living world?' I gasped.

'Of course you can,' Sam said, smiling, 'isn't that what wars are?'

I continued with my questioning. 'Setting aside the Redeemed Angels, do all the Angels know what those other evil entities are capable of doing?'

'Of course they have a good idea, but no one really knows what an entity is capable of. That is why we too are sometimes caught off guard. All I can tell you is that goodness always supersedes evil. For instance, look at the damage a family has to endure after experiencing the death of a child such as your friend Janet. Because of one murderous person's wicked act other innocents are affected and the perpetrator gets a kick out of inflicting pain not only on the victim, but also on the victim's family as they know it will disrupt and destroy the family unit. When a family can unite despite such sadness and sorrow, then goodness prevails.

My mind was now working overtime. I had so many more questions needing answers. 'What would that child who was murdered feel when they entered into the true light of the spiritual world? What would my friend feel? Would she automatically float into Heaven's gates or would she be trapped in some sort of middle ground, like limbo?'

'Where do you get these notions from?' Sam replied. 'On most occasions when anyone passes into spirit, even in such a tragic way, they would enter into the light straight away, generally being met by a member of their family or a Guide to assist them on their way. There are rare times, however, when this does not happen straight away. In these cases it is usually because of a traumatic death, like an accident or murder. Because death happened so quickly, the traumatised spirit sometimes tries to seek an answer as to why they are dead. The person concerned may want to see for himself or herself what has happened to them, so that the spirit can be at rest. But they are not in some "middle ground"! They are wrapped in the light of protection, in a place of spiritual goodness. What they are not doing is progressing, by moving on within that new world of spirit. They are basically standing still, staying near the death scene.

'In general, hearing from those souls who are departed helps heal not only the person who is grieving in your earthly world, but also the spirit who has just passed. It helps everyone concerned come to terms with where they are now. You are a sort of therapist to all, my dear. When loved ones on the earthly plane accept that those in spirit are safe, and vice versa, they realise they will never truly be parted. It is the knowledge that we never completely die that comforts and allows earthly folk and spirit alike to adapt to their new lives. It is the knowledge that one day they will all meet again that completes the love bond, which is inextinguishable.

'Remember, love is a bond that is unbreakable; that is why your heart aches when you lose someone dear. Your gift of spiritual sight is yet another way to heal people, Helen, and it is as important as any physician's operation or the laying on of healing hands.'

At these words I couldn't help but think how lucky I was that none of my own dear family had had to endure such heartache and hurt. Although I had experienced deep grief within my own family, I was grateful it had come in the way it had and not an even worse scenario.

I said to Sam, 'How do I know the help I give to people who have lost dear ones in such a way is enough? They mourn so deeply. Living with that type of anguish must be unbearable.'

He replied, 'You don't know whether it is enough . . . but what you are always capable of doing is releasing a bond of hope within that person's heart. Hope comforts them with the knowledge that they will meet again one day as a complete family, and that meanwhile their loved one is safe and comforted in the arms of other family members, Guides and Angels.'

By now tears had welled up in my eyes and were running down my face. Sam's words echoed deep within my heart. I kept hearing them in my mind over and over again . . . We will meet again.

'Surely faith in their religion should offer comfort to those who grieve here?'

'Oh, chile,' Sam smiled at me. 'Yes, sometimes religion is a healer and helps the sufferer to refocus their life. All religions try to be near what you may call the source or creator. Every religion has the belief that its roots are connected to the God-energy. There are also those who "know" that most religions are made purely by man, titles assumed to show what faction you belong to. The religion you observe is generally dictated by your culture and the country you reside in. The rules of that religion are not made by God, but by men bent on control. For people who understand this, religion only leads them further away from the source or creator.

'As I have said before on many occasions, there is only one true God and that is love. If you believe and have love in your heart, then you are close to and part of God – or the creator of light, as I call this energy. Sometimes I hear people ask why God allows violent and sudden deaths to occur? How could someone dear to them have been taken from their lives? Would a God of love do this?

'The answer, my dear, is that the creator has not taken them. It was an accident or caused by another person's hand. Or in the case of serious illness it is the body's mechanism breaking down. The creator is bonded to you by pure love. This is why there are always tools around with which to connect to that love.

'One of those tools is *you*, Helen! Your messages are the hope and love needed to thread that essence back into a person's life when it seems all is lost. Love is the force that drives all of us, and you are the living proof that life exists in another realm. The messages you give help the healing process so that an individual or family can continue on their life's journey. The gift you bring is as valuable as any precious stone. In fact, it is priceless.

'You have chosen to spread this message because you have a natural empathy, reaching into the hearts of those to whom you speak. Your gift goes beyond the message you are relaying. It is a unique ability to touch a person's soul. Once they have received your voice, in doing so they have taken the first step towards the knowledge that those they love are still around them and they are not alone. Granted, you cannot take the pain of their loss away, but you can help awaken them to the power of love. Once they have that, no one can ever take it away again. Love binds. The belief that their loved ones will be waiting on the other side when they pass is the greatest comfort of all.'

Flippantly I remarked, 'Gosh, some people will think I am writing a film script when I tell them all this!'

Sam was not insulted by my comment but laughed out loud. 'Where do you think an author's inspiration comes from in the first place?' he chuckled. 'Of course it's from spirit! All gifted people tap into the source of spirit.'

After hearing this answer, I decided then and there that I had to try and get the message of the need for change out to normal people. By that I mean spiritual change, one that penetrates deep into our hearts and consciousness. Only then can we begin to build a better world for us all to live in.

16

Tough Love

Now that we had two young children to provide for, money was tight. It was at this time that my husband decided to go abroad and work in Saudi Arabia. The salary was fantastic and he could come home every four months, paid for by the company. His wage would be supplemented by a huge bonus if architectural plans were completed within the project's stipulated timeframe.

My husband loved the idea of this extra earning capacity, explaining to me that it would put us on our feet financially, but giving little thought to how I would cope all alone with two small children. But since our finances were in such a bad state, I had to agree to his leaving.

Four months soon passed, and the time had come for me to pick my husband up from the airport when something strange happened.

Although Manchester Airport was only an hour away by car, the prospect of disturbing two children from their sleep very early was unappealing, especially as one was a baby, so I decided to stay with my parents the night before. It seemed preferable to leave Fiona and Anthony with them while I travelled to the airport the next morning.

My parents had built a huge extension onto their bungalow, knocking down the original garage and building new bedrooms where it once stood. It looked gorgeous and they had so much more space. Fiona and I shared a room with twin beds, while my mum took Anthony with her to feed him in the night, so I could have a proper rest.

However, while I was in a deep sleep in the middle of the night, I was woken by a nudge to my side. I thought my mother had come into the room as there was a problem with Anthony. I looked around and saw no sign of her. But there was a woman standing by my bedside dressed in a Wrens uniform, complete with peaked cap. She said nothing, just looked at my daughter and me lying in bed. I know I see spirits all the time, but the thought that there was one now physically prodding me in the side to wake me was shocking. I wondered if I had dreamed this one so I turned on the bedside lamp and there was no one there. The apparition seemed to have vanished. Satisfied that I must have been imagining things, I turned the light back off. As I did so the woman in spirit appeared again, standing directly beside me, still in her Wren's uniform. Without thinking I shouted at Fiona to wake up and look, but she seemed still to be sleeping peacefully. A light appeared beside the woman in uniform as she stood silently. I had a sense that the light was a Guardian by her side.

The apparition was so close to me and I could see her overall appearance. Then the strangest thing happened. She pointed to a tin she was holding in her hand. The tin looked rather like one of the old tea canisters my nana had had on her pantry shelf. As if trying to attract my attention further, she shook the contents, as though something would jangle inside.

That was when I yelled out in shock, as even in those days spirits who caught me unawares managed to pump up adrenalin in me and make my heart race. In response to my screams, my parents came rushing in from the other room, but Fiona was still fast asleep, which was strange. I told my parents about the woman dressed in uniform and the tin she'd been holding. My father kept silent and I could see denial written across his face. Despite all the talking, Fiona didn't wake.

The next day nothing was said about the strange night-time activities – in my father's eyes they hadn't happened anyway – and I left, as arranged, to pick up my husband.

Naturally I was pleased to have him home. Life as a single mother was very difficult, not to say lonely. We returned to our own house.

Out of the blue, a couple of days later, my mother telephoned me to say they had found an old tin resembling the description I'd given. She said that the canister had been sitting on a rafter up in the roof space. Despite my parents having had a whole new roof put on during the alterations, Dad had gone up to check something to do with the plumbing and had found it. No one knew why it was there or who had left it.

'We opened it up,' Mum said excitedly, 'and lo and behold, there she was! A picture of a woman in Wrens uniform.'

What the significance of it was we will never know, but now I felt I had an inkling who my ghost was. Perhaps she had lived there before my parents did and wanted to make herself known to the family. As much as I discover about the spirit world, with every new experience my mind is filled with further questions. Sam said that the spirit woman had died in an accident while on duty. I felt she might be confused as to where her earthly family were now living. I sensed that it was as though she had to see for herself that her parents no longer lived in her previous home and she needed to be guided elsewhere to where they were. I was sure she wanted to speak to me, but somehow she had yet to learn the art of spiritual communication. I can only hope that she managed to find her way, although I am sure her Guide would have directed her.

My husband's home-stay over, he had to return to Riyadh. A couple of weeks prior to his next leave, I had a phone call from him to say that he wasn't going to come home on this occasion as the travelling was too tiring. Instead of making the journey back to the UK, some of his team were going to stay in Saudi Arabia and have a good rest as the workload had been extreme.

I believed his story and encouraged him to take a well-earned rest. I trusted him, and in my mind felt that everything was still OK between us. Soon after that, the housekeeping money that he regularly sent home seemed to shrink at an alarming rate, and it made me anxious. He did send me letters full of words of love, but why didn't he come home to be with us? Maybe words in a letter are easy to write, actions harder to perform.

I felt like a single parent as my partner only seemed to come when it suited him, he obviously thought that working abroad was the right thing for all of us. Needless to say, our marriage started its decline from then on.

I was already giving spiritual guidance sessions at home; it helped me cope with the loneliness of the long, empty nights. Most of the people I saw were mums from school. If it wasn't for the fact that people were continually asking to make appointments to see me, I don't believe I could have made ends meet at that time. I couldn't understand why our finances still seemed so bad and often queried my husband's wages, but had to believe him when he said he was sending home every penny he could.

It was then that the gypsy's words from years ago started to prey on my mind: *'Your man is about to leave and travel a long way from you, possibly abroad. All will change when he does and the life you know here will be no more. He will not be your husband for ever. You are destined for someone else.'*

Having remembered those words, I told Sam that I felt scared and unloved. Oddly, he never said anything negative about my relationship; in fact, I have never heard him say anything negative at all. I wanted to hear from him that my husband really loved me and everything would be fine. But he said nothing.

I think my parents had already started to realise that things were not right and they would often take the children out for days to relieve me. Even my dad seemed worried about me as I became very thin. I had lost over two stone in weight and weighed a mere seven and a half stone. I looked pale and weak. I had never been so thin before, I like my food too much, so seeing me in this gaunt state alarmed my family, but I just said it was because I was running around after the children, and they accepted this explanation.

Sam also was growing concerned and would say to me that I needed to be true to myself and that I was hiding from the truth. I learned many years ago you can't hide anything from him! He is a true Guardian Guide, always steering me along my life's path.

Sam was now calling on me all the time, popping his head round the door continually as if to check on me. Although he never said very much, I knew he knew what was going wrong with my health. Although I had not admitted it to anyone, I had become bulimic. I thought that my husband didn't love me because I looked too fat, so I was trying to become thinner for him. Maybe then he would fancy me more and want to come home more often. I became withdrawn and reclusive despite pretending to outsiders that everything was fine.

Eventually I cracked. I felt so miserable and depressed that one day I could not be bothered even to dress myself. I wouldn't eat, talk, wash . . . in fact, I didn't want to do anything. It was almost as if I had switched off completely. My mother came round to the house and, seeing me like this, immediately called the doctor.

I had what is known as chronic post-natal depression. It took me a while to overcome the illness, but I fought hard and with the help of Sam eventually discovered a new, more confident me. Once back on my feet, I had the courage to explain to my husband how sad I was about him being away, and said that if our marriage was to succeed he needed to be a husband and father at home. Eventually he did return and managed to secure a job near where we lived in Wales.

Despite going through the charade of married life for many months, I knew deep inside that our marriage was failing. It is not my intention here to discuss the intricacies of a dysfunctional relationship, but it's an experience many have had. We decided to separate officially and my husband moved back in with his parents while I lived in the family home with the children.

It was the summer of 1985, I was twenty-six years old and once again living the life of a single mother. Despite developing quite a reputation as the person to see if you wanted to sort out life's problems, I was separated from my husband and desperately confused about my own future. Especially as spiritually I felt important changes were about to happen for me, whether I wanted them to or not.

One of my clients had left me the telephone number of an old lady who also had a reputation for spiritual guidance. I'd left it under a jar in the cupboard, in case I needed it one day. Perhaps that day had now come. Despite seeing clearly for others, I was refusing to accept my spiritual awareness about myself.

I finally plucked up the courage to call the number. The lady's name was Mrs Gordon.

An elderly-sounding voice answered the phone to me. She did

not ask my name but said: 'You sound like you are in great need. You'd better come tomorrow. I have one appointment free which must obviously have your name on it, love! Be here for eleven.' Mrs Gordon gave me her address and directions, and put the phone down.

I had no idea what she was like, where she lived other than her directions, or even if she would tell me anything to confirm my inner feelings. However, something inside kept telling me that I needed to go, I would definitely learn something from her.

Sam smiled, and said that help was being guided to me.

I arrived at Mrs Gordon's house and rang the doorbell. A woman answered the door. She looked to be in her late seventies, small and buxom, with brown hair in tight curls. She gave me a big smile.

'Good!' she said as I walked through her front door. 'I have been waiting for you!'

I felt a little reprimanded, as though I was late, but as it happened I knew I was five minutes early – by my watch at least.

'Your name is Helen and they have told me that you are special,' Mrs Gordon proudly announced.

I started to frown, a little puzzled. 'Mrs Gordon, I specifically remember not telling you my name when we spoke yesterday. Who has told you that my name is Helen?'

'Do you mean someone alive or dead?' she enquired, a little sardonically. 'As it's the dead who speak to you, isn't it, dear? They speak to me too!' I knew they had to because no one else knew I was going to see her. This gave me confidence in her that she may have the answers to my questions.

Although Sam was around, he had not spoken a word to me about my personal life for months and I was beginning to think that all in spirit were turning their backs on me. At last I might find some answers.

Mrs Gordon invited me into her kitchen, but as I went to sit down she started to plead with me. 'Oh, I have been waiting for you to come for so long! They have told me you are very special and I would love to hear something for myself.'

I smiled at her graciously.

'You have the true gift of enlightenment,' she continued. '*Please* would you sit for me? Tell me what you can see for me! I am waiting to hear from my husband.'

I was speechless. Here I was, meant to have an appointment with this lady, and she wanted me to sit for her! The truth was I could see someone wanting to talk to her, one person actually came for her. Her husband Edward had walked in with me from spirit to say that he wanted to tell her that she would soon be joining him. I didn't know what to say or do as I didn't want to upset my hostess. But she was so disappointed that I told her that her husband and Guide had walked into the house with me, but because of my confused state of mind, I couldn't interpret the communication.

She finally accepted that I could not sit for her that day, and duly sat down opposite me across the kitchen table and began sitting for me.

It was hard to listen to details about my life from a stranger, as she coolly described my marriage breakdown and how, despite our efforts at a future reconciliation, the relationship was still doomed to failure. I was devastated because it confirmed what I had been feeling, but all the same no one really wants an important relationship to end, especially where two children are concerned.

When someone you don't know bluntly tells you accurate information, it is a bitter pill to swallow. I didn't want my marriage to continue the way it was, we were separated for that reason, but now she was telling me it had no future. It was definitely over.

She could see a long-haired woman causing a problem in my marriage. She went on to explain that my father would die young of a breathing disorder.

As if to question my being there at all, Mrs Gordon said: 'But you know all of this, they have shown you and you have seen it!'

This was true, but as with any devastating news there is always a certain amount of denial – that is normal. But from a stranger's lips, such messages have the air of truth about them, and to deny them then is foolish.

Mrs Gordon paused and looked at me hard across the kitchen table. I could tell she was thinking something deep as she had been silent for many minutes – listening and thinking. She took a deep breath before addressing me again.

'You know, I have not given a sitting to anyone quite like you before, Helen. I see many things happening to you – so many that it would be night-time before I could tell you all of them.'

I heard what she said, but all I wanted to hear about was my marriage, about being happy, about my children being happy, about being settled at home and being a good mother and wife. Please tell me these things! I thought.

She continued: 'I see you being famous and going to the very top of a profession. You are going to touch people's hearts . . . many people in many countries. You will write books and talk to people on platforms and stages.'

She paused then added, 'Oh, Helen, please sit for me and tell me what you see?'

I felt sad because I knew she was desperate to hear from her beloved husband in spirit. How could I tell her that he was talking of her own death? Sam smiled and said to say to her that her husband was with her constantly and when it was her time to enter the Spirit World, he would be with her. So at least I passed that message. I was so surprised when she ecstatically answered me. 'Oh Helen, that's wonderful. I feel Teddy my husband around me all the time, but for some reason I cannot see him. Thank you so much, I am happy to know that he is here with me.'

Mrs Gordon sighed contentedly. There was another few minutes of silence followed by a deep breath as she turned to address me: 'First you will meet a man with the initial R. In fact, he comes from a family of initial Rs and he has lots of socks . . . far too many . . . not pairs of socks, but single socks. I see him wearing a tweed jacket, but not like a farmer's or workman's . . . a more modern jacket.'

It had all got too much for me so I started to bring the sitting to a close. Funny that I decided to leave when the lady wanted to go further, but I couldn't listen to any more. I wanted to go.

Hearing that my dad was going to die and my marriage was on the rocks was enough information for one day. I knew she was right about Dad, Sam had told me so for years, but I didn't want to face the added complication of having someone new coming into my life. I had enough stress already. Meeting someone else was the last thing I wanted or needed right now.

Mrs Gordon escorted me out of the house, walking me to the street where my car was parked. 'Are you sure you can't give me a proper sitting, Helen?' she said in a final plea before I left.

Gently I responded, 'I would love to have given you a proper sitting, Mrs Gordon, but as I told you earlier, I can see your husband alongside of you. With him is your Guide and over your right shoulder I can see a bright light which I feel is an Angel bestowing much love upon you. I can see what I can only describe as glistening snowflakes showering over your head and shoulders. I believe those in spirit are trying to say they are all around you and sprinkling you with their love and energy.'

Mrs Gordon smiled at me. 'You are very kind, my dear, but I feel you are holding back on me and you are trying to protect me from sad news. I fear that my own time here is soon coming to an end and I was hoping that you might confirm this for me.'

I looked at her, bewildered: how could I even confirm or deny this suggestion? 'In all honesty, Mrs Gordon, my ability to communicate with the spirit world today is very much marred by my own personal problems. Maybe I could sit for you another time.'

As I finished speaking, a beautiful-looking spirit person appeared by Mrs Gordon's side, looking into her face. He looked healthy even though he was pale, tall and broad and dressed in a simple white gown interwoven with some sort of silver thread, a silver-cord hanging at his waist. The cord seemed to have an energy of its own, as if it served another purpose than merely tightening the robe around the body. There were no sleeves to his gown, exposing strong arms that had a luminescent white glow, and the neckline was also scooped away, revealing his neck and the top of his chest. I would say he was a man, but he was so pretty he could quite easily have passed for a woman, especially as his hair was thick and long. The spirit put his finger to his lips the way we do when we don't want others to talk. I never said a word, just smiled and thanked Mrs Gordon as the spirit nodded in a respectful way.

As I drove away Sam suddenly appeared beside me. He never comes as a social visitor just to pass the time of day and have a chat; his visits have a purpose and always include some form of enlightenment for me.

'That was one of the Angels of Death,' he announced.

'How many are there?' I asked, surprised.

'Many,' Sam said knowingly.

A month later I read in the local paper that Mrs Gordon had died. It seemed that without my confirmation she knew her own destiny.

I cried: not for myself, but for Mrs Gordon, and thanked spirit for taking me to her. Now I prayed that she was safe and happy with her family in the spirit world. There was no real need for tears, though, as a passing into the world beyond is often a joyous occasion and I had no reason to doubt this was true for Mrs Gordon.

I needed to talk to someone after my visit to Mrs Gordon as my marital situation continued to make me miserable. On this occasion I felt the only person I could trust was my mother. Although she didn't give much credence to my spirituality, she was after all my mum and she was very good at giving practical advice. Since John had been abroad for extended periods, I would meet up with my mum and dad more regularly so that they could enjoy some extra time with the children.

So one morning, as we drank tea in her kitchen, I told her that I had visited Mrs Gordon as spiritually I felt great changes in my life and I needed someone physical to confirm they were true. To my surprise Mum showed a genuine interest and didn't discount what I had to say.

'What did she tell you?' was the first question my mother asked. Not unreasonable under the circumstances.

Naturally, I held back the message about my father. I suddenly realised that my mother was curious and was maybe even starting to accept that the spirit world did exist. I considered whether all the time it had not been the spirit world she'd doubted but whether *her* daughter could see that spirit world. Maybe it was just me she doubted!

I spoke candidly with her. It was the first time I had actually discussed the possibility of divorce. I had previously felt separation was what we needed, to give my husband a jolt and stop him taking me and the family for granted. Although we had spent much time apart while he was abroad, he was content in the knowledge that I was waiting for him at home. However, separation implied the possibility of a permanent parting if husband and wife failed to resolve their differences. Innocently I'd believed that by not making myself so accessible to him, I might make him fight harder for our marriage. I thought that because we'd had children so early on, it was a contributory factor that also needed addressing. Maybe time apart to reflect on it might bring us closer together.

Or maybe it had been too soon for me to marry at nineteen years of age and take on such responsibilities. Mum and I sat with mugs of tea in our hands; I was shaking with nerves at the prospect of ending my marriage and having to break the news to my children. If only it could still be saved! Perhaps if I prayed for a miracle our marriage might not be lost.

My mother had no doubt that I was deeply unhappy, and living as a single parent separated from my husband was not the answer – she could see as much. But if the break became permanent and a divorce was sought, where would I live and how would I survive on my own with two small children? She pleaded with me to take some time before I made any decisions I would later regret.

It was a conundrum. I had ultimate faith in my guidance from the spirit world, and yet what my mother advised also rang true!

We had been separated many months by the time Christmas came around, and the children missed their father very much. This would be their first Christmas without their dad and the thought was painful to them. Like every mother I wanted my children to be happy, so despite the spiritual guidance I had received, I listened to my mother's advice and pleaded with my husband to give our relationship another chance, for the sake of the children.

Maybe men think differently from women when it comes to looking after a family. I knew it was an easier life for my husband, not having the worries of childcare to deal with, and I remembered him telling me that he could live a bachelor's life again quite easily. If we were going to get back together, then it had to be done quickly, before he started to make a new life for himself.

So we tried again, for the children's sake, to make our relationship work.

The first few weeks both my husband and I were on our best behaviour and married life seemed tolerable to me at least. Actually we had an immaculate home with a pristine garden in a lovely area . . . on the surface, it was a life many would envy. I had a little independence from my appointments with people who were being recommended to me for spiritual guidance, so my confidence was improving. Emotionally, despite the stress of the separation, I was fully in control of myself and my eating habits once again.

Christmas 1985 was almost upon us. Then one day while out shopping, as I came out of a cake shop after buying all sorts of Christmas goodies, I saw an Angel poster in the bookshop window next door. This attracted me to such an extent that I went inside. Sam appeared to be walking around the shop with me and I thought it strange that he had suddenly become an expert shopper! It was quiet in the shop and I walked to the very back where the children's books were kept. As I approached the children's section, another poster of the same Angel was hanging on the rear wall, and I noticed that wherever I went within the vicinity of the poster, the eyes of the Angel always seemed to follow me. Then, out of the blue, I heard a voice telling me to turn into the next aisle.

Out of curiosity and a lifetime of faith in my spiritual voices I turned into the aisle and started to scan the bookshelves. I looked up and noticed the words *Spiritual and Religious Books*. The voice came back – *third shelf down* – and as if it was planted there for me to see was a book by Doris Stokes, entitled *Whispering Voices*, and I knew there and then that I had to buy it. While I was taking the book off the shelf the voice returned. *Now read that, my love – you need to read it.* Sam came to the cash desk with me. He was smiling.

As soon as I arrived at home I sat down and started to read the Doris Stokes book. Once I'd started, I couldn't believe what I was reading as so much of her life was taken up with seeing spirit guides and people. At last I realised that there was somebody else out in the world who was similar to me. Despite the fundamental difference that my spiritual communication centred upon healing, we were in essence very similar.

Reading this book gave me the confidence to believe that once both children had started school, I could offer my services to the spirit world on a full-time basis, and devote my life to expanding my healing abilities for the benefit of others.

Finding that book became my epiphany.

What my spiritual guides and messengers failed to warn me of was the loss of my dear Granddad Joe. He was still an integral part of my parents' household and a confidant to me when I needed a listening ear. He was now in his eighties and although he was a relatively lively old soul, going on holiday with his seniors club, enjoying his days playing cards and having sing-songs with his friends at his card club in the local community hall, Granddad still had only one woman in his life: my Nana Ada.

After a serious chest infection had hospitalised him for several weeks, Granddad was allowed to come home for Christmas. He was like me as he loved Christmas, and now my family was reunited it made for an even more special festive time.

A few weeks later, in the New Year of 1986, he was admitted back to hospital again. On a visit to him there, I was startled when

I saw the same Angel of Death who had attended Mrs Gordon. I knew by the presence of this Angel that Granddad must not have long before he joined Nana Ada. His silver-cord was already showing itself to me. It extended outward from his body, becoming thinner, like a stretched piece of smoky elastic.

The Angel, so pale and beautiful, with sea-blue eyes, looked at me sympathetically as if there was something that must be done for my granddad that only I could do. I knew what that something was. I sat with him, holding his hand, while Mum sat the other side and my dad was at the foot of the bed. I knew my father was scared. Granddad was dying of emphysema, the same disease that kept my father housebound for long periods of time, and he was not yet fifty years of age.

'Please let me give you some healing, Granddad,' I whispered into his ear. My mum heard. With tears in her eyes, for the first time ever she nodded in acknowledgment that I could do so.

'It's too late, Helen, my love,' Granddad said. 'I can see them all waiting for me. I need to go with them, my love. They are here now. I love you. I love all of you.' He squeezed my mother's hand and mine. I told Mum that I could see his spiritual silver-cord and that it was stretching.

'Please don't leave us, Granddad!' I cried.

He smiled, then in a whispering voice said, '. . . never leave you.'

I saw his cord stretch further. I knew the Angel wanted me to break it to expedite Granddad's passing. It would be easier for him that way. In the moment I concentrated on it, the cord became so thin it snapped. Granddad had passed away in front of our eyes. The Angel of Death smiled. His job was complete. His pale face turned to look at my father. I knew his time was near, too near. But, please, not yet, I thought.

Before my eyes the Angel of Death faded and disappeared.

There at the end of the bed next to my father I saw a group of onlookers from the spirit world. Their outlines were very faint but I could certainly make out some of their features. They must have been Granddad's family and friends because I didn't recognise most of them.

There was one face that I did recognise. She pushed in front of the others because she knew that any second they would be taken back from whence they came. At that moment I saw my Nana Ada. She looked younger and more beautiful than I remembered her, but it was her. She blew me a kiss then in an instant they had all gone.

Granddad's physical body was still lying on the bed and Mum and I were still holding his hands and yet we both knew he had gone. He was not there, only his shell. He had found Ada again. Although I cried, I was happy that he was with her, the love of his life.

They had been married over fifty years and now it was their time to share a new adventure in the spirit world.

Why didn't I feel I was married to my own soul-mate? Holding Granddad's hand, I selfishly cried for myself.

17

Time to Move On

My life seemed to be in complete flux.

My husband was at home decorating the house ready to sell it. Another sale! How many houses did we have to buy and sell before he would finally settle down? His plan was to move back to Chester as it was nearer to his new job, release the equity in our current home and buy a house in need of modernisation on a maximum mortgage, using the cash to pay for the renovations. Naturally I wasn't consulted to any great degree as John felt as he was the breadwinner and he needed to be nearer his work, then it was his decision to make. Breaking the news to Fiona that she was to change schools and leave her friends was very difficult for me.

Knowing he was decorating, my mother and I thought this an ideal opportunity to go out shopping, taking Fiona with us but leaving Anthony at home in his father's care. Any mother will say the same: it is easier to shop with one child rather than two. We felt a man could manage for an hour or so with a little boy of three playing peacefully in his bedroom. Besides, it gave us a chance to have some mum and daughter time in town. Since talking to my mum about Mrs Gordon and how unhappy I had become in my marriage, we had become very much closer. Mum was aware I was offering consultations professionally and started to take a genuine interest in my spiritual experiences, sometimes even asking me about Sam. I remember one afternoon Mum becoming very emotional when she told me she felt she had missed out on so much during my growing years. Little did she know I felt the same! I did have enormous respect for my parents still, though, despite not understanding their lack of support for me then.

Happy after our time together that morning, we returned home from shopping. As we started to walk up the drive we could hear Anthony screaming inside the house. I dropped my shopping bags and ran up the drive as fast as I could and in at the back door. Anthony was upstairs, yelling at the top of his voice.

Where is my husband? I thought. Why isn't he looking after Anthony?

When I reached the landing I saw my husband working in Fiona's bedroom while Anthony continued to sob, catching his breath intermittently between crying out, 'Mummy! Mummy!' He was in the toilet with the door closed. I couldn't believe that my husband seemed oblivious and could continue painting as if nothing was wrong while our son cried out for attention.

Anthony was sobbing so much and when he saw me he couldn't get his breath but reached out with both his hands, begging for rescue. I lifted him up to cuddle him. My husband kept apologising, saying that Anthony had wet himself and wouldn't sit on his potty. He had to learn, didn't he? And he should have learned by now!

My eyes were fiery with temper as I blazed out my wrath, screaming at my husband that Anthony was a special child and we were lucky to have any children at all! John was a good father, but obviously on this occasion, his patience had worn thin.

At that moment, I knew I was not going to last with this man. As soon as I felt strong enough to take the children and look after them myself, I would leave him for good.

*

After about twelve months on the market, the St Asaph house sold. Meanwhile my husband had found a semi-detached house in Chester that needed total refurbishment. We were leaving our lovely detached home, where, if we weren't happy, we were certainly settled, and moving to another building site forty miles away from my friends and family. Once again, I had to face camping on floorboards while the house was stripped out – this time with two young children. It was going to be a tough move.

As I had to be home for the children, I mainly worked in the mornings or afternoons, never all day. Anthony's nursery hours varied week to week and Fiona was in full-time school so my time was limited depending on how far I had to travel to see the people who wanted a sitting. My parents had just moved to Kinmel Bay, into a smaller brand new bungalow after selling the huge one in Chester. This was mainly because my father's health had deteriorated to such an extent he had given up work and was now officially disabled. My mother was his nurse and carer. No sooner had they settled into their new home, to be nearer the grand-children and me, than my husband was moving us back to Chester.

Fortunately, my diary was generally full, which kept me busy and my mind off our marital disharmony. Today's appointments were in a bungalow just around the corner from my mother's new home, where four female friends had made arrangements to see me. I knew this particular day was somehow life-changing because Sam was on full alert. As usual, though, he knew when to keep silent.

It was one of those beautiful, bright May afternoons that fill the soul with optimism. The summer had started early and promised to be long and warm. Britain at its best with smells of grass cuttings, strawberries and cream teas! Periods of good weather are unusual on the British calendar, so I naturally assumed Sam's optimism was due to the sunshine, not because of the surprise he had secretly waiting for me.

This was the day I met Elsie, a very formidable lady, overweight in a middle-aged way, and expensively dressed. She was ushered into my make-do office, very confident in her manner. After introducing herself, she gave me a warm maternal smile. She sat down heavily on the chair provided and plunked her over-sized handbag on the desk between us. I realised from the outset that this was not a lady to be trifled with.

Sam always stands guard in the room when I am working and I could see him from the corner of my eye, watching my visitor intently. He does this quite often, so at first I took little notice. However, today was different. He was actually observing Elsie like a surveillance camera.

At first I felt a little put off, almost scared to speak to her, until Sam told me to go right ahead and not spare the horses. 'Be honest, be blunt,' he said, 'this lady needs to hear what you have to say. In the future you will be of great comfort to her.'

I took a deep breath and gritted my teeth, knowing this was going to be a tough session. You see, what I have learned over the years is that when I conduct a sitting, quite often the spirits pass on messages that cannot be confirmed there and then. This will sometimes be because the person I am sitting for has little or no knowledge of their family history, or sometimes because spirit has brought them to me to prepare them for a future event. All I know is that there is always a reason behind every message, whether we connect to it straight away or not. And despite a message being accurate, there are times when a person glibly says no to it. It's almost in defiance, as if to say, 'OK – now tell me something I do know.' But how can a person grow and learn if you only ever teach them what they already know? Often it takes time for the message to connect – as Elsie was going to find out!

With a gulp I proceeded to tell her about her business with her husband and the complexities within it. She nodded and smiled. Then I went on to talk about her two adult sons and described them both in detail. I correctly gave both their Christian names, which again she agreed with totally, bobbing her head up and down. In fact, she was looking pretty awestruck by the accuracy of everything I told her. So far, so good. Perhaps I was worrying about nothing and this sitting was going to be straightforward after all.

Relieved that I was on the right track, I could at last lighten up before the strong personality sitting opposite me. Then it happened: the messages changed in tone and the energy altered into a more serious one as I explained what was happening in the life of her eldest son. I explained that he had just left his wife, maybe even that week, and his three children were living with their mother in the matrimonial home. I said that he was very concerned about telling his parents at this time because he didn't want to cause them worry, so he was keeping his feelings to himself for now. I then went on to tell her that despite having made changes in his life, he was at a crossroads and didn't know what to do. However, he would decide to divorce his wife. He wanted happiness, but it would come at a great cost.

Elsie's face changed from politely friendly to positively aggressive. 'That's utter rubbish!' she shouted loudly, and told me in no uncertain terms that I didn't know what I was talking about.

She rose to her feet and towered over me. She spread both her hands on the desk in front of me and lowered her head defiantly.

'I do have two sons, and the one who is married does have three children. But he is *happily* married, has a beautiful home with a swimming pool, and *no way* will he leave his wife. He is not that sort of person! This whole sitting is rubbish. I am leaving!' She stormed out of the room and slammed the door behind her.

I was reduced to floods of tears. This had never happened with anyone before (or since, I am happy to add). Why would I sense such a scenario for her son unless spirit wanted me to relay that information?

Sam smiled and in a calming voice said: 'Well done, you have given accurate information.'

I was totally bewildered as to how he could say such a thing when the woman had just slammed the door on me in a rage. I could still hear her ranting in the next room.

Jean, the lady of the house, rushed in to ask what the problem was. I sobbed as I told her I didn't mean to upset her guest, I had only told her what I could actually see for her. Poor Jean didn't know what to say so, as we do in such circumstances, she put the kettle on and made a cup of tea.

My anxiety eventually eased after about half an hour and I continued with the next lady – my last client before leaving Jean's home. Once I'd finished, I apologised to her again for her other friend's sitting. 'Don't worry,' Jean said as she hugged me goodbye. 'Elsie will get over it.'

Despite the problems within our marriage, we had booked a holiday in Marbella at the end of September. My parents had suggested that they should have the children for a week so that I could have some desperately needed time with my husband, to try and repair our failing marriage. I was excited at the prospect of going away as it had been a long time since I'd had a holiday. In fact, the last holiday I'd had with my husband on our own was our honeymoon. There was a small snag with the arrangements, though: we were to be joined by two friends of ours, or rather recent acquaintances. I did think it strange that my husband suggested they should come with us, especially as they were not married, but nevertheless I was glad just to get away. Deep down, I knew it would have been better for us to go as a couple, but I was assured that it would be fun and less stressful if we had friends with us. So I went along with my husband's arrangements – yet again.

Actually our marriage had seemed to pick up that spring after making friends with the young couple. They would invite us for a meal one weekend, then I would return the compliment the next. I have always loved cooking so becoming a good hostess was second nature to me and my husband seemed to enjoy my dinner parties. However, it was at one of these that I discovered him on the doorstep kissing our female friend in an overly friendly way! Naturally he tried to pass it off. 'Oh, it's not what it looks like!'

From that moment on, I knew there was no hope for us.

We had already booked and paid for the holiday to Marbella. Should I cancel? Needless to say another argument ensued when I said I didn't want to go, and once again my other half convinced me that there was nothing to worry about. It was just an innocent kiss.

Meanwhile . . . about six weeks had passed since the encounter with Elsie. I had not expected ever to see or hear from her again. So I was shocked when Jean asked if I would see Elsie's son. In fact, she begged me to see him. Why was that? I wondered. What had I said that had now struck a chord?

So the appointment was made. My stomach churned all morning at the prospect. I kept asking myself why I was consenting to see the offspring of the dreaded Elsie? I had enough trauma in my life right now.

It was the last week of July and the summer so far had been

gorgeous. Today was no different. The sun was warm and the air fresh, full of expectation. Why did I feel this was going to be a day to change all of my days? A day when life would alter for me for ever? I brushed aside my thoughts and prepared for the prospect of being verbally attacked again by one of Elsie's family.

Jean did assure me, though, that this time it would be different. Elsie's son was not like his mother. Something had clearly brought him to me so quickly after his mother's sitting.

I walked into the lounge to greet my appointment and felt quite taken aback as I noticed the very good-looking man sitting nervously on the sofa's matching footstool. This couldn't be him surely? He looked so nice, so normal, and definitely not as terrifying as his mother! He was wearing a canary yellow shirt, which lit up his dark-tanned features and smiling face.

As I entered the lounge, Jean's over-sized dog decided to follow me and join in with the meeting and greeting. I walked over to the stranger – so did the dog – except he reached the man well before me. As the man tried to stand up in a gentlemanly way and introduce himself, the dog jumped up on to him, sabotaging any move towards a gracious introduction. I laughed out loud, it was such a funny sight as the weight of the dog continued to hurl his front legs on to the lap of the poor man, covering him with doggy slobber and stray hairs in his demands to be petted.

Elsie's son was being showered with doggy love, which I am sure he could have well done without. Every time he tried to stand up, the dog hurled itself into his lap over and over again.

That's how I first met Richard Bull.

He looked up at me and burst out laughing. I sensed by the way he stared that he was surprised by my appearance. Perhaps he'd expected to see a dark-haired old gypsy with gold earrings.

He cheerfully spoke, 'Hello, I'm Richard. Thank you for meeting me – I am very pleased to meet you.'

Encountering this handsome man, I was glad I had put on my best outfit today! He seemed a nice enough chap, and not a bit aggressive like his mother, so I smiled back. Extending my hand to him, I managed to say, 'Hello, I'm Helen.'

As his hand touched mine it was as if a jolt of energy passed through the whole of my body. I looked into his hazel-coloured eyes and felt I was touching this man's soul. Within a second I felt I knew him . . . that I had always known him. His eyes, the gateway to the soul, captivated me.

I stepped back. Pull yourself together, Helen, I said to myself.

Even though that first moment was over, strangely the room felt as though it was still full of magic. Sam stood in one corner, smiling at the indefatigable animal now rolling over on the carpet with its paws in the air, still demanding to be petted by anyone who would give him affection.

As if to change the energy of our meeting, we all laughed as the soppy creature was told by his owner to behave and go and lie down.

I invited Richard into the quiet room from where I worked in this house, but he had to go and freshen up from the slobber and hairs first.

This appointment was going to be powerful, I thought. A bright glow had filled every corner of the room when I entered it. I knew then that authoritative Guides and Angels were preparing me to say something important to this man. A few minutes later he walked in and sat down, ready to start the appointment.

It was then that the emotion hit me.

I was gripped with sadness as I saw poor Richard's life unfolding before me. As I looked into his eyes, I could feel the overwhelming lack of self-esteem that even his confident smile could not hide. I felt his desperate loneliness as I pictured him driving his car miles and miles to work each day. In my mind's eye

I received spiritual visions of different scenarios. I shared his thoughts, which gave me chills. His imagination was running wild as he was plagued with graphic details of his wife's affair. I found it hard to concentrate as I saw him clinging to the vain hope of his nightmare vanishing and everything going back to normal. If only that could happen, I thought, if only I could turn the clock back for him, before his wife leaped into something that altered her life for good. I scanned my inner vision for the slightest sign that the impending divorce I could see would somehow not happen. He was desperate to hear all would still be well. What could I tell him?

As if in answer to my plea for guidance to help this man before me, Sam my ever-faithful Guide stepped in. 'Advise him that if he stays in his present relationship, it is as good as it will ever be. The levels of loyalty, affection and honesty will only be what they are now. If this is not enough and he wants more, then look into your heart, Helen, and see what lies ahead for him. You can do this. Be brave and answer him honestly. That's what this man needs and wants . . . honesty.'

With no hesitation I accessed that spiritual part of me that unites me with the spirit world. Today was very important for this man before me. I must look and listen very hard to my Guides. I took a deep breath and allowed the essence of spirit to fill my body: 'My Guides are saying you feel you are at a crossroads in your marriage. They say that you have already left your wife and are undecided what to do next. However, if you truly look deep into your heart, you know what you are going to do . . . though you haven't faced the truth and done it yet. The spirit world wants you to know they can feel your pain. You are not alone and they are there to help you.

'I am being told that you have three children. If you choose to go back to your marriage you will make it work, but it will only ever be what it is now. Nothing more. If you are content to accept that, you will be fine, there is no one to judge you other than yourself. However, one day as you grow older, you may look back and question your choice and say, *What if – what if I had made the break? What sort of life would I have had?* However, if you stay with this marriage, it will be you who makes the sacrifices to keep it together. You ask the question, *will it work?* You will make sure it works – but at what emotional cost?

'If you do make a clean break, there is a second marriage for you and it's just around the corner. The Guides are telling me about the new love of your life. You are going to meet her very soon. They say very soon, like yesterday or today or tomorrow – that imminent. They are telling me you might even have met her already. This lady you are going to meet is twenty-seven years of age and has two children. It's all happening immediately. I don't know why, but my Guides keep pointing to me. I can only assume what they mean is that the person you are going to meet is called Helen too. This new person has the same name as me. That's a coincidence!'

The next second I broke away from the spiritual to the physical world and saw the man concentrating on my every word, his eyes fixed on mine. We broke into laughter together at the coincidence about the name. As if to confirm the situation, I told him that I didn't mean myself, of course. It was just the same name as mine. 'Do you know anyone called Helen?' I asked, to divert any association from me.

He explained that he employed a lady called Helen at his city centre store in Chester, but had no intention of having a relationship with her. He laughed, saying that although she was attractive and in her twenties, she was much taller than him and she smoked – that would never work, he joked.

Apart from that, throughout his appointment he barely said a word to me, which I found rather off-putting because I generally need at least to hear a 'yes' or 'no'. It's not the words I need, it's the actual energy from the voice I use to create a more accurate link with the spirit world. As an artist uses paint, or a potter uses clay, in my case I need emotions as my raw material, to create an accurate spiritual link. So, if the artist is denied a full palette of paints and is restricted to, say, black and red, his creation will be limited to and represented by only those two colours: it can't be anything more, however good the artist. The more someone restricts their emotions and even the intensity of those emotions at the time of the sitting, the more the quality of it will be affected accordingly.

Although Richard remained silent during his sitting, it was as if he had surrendered his soul to me so I could see everything there was to know about his life through his eyes. This was the first time during a sitting I had been offered access to such heartfelt emotion. For me, at that time, I had never been offered such a range of emotion to work with.

The spirit world had said enough for now. This man could go forward and decide for himself what he must do next. However, I consoled him by saying that I was sure it would sort itself out. Tears welled up in his eyes, but I didn't dare tell him I understood his unhappiness. How I could relate to his hurt and suffering. Our lives were very similar. Fortunately, he had true love just around the corner for him. For me it seemed a distant prospect and not one I wanted to think about.

After about an hour I brought the session to a close, reiterating that Richard needed to think about his time with me, and what the spirit world had said. He suggested another meeting in the next couple of days but I explained it was inappropriate. He needed longer, to take time over his choices. I explained he needed to digest what he'd heard and maybe in a couple of weeks he could call Jean, the lady who'd arranged the appointment, and we could talk again.

We said our goodbyes. Through the window I saw him open his car door and then he drove away. I wondered whether I would ever see him again.

During the ensuing days, fate really did play a prominent role in my life. I was driving back from Chester with my husband as we were ready to exchange contracts with the buyer of our home in St Asaph and for the new house in Chester. Strangely, I saw Richard's car parked at the side of the road in the village of Northophall. He was in a roadside phone-box. My heart raced, I had no idea why. Why did I feel this rush of adrenalin and feelings towards a man I had met only in a sitting? I had never had any such feelings towards anyone other than my husband, so why now and why him?

The next day I was driving to my mother's and couldn't believe it when we stopped opposite each other at a set of traffic lights in Kinmel Bay! It happened again, and then again. I had never seen this man before and now it seemed that everywhere I went, I bumped into him. Not only that, no matter what I seemed to be doing at home, I kept seeing his face smiling at me. I couldn't get him out of my mind.

My longed-for holiday was now only a few weeks away, but it was starting to bother me because I felt I couldn't go away and pretend that everything was hunky-dory with my husband. My appointment with Richard had made me reflect that maybe I should start making some life choices of my own. Dishing out the medicine is easy, but when it comes to taking it yourself – that's a different matter.

The sitting I'd had with Mrs Gordon almost two years before was still floating around in my mind. All the details of what she'd said came flooding back. Question after question filled my head. In the end I applied my own brand of therapy to my situation.

I had learned a long time ago that Guides like Sam and the many others who influence my life don't make decisions for us. That is not their role. We have to take full responsibility for that and ultimately use our own freedom of choice. This is a shock for some people as they sometimes come to see me for advice with the misconception they are going to be told what to do for the best. A good parent doesn't dictate to their children how to live their lives and what to do with them; a good parent will offer advice and wisdom and trust their children to make choices based on that. As a spiritual communicator, I verbalise the message of guidance from the collective consciousness of my Guides. It is up to the recipient to make their own life choices based on that guidance, if they so wish.

Choices – decisions! Who was I kidding? I had to be honest with myself. I didn't need another person to fill my life, I needed to find a life that could fulfil me. When I'd married and had children, I'd thought that would be enough fulfilment, but it wasn't. I didn't feel special to my husband, that I mattered, that I was loved and cared for in the way I wanted and needed. I suppose he was a good man – a good man for someone else – but not apparently for me. Why was I even thinking this?

I could not live with the emotional charade any more, and talked to my mother very seriously about leaving with the children. She knew how unhappy I had been for a good while. She was sympathetic but practical. 'Where will you go?' she asked. I was rather hoping she might have invited us to stay with her, but she was right, where would I go and live with two children? So I started looking in the daily newspapers for rental houses. Maybe soon . . .

The sale of our beautiful St Asaph home had gone through

and we were shortly to face camping on the floorboards of the new one. Two children living in a building site . . .

Jean had been on the phone several times to me, trying to organise another appointment for Richard. I had been very evasive as there was so much going on in my life. We were trying to sort out the house for our move to Chester, I had been helping my mother as my dad had had some bad bouts with his emphysema, and I'd had my twenty-eighth birthday, which went with a blip rather than a bang! As strange as it may sound, I was going to tell Richard I couldn't sit for him. He had been running through my mind so much lately and in my present predicament I felt too close to him to offer a constructive sitting. Even though with everyone else I could detach my feelings, with him it was different. I couldn't understand why.

Eventually Jean did tie me down to a date and time for Richard's next appointment: from memory it was 11 August.

Richard arrived on time, smelling of lovely aftershave and looking immaculate in a white linen shirt and navy trousers. Thankfully the dog had been locked in the kitchen that day, so another robust greeting was ruled out.

We sat down on either side of the desk as we had on the previous occasion. Granted Richard was handsome, but I doubted he would ever be interested in me. Pull yourself together, I thought, concentrate on the job in hand!

My intuition kept me from telling him how I had 'bumped' into him and been seeing him in my thoughts. The prospect of rejection while I was feeling so fragile was intolerable – anyway I didn't need to complicate things. I just needed to sort out my own problems and lead a more peaceful life.

Before I could open my mouth, Richard asked politely about my welfare during the last couple of weeks. Despite my shyness we looked at each other directly as he started to say: 'Helen, I don't know why I am telling you this, but since I saw you three women have asked me out on a date. I have even been propositioned to spend a weekend away by two of them.'

My heart sank right through the floor. Now I had met him for the second time, I realised how truly attracted I was to him, and how gorgeously handsome he was.

He continued by saying something strange: 'I couldn't go. Even the thought of going filled me with guilt. For some reason, something inside was telling me you would not like me socialising with any of these women and would be upset if I did. So naturally I declined all their offers and felt better for doing so!'

I paused for a moment, trying not to let any emotion show, but my heart was pounding. 'Speak from the heart,' Sam pleaded as he stood watching.

Looking into this man's warm and caring eyes, I said: 'There was no need for you to show such loyalty to me. You don't really know anything about me. But I have to say, you have been constantly on my mind. Every time I closed my eyes, all I have been seeing is your face. Even doing the ironing, all I did was think of you. You are continually in my thoughts. When I was driving around, I kept seeing your car.

'What you have done is make me reflect on how my own relationship has failed. I know I cannot carry on with my husband. A short while ago I accused him of having an affair and we mutually seperated for about six months. We decided to get back together around Christmas time as I was feeling so guilty about the children not having their father at home . . .'

Once I had started to open up, I didn't seem able to stop. 'Please don't think your interest in me is compromising as I fully recognise the unhappiness in my own marriage. It is all but over, has been for a while. But in all honesty, Richard, you and I don't know each other. Although I am not happy, I won't do anything behind my husband's back, so unfortunately I am in no position to see you.'

Richard never said a word, just listened. He was a good listener for sure, but I needed him to talk right now. Eventually, after I'd talked to him about my own marital breakdown for another ten minutes and why I felt I couldn't sit for him today, he smiled at me.

'I really don't expect anything from you, Helen. I have no right to have any expectations whatsoever. I was just sharing with you what had been happening to me. Knowing you have even thought about me fills my heart with happiness. Your life sounds just as complicated as mine, and you certainly don't need any further difficulties right now. I want you to know I am very patient and will wait as long as it takes.'

Wait for what? I thought.

As I focused back on Richard's sitting, what happened next sent shock waves through my mind as I started to write down names on a piece of paper. 'Do these mean anything to you?' I said. I noticed that they all had the initial R. That was when Richard mentioned he came from a family that had a lot of initial Rs to their Christian names. I started to write down at least eight names other than his, all beginning with R: Rachel, Rhian, Reece, Robert, Ralph, Roy, Robina, Royston. 'Who are they?' I stammered as I registered that I had previously been told by Mrs Gordon I would meet a man with a family line of initial Rs.

'Oh, Rachel, Rhian and Reece are my children, the others are my father, brother, uncle, auntie and cousin. We seem to have a thing about the letter R in our names!' I was totally shocked but kept my feelings to myself

Once I'd gathered my composure we chatted, nothing heavy or serious, just friendly. As Richard stood up to leave I shook his hand and the same tingle of energy as before jolted my soul. Then he lifted my hand and touched it with his lips, gazing adoringly into my eyes. My mind was wary, realising all the implications of allowing this man any nearer to me emotionally, and then he smiled and my heart melted at the thought of seeing him again.

To be friendly yet non-committal, I made a suggestion: 'Maybe I could meet you for a coffee the next time I am in Chester and you happen to be there,' I said, knowing this was a move that could end my marriage for good. 'I am going there in three days' time to do some shopping. I'll say hello if you are around, and if you want we could go for a coffee and just chat?'

Chat! What was I thinking?

We said our goodbyes and parted. At that moment our future could have lain in any direction. Richard might have decided not to go to Chester that week, or worse have succumbed to the advances of someone else. Meanwhile, my own freedom of choice might have decided for me that any emotional risk at this time was unacceptable. I had no real idea of the long-term intentions of this man. I could be left stripped of everything.

Decisions – complicated choices!

The three days ticked by and at noon on the day I'd arranged I knew this was going to be a life-changing moment. Without any hesitation I walked into Richard's shop. Something inside me felt I had found my soul-mate. He was dropping something into a display basket down the centre aisle when I entered. I could see him at the far end. I walked over and he gave me a startled but happy look. Little did I know he had positioned himself so that he could see me enter the shop the moment I came in! Our eyes met, and then we gave each other a brief hug and a kiss, like long-established friends. That was it, greeting over. The ice was broken. Now we needed to get to know one another properly.

In the middle of the aisle, we held hands as if forming an

invisible circle. Without moving, Richard whispered under his breath, 'Do you realise there are about ten pairs of eyes on us?' All the staff stood staring as if witnessing an illegal act.

We smiled lovingly at each other. It felt as if our being together was the most natural thing in the world.

Richard linked my arm in his and in one sweeping motion ushered me towards the door. 'Come on! We can't stay in here. Let's go down the road and have that coffee you promised me.'

Had I found my soul-mate?

Now my story really begins . . .

A Note About Censorship

It is hard to believe, in this day and age, that my working life, and that of other genuine spiritualists, has been governed and restricted by censorship and prejudice that for most other walks of life has long since been swept away.

Even now, the radio station I do a show for cannot say that I am a healer, nor that I am able to pass on messages from the spirit world. It is a constant frustration for me and others in my situation, because the simple fact is that communicating with the spirit world is not a lifestyle choice: it's the way I was born! I see them whether you want me to or not.

Don't get me wrong, attitudes have changed considerably during the 30 years I have been working, otherwise I would not be eligible to present my own radio show. However, you might not understand how difficult it was for me to practice my work during the early years. Even in the 1980s and 90s spiritualists like myself who communicated with the spirit world were severely restricted. Our work was regulated by the 1951 Fraudulent Mediums Act, which replaced – but was very similar to – the 1735 Witchcraft Act! Yes, the Witchcraft Act! Granted the outdated Act was probably enforced to protect the public against charlatans, and rightly so, but it made life very difficult for those of us who offered genuine physical and/or emotional healing in a professional therapeutic environment. We were not allowed to publicise our work nor were we given any opportunity of proving our genuine abilities.

In the early 1990s this outdated act put tremendous fear and pressure on even the more liberal and rebellious broadcasters who wanted me to have a platform to showcase my abilities. There was only one television broadcaster who dared showcase my work and that was the iconic Gay Byrne in Ireland. Gay invited me on the *Gay Byrne Late, Late Show* on RTE television in March 1996 and his gamble paid off as he had me back later that same year in October, telling the audience, 'The response to her last time was phenomenal; and I do mean phenomenal; we have been at this a long time now and we know the difference between phenomenal and *phenomenal!*' TV presenter Ceidiog Hughes reported on British news that my second appearance caused the programme ratings to 'beat that of Coronation Street!'

Newspapers and magazines were accountable to the same outdated rules and would not take any form of advertising or promotional material about my work. Any features were written with the emphasis on doubt, ridicule or debate, but never to showcase. As a result, I was completely reliant on word-of-mouth to spread the word about my work and the help I could offer. I had no huge media machines urging me forward, pushing me out in front of the public. I am only known as well as I am today through thirty years of word-of-mouth recommendation.

Finally, following a directive from the EU on the 26th May 2008, the old Act was replaced by some new Consumer

Protection Regulations. However, I have read the new EU legislation and in my opinion certain regulations still remain unclear, yet to be clarified by a judge in a future prosecution. Since the new regulations you have seen a glut of spiritual TV, but the programmes are still tainted with incredulity and billed as entertainment rather than as programmes of real substance and truth.

Now I have been lucky enough to be given my own platform on radio in the form of the *The Sunday Session* with Helen Parry Jones, and my objective with both the show and this book is to reach out to as may people as possible, and spread the truth of how the spirit world appears to me, and how the wonderful gifts of healing I have inherited can help so many people in need.